T0332116

Demystifying Federated Learning for Blockchain and Industrial Internet of Things

Sandeep Kautish
Lord Buddha Education Foundation, Nepal

Gaurav Dhiman
Government Bikram College of Commerce, India

A volume in the Advances in
Computational Intelligence and
Robotics (ACIR) Book Series

Published in the United States of America by
IGI Global
Engineering Science Reference (an imprint of IGI Global)
701 E. Chocolate Avenue
Hershey PA, USA 17033
Tel: 717-533-8845
Fax: 717-533-8661
E-mail: cust@igi-global.com
Web site: http://www.igi-global.com

Library of Congress Cataloging-in-Publication Data

Names: Kautish, Sandeep, editor. | Dhiman, Gaurav, 1993- editor.
Title: Demystifying federated learning for blockchain and industrial
   Internet of Things / Sandeep Kautish, and Gaurav Dhiman, editors.
Description: Hershey, PA : Engineering Science Reference, an imprint of IGI
   Global, [2022] | Includes bibliographical references and index. |
   Summary: "The purpose of this book is to rediscover, redefine, and
   reestablish the most recent applications of Federated Learning using
   blockchain and IoT to optimize data for next-generation networks"--
   Provided by publisher.
Identifiers: LCCN 2022001860 (print) | LCCN 2022001861 (ebook) | ISBN
   9781668437339 (h/c) | ISBN 9781668437346 (s/c) | ISBN 9781668437353
   (ebook)
Subjects: LCSH: Blockchains (Databases)--Industrial applications. |
   Internet of things--Industrial applications.
Classification: LCC QA76.9.B56 D46 2022 (print) | LCC QA76.9.B56 (ebook)
   | DDC 005.74--dc23/eng/20220401
LC record available at https://lccn.loc.gov/2022001860
LC ebook record available at https://lccn.loc.gov/2022001861

This book is published in the IGI Global book series Advances in Computational Intelligence and
Robotics (ACIR) (ISSN: 2327-0411; eISSN: 2327-042X)

British Cataloguing in Publication Data
A Cataloguing in Publication record for this book is available from the British Library.

All work contributed to this book is new, previously-unpublished material.
The views expressed in this book are those of the authors, but not necessarily of the publisher.

For electronic access to this publication, please contact: eresources@igi-global.com.

Advances in Computational Intelligence and Robotics (ACIR) Book Series

ISSN:2327-0411
EISSN:2327-042X

Editor-in-Chief: Ivan Giannoccaro University of Salento, Italy

MISSION

While intelligence is traditionally a term applied to humans and human cognition, technology has progressed in such a way to allow for the development of intelligent systems able to simulate many human traits. With this new era of simulated and artificial intelligence, much research is needed in order to continue to advance the field and also to evaluate the ethical and societal concerns of the existence of artificial life and machine learning.

The **Advances in Computational Intelligence and Robotics (ACIR) Book Series** encourages scholarly discourse on all topics pertaining to evolutionary computing, artificial life, computational intelligence, machine learning, and robotics. ACIR presents the latest research being conducted on diverse topics in intelligence technologies with the goal of advancing knowledge and applications in this rapidly evolving field.

COVERAGE

- Heuristics
- Computational Logic
- Evolutionary Computing
- Synthetic Emotions
- Artificial Intelligence
- Cognitive Informatics
- Natural Language Processing
- Cyborgs
- Algorithmic Learning
- Fuzzy Systems

IGI Global is currently accepting manuscripts for publication within this series. To submit a proposal for a volume in this series, please contact our Acquisition Editors at Acquisitions@igi-global.com or visit: http://www.igi-global.com/publish/.

Titles in this Series

701 East Chocolate Avenue, Hershey, PA 17033, USA
Tel: 717-533-8845 x100 • Fax: 717-533-8661
E-Mail: cust@igi-global.com • www.igi-global.com

Editorial Advisory Board

Table of Contents

Detailed Table of Contents

Chapter 1

Sushma Malik, Institute of Innovation in Technology and Management,
    Janakpuri, India
Anamika Rana, Maharaja Surajmal Institute, Delhi, India

The internet of technology (IoT) refers to the connectivity of smart devices with the internet to accumulate data and transfer it to smart devices. But with the lack of built-in security measures, IoT is vulnerable to privacy and security threats. Blockchain technology assists in the security needs of IoT devices. The main characteristics of blockchain technology like immutability, transparency, auditability, and encryption of data sort out the inadequacy of IoT devices. This chapter represents an inclusive survey on blockchain and IoT technologies with the integration of these technologies to overcome the shortfall. This chapter includes an overview of both technologies with their advantages and disadvantages. It also highlights the domains of their applications and represents the advantages of integration of blockchain and IoT technology to develop BIoT (blockchain-based IoT). Also, it analyzes the main challenges faced during the smooth integration of blockchain and IoT technologies.

Chapter 2

S. B. Goyal, City University, Malaysia
Pradeep Bedi, Galgotias University, India
Jugnesh Kumar, St. Andrews Institute of Technology and Management,
    India

With the rapid development of big data technologies, their applications are growing rapidly. Conventional big data management is vulnerable. If any tampering occurs over stored database or sometimes untrusted data gathering occurs, then it causes serious issues with conventional data management. To resolve these problems, this chapter is focused on the development of blockchain technology for secure educational big data (EBD). Blockchain techniques divide the data blocks into secure data blocks using cryptography algorithms. The secure data blocks are connected in the chain with each other. This ensures security as well as flexibility. So, in this chapter, the proposed methodology had adopted blockchain technology and ensures its efficiency due to its decentralized and flexible approach.

Edge computing is a type of distributed computing that was designed especially for internet of things (IoT) users to provide computational resources and data management nearby to users' devices. By introducing edge computing for IoT, networks have reduced the bandwidth and latency issue while handling real-time applications. The major benefit of edge computing is that it reduces the communication overhead between IoT user and server. With integration of IoT in our daily lives, it has attracted researchers towards its performance management such as complexity minimization, latency minimization, memory management, energy consumption minimization, etc. In this chapter, deep reinforcement learning is focused to minimize the computational complexity at IoT user end. The task offloading decision process is designed using Q-Learning, which minimizes the system cost and curse of high dimensional data. In addition, the proposed methodology will perform better as compared to existing algorithms with respect to system costs.

Chapter 4

Although telemedicine is still practiced today, high-speed connections and improved organizational capability have enabled remote operation of medical equipment, known as telerobotic surgery. The technologies have a number of benefits, including enhanced performance and the ability to reach complex operations to geographically isolated places where trained surgeons are unavailable. This study proposed an early robotic solution for limited teleoperation tasks in a complex and unpredictable environment. So, the research is inspired by future human-robot collaboration. It focuses on limiting or preventing accidents between the robot and its environment. In order to enable access to robotic surgery equipment in a confined area, a fuzzy control method is used. We may infer that an adaptive robotic system capable of accomplishing limited tasks while also responding to external factors in an unpredictable and dynamic environment is potentially feasible.

Pawan Whig, Vivekananda Institute of Professional Studies, India
Shama Kouser, Jazan University, Saudi Arabia
Arun Velu, Equifax, USA
Rahul Reddy Nadikattu, University of Cumbersome, USA

Increased agricultural activity is intended as intelligent agriculture or precision agriculture to be of critical importance. The fast growth of networking has resulted in IoT-based farm management systems. Increased agricultural activity is intended as intelligent agriculture or precision agriculture to be of critical importance. The established cloud-based platforms cannot cope with the huge quotas and diverse data provided by the connected IoT devices, which are based on conventional cloud models. It is important to get data processing closer to the origins of their output to reduce lag in aiding real-time decision-making based on the data generated. The adoption of fog-based models will solve this and will be discussed in this chapter. To ensure optimum bandwidth usage and low latency for real-time decision-making, an IoT-Fog farm management system may be more capable.

Pawan Whig, Vivekanada Institute of Professional Studies, India
Arun Velu, Equifax, USA
Rahul Ready, University of Cumbersome, USA

Today, attempts have been made to overcome entertainment objectives in the production of video games. In reality, much work has gone into seeking tools in computer science using AI and advanced technologies to develop games so that they can be used in educational, industry, or political processes. For these goods to be successfully introduced into society, they must be crafted to be as available as possible to all people, including those who belong to minorities with special needs. Adaptability and compatibility need to ensure better quality and adoption of goods to meet accessibility requirements. With demystifying federated learning in artificial intelligence, the possibilities of combining human-computer interaction with artificial intelligence to enhance usability in games, and thus to make them more democratic and useful to society, especially for those who rely on assistive technology services, are discussed in this chapter.

Chapter 7

Pawan Whig, Vivekananda Institute of Professional Studies, India
Arun Velu, Equifax, USA
Ashima Bhatnagar Bhatia, Vivekananda Institute of Professional
Studies, India

The cumulative amount of greenhouse gases that are shaped by our actions is a carbon footmark. In the US, the total carbon footmark of a humanoid is 16 tonnes, one of the largest amounts in the world. The average is closer to 4 tonnes worldwide. The average universal carbon footmark per year requirements is to drop below 3 tonnes by 2050 to have the utmost chance of stopping a 2°C point rise in worldwide temperature. Rahul et al. already predicted that the carbon footprint reduced by 17% with the use of IoT-enabled services. In this research study a novel approach to reduce carbon footprint using IoT with reinforcement AI learning is presented, which further reduced carbon footprint by 5% when using and nearly 7% when it is done using Q-Learning. The detailed findings are included to demonstrate the result.

Chapter 8

Pawan Whig, Vivekananda Institute of Professional Studies, India
ARUN Velu, Equifax, USA
Pavika Sharma, Bhagwan Parshuram Institute of Technology, India

Blockchain genuinely has the power to revolutionise the energy market mechanism by introducing smart PPAs (purchase power agreements), smart micro grids, and REC certificates. By converting energy resources into digital commodities that can be exchanged on a blockchain, new investment and trading possibilities that allow new players to join easily and encourage innovations will be enabled. It may also contribute to a shift driven by the organisation to address the issue of last mile connectivity. While recent grid developments have broadened the use of advanced control techniques, the next-generation grid requires technology that makes it simpler to connect distributed energy services (DERs) for users who both acquire and sell power seamlessly. This chapter will present a case study of a blockchain-based optimization paradigm and framework for crowd-sourced operations.

Chapter 9

This chapter is written with the intent to explore the history, architecture, applications, and challenges in the implementation of digital twin with IoT competences. Digital twins are considered to be a fundamental starting point for today's smart city construction. The chapter initiates with a brief description of the concepts of digital twins and digital twin for cities and smart homes, discusses the relationship between digital twins and smart cities, analyses the characteristics of smart cities and homes based on digital twins, and focuses on the main applications of smart cities based on digital twins. This chapter sheds light on the future development of smart cities and smart homes based on digital twins.

Chapter 10

The wellbeing of a country depends mainly on its healthcare and is also one of the most impacted frameworks from the viewpoint of decision-making with multi-objectives and inclined more to mistakes in the various activities, and multi-decision criteria analysis (MDCA) helps a lot as a tool for this interaction of various independent actions. Therefore, the present study helps to break down and incorporate articles found in the literature involving MCDA along with assessing their general issues and various strategic angles and organizing them. Investigation in the bibliographic data sets of PubMed showed 85 journal articles regarding the subject of multi-decision criteria analysis, and after a cautious verification, 85 journal articles examinations were chosen to be studied in detail.

Preface

INTRODUCTION

In recent years, countries all-inclusive are more focused to the development of Industrial Internet of Things (IIoT). Industrial Internet is an important keystone of the Industry 4.0 and a key element to transform old kinetic energy into a new era. With the help of latest development of IIoT, a single form of equipment and different types of enterprises have been connected by the Industrial Internet, which allows the resources of different links to be organically combined. The Industrial Internet system architecture consists of four aspects: network connection, platform, security system, and identification analysis system. Among them, the network is used to realize the connection of people, machines, and things, and it is the foundation of Industrial Internet. The security system is responsible for providing security protection and guarantee, and the purpose of the platform is to open up operational data and Internet data to integrate resources. The identification analysis system is an important hub for the realization of Industrial Internet.

Mobile technology and the internet of objects have been used in mobile networks to meet new technical demands. Emerging needs have centered on data storage, computation, and low latency management in potentially smart cities, transport, smart grids, and a wide number of sustainable environments. Federated learning's contributions include an effective framework to improve network security in heterogeneous industrial internet of things (IIoT) environments.

Demystifying Federated Learning for Blockchain and Industrial Internet of Things revives, reassess, and regenerates the most emerging tenders of federated learning using blockchain and IIoT to elevate data for future networks. The book will provide an insight to its readers in a way of inculcating the theme that shapes the next generation of secure communication. Covering topics such as digital twins, advance applications of Blockchain integration, this premier reference source is an essential resource for computer scientists, programmers, government officials, business leaders and managers, students and faculty of higher education, researchers, and academicians.

Federated Learning is a platform that promotes the connectivity of intelligent systems with increased network capacity, service quality, accessibility of the network, and user experience. Blockchain is a technology that is exposed and can contribute to stability in IIoT. Blockchain appears to be a mechanism to preserve IIoT and retain the confidentiality of user/data, and the capacity to provide unauthorized reproductive and information services. The emerging needs have centered on data storage, computation, and low latency management in potentially smart cities, transport, smart grids, and a wide number of sustainable environments.

The book *Demystifying Federated Learning for Blockchain and Industrial Internet of Things* has 10 chapters focused on various dimensions of Federated Learning for Blockchain and IIoT from different perspectives, i.e., introductory topics, uses of big data in Blockchain and Federated Learning, Edge computing and many more. The main objective of this book is to rediscover, redefine, and reestablish the most recent applications of Federated Learning using blockchain and IIoT to optimize data for next-generation networks. The book contains 10 chapters in total which covers variety of topics, i.e., Federated based traffic offloading prediction and optimization, Blockchain and IoT applications.

CHAPTER DESCRIPTIONS

Chapter 1 discusses the introduction to Internet of Things (IoT) which refers to the connection of smart devices to the internet to collect data and send it to other smart devices. Due to the lack of a built-in security mechanism, IoT devices are prone to privacy and security concerns and this problem is sorted out with Blockchain technology. The key features of blockchain technology, such as immutability, transparency, auditability, and data encryption, eliminate the shortcomings of IoT devices. This chapter contains a comprehensive analysis of both Blockchain and IoT technologies as well as their integration to overcome the shortage of these technologies. Demonstrate the benefits of using blockchain and IoT technology to produce BIoT (Blockchain-Based IoT). Examine the major issues that arise during the seamless integration of blockchain and IoT technology.

Chapter 2 discusses the use of big data technologies and applications which is quickly expanding as a result of their fast growth. Big data management as it is now practiced is fragile. When a stored database is tampered with, or when untrusted data is gathered, it poses major problems with traditional data management. This article focuses on the development of blockchain technology for safe educational big data to address these issues (EBD). The blockchain approaches partition the data blocks into safe data blocks using cryptography algorithms. The encrypted data blocks are linked together in a chain. This guarantees both security and flexibility.

As a result, the suggested technique in this study uses blockchain technology and assures its efficacy through its decentralized and adaptable approach.

Chapter 3 examines Edge computing technologies which is a sort of distributed computing that was created with Internet of Things (IoT) users in mind, providing computational resources and data management close to their devices. Edge computing has decreased bandwidth and latency issues for IoT networks while handling real-time applications. Edge computing's main advantage is that it lowers the communication overhead between IoT users and servers. With the widespread use of IoT in our daily lives, academics have been drawn to issues such as complexity reduction, latency reduction, memory management, and energy consumption reduction. Deep reinforcement learning is employed in this work to reduce computational complexity at the IoT user end. Q- Learning is used to build the job offloading decision process, which reduces the system cost and the curse of high dimensional data. Furthermore, when it comes to system expenses, the suggested technique will surpass existing methods.

Chapter 4 discusses remote healthcare research which is increasing as the world moves from remote surveillance to real- time and rapid disease identification. Robot assisted surgery is enhancing traditional surgical procedures, particularly in long-distance surgeries. Telerobotic surgery provides a variety of products and services, including high-quality assistance for people in developing countries and military surgical needs. It can also overcome the limitations and inconsistencies of public health systems in developing and developed countries and regions. Due to the lack of a system for device identification, the major problem in performing telerobotic surgery is reliability. A fuzzy control system is utilized to allow access to robotic surgery equipment in a constrained environment. Here an adaptive robotic system capable of performing constrained tasks while also adapting to external influences in a dynamic and unpredictable environment is possible. The proposed model uses a fuzzy logic-based selection strategy to detect relevant features and provide access rules to surgical equipment.

Chapter 5 includes various aspects in which Fog computing is connected with IoT and helps in the various sectors particularly in Agricultural Sector. Increased agricultural activity is intended as intelligent agriculture or precision agriculture to be of critical importance. The fast growth of networking has resulted in IoT-based farm management systems. This chapter is very useful for researchers working in the same field. With the advancement in technology soon we have a new revolution in the agriculture sector which is known to be agriculture 4. O.

Chapter 6 has explored seven major difficulties that exist in today's socio-technical world, to use the growing availability of interaction intelligence to meet pressing human and societal demands. Despite being sparked by current technology breakthroughs and intelligence, the conversation has mostly argued for a future technological fabric in which intelligence would be used to better serve and empower humanity. In this environment, the HCI community is called upon to perform a significant task: to create a future in which intelligence integration does not undermine human self-efficacy and control, but rather enhances it.

Chapter 7 introduces a carbon footprint may be a large measure that can be attributed to an individual's behaviour, a family, a case, an entity, or even a country as a whole. Tons of CO_2 corresponding gases, counting methane, nitrous oxide, and other greenhouse vapours, are typically measured as tonnes of CO_2 produced each year, an amount that can be augmented with tonnes of CO_2 corresponding vapours This book chapter presents a novel approach to reduce carbon footprint using IoT with Reinforcement AI Learning is presented which further reduced carbon foot print by 5% when using and nearly 7% when it is done using Q-Learning. The detail findings are included to demonstrate the result. This Book chapter is very important for the researchers working in the same field.

Chapter 8 will present a case study of a blockchain-based optimization paradigm and framework for crowd-sourced operations. Energy networks, peer-to-peer energy trading through purchases In this Chapter, we leverage the block chain to develop a novel trading mechanism for unlocking fresh energy resources that might be employed in the future. Blockchain is an open leader in which all online transactions are logged and all transactions can bind, submit, or check. Blockchain is a digitalized accounting records scheme in which all transactions are documented in full in accordance with a set of cryptographic rules to prevent unauthorized intervention.

Chapter 9 is written with the intent to explore the history, architecture, applications, and challenges in the implementation of digital twin with IoT competences. Digital twins are considered to be a fundamental starting point for today's smart city construction. The chapter initiates with a brief description of the concepts of digital twins and digital twin for cities and smart homes and the relationship between digital twins and smart cities, analyses the characteristics of smart cities and homes based on digital twins, and the main applications of smart cities based on digital twins. This chapter shed light on the future development of smart cities and smart homes based on digital twins.

Chapter 10 emphasizes that wellbeing of a country depends mainly on its healthcare and with its various decision-making frameworks. Nowadays even the healthcare systems are exploiting the latest technologies such as artificial intelligence (AI), blockchain and AI federated technologies. The multi-criteria decision analysis (MCDA) techniques still assist the other technologies while making important decisions. Therefore, the present study helps to incorporate articles found in the literature based on healthcare systems which are exploiting AI federated learning and multi-criteria decision analysis for supporting healthcare systems and for proposing different healthcare frameworks. The research study is utilizing MCDA method for assessing healthcare general issues along with various strategic angles and perspectives. The bibliographic PUBMED data has been investigated which has utilized 85 journal articles distributed from 2008 to 2021 regarding the subject of multi decision criteria analysis for bibliometric analysis. From the study it can be observed that multi-decision criteria analysis techniques are widely used in healthcare along with the AI federated tools in healthcare applications for solving various health related problems.

CONCLUSION

The Industrial Internet of Things (IIoT) can be referred to as the millions of physical devices (such as, instruments, and interconnected sensors and different devices). These devices are connected to the internet without requiring any interventions, i.e., human-to-human or human-to-computer interaction. It is beneficial in low deployment cost and wide terrestrial exposure and has found various beneficial applications in varied areas, including, environment monitoring, smart city and networks, drones, robotics, transportation, smart solutions in healthcare, etc. Low-cost computing can enable cloud, big data and SaaS, business analytics, and mobile computing technologies, IIoT devices can share and collect data with no human intervention. The data collected by IIoT devices can be transmitted to the central cloud server for storage. By using data encryption techniques, the security and privacy issues can be easily solved. However, IIoT-based systems sometimes faces severe security and privacy related issues, particularly during data processing and analytic. Federated learning (FL) is referred to as a new computing model that trains a machine learning algorithm on multiple local datasets in local mobile nodes without explicitly exchanging data samples. The general principle consists of training local models on local data samples and exchanging parameters (e.g., the weights and biases of a deep neural network) between these local nodes at some frequency to generate a global model shared by all mobile nodes.

However, federated learning solutions still face many new security and privacy challenges when it needs to meet the mobile IIoT paradigm. Many new paradigms are emerging which advocates for the combination of Federated learning with Blockchain in order to achieve the true objectives of Industrial Internet of Thing (IIoT). Federated learning (FL) is a realistic solution to solve the problems of data sciences, break data barriers and challenges, and provide best protection in terms of high end data security and privacy, especially in the context of the Internet of Things (IoT), and big data. The development and evolution of modern information and communication technologies is leading us to the fourth industrial revolution, in which the Industrial Internet of Things (IIoT) is assumed to be one of the key aspects to realize Industry 4.0. With the increase of both quantity and type of IoT devices, a critical mass of data is collected from the real-world environment every day. The data need to be processed and analyzed to derive intelligence for further use in efficient, secure, and economic ways, and machine learning has been adopted in academia and industry to scrutinize and study the data for business decision-making. Nevertheless, data hungriness may hinder the development of machine-learning-enabled systems, with another growing challenge on protecting data privacy. To address the above issue, Google proposed the concept of federated learning in 2016. As an emerging machine learning paradigm, it allows clients at edge to perform model training locally and only send model parameter updates to a central server for the aggregation of the global model. All raw data are kept in respective local storage and not transferred to other clients.

Information technology is a key enabler in the industrial evolution and revolution of societies around the world. We are now in the midst of the fourth industrial revolution – Industry 4.0 – and one of the biggest drivers has been the Industrial Internet of Things (IIoT) and Wireless Sensor Networks (WSN). The IIoT and WSN is the result of widespread use of computers and the interconnectedness of machines and connected electronic devices. It has made software a crucial tool for almost every industry, from bakeries and arts to manufacturing facilities and banking systems. Computers can be mobile or geographically separated over large a distance, which exposes them to network disturbances, Quality of Service (QoS) degradation, and security vulnerabilities. The IIoT is a complex network at a large scale and there is a dire need for network architecture and protocol design that will accommodate these diverse domains and competencies and handle the increasing levels of complexity.

Sustainable computing using federated learning in IIoT environment, providing the environment for reduction of energy requirement, is a key factor for energy constrained IIoT devices. However, the WSN paradigms were not originally developed for this kind of IoT environment. Both technologies are computationally expensive and can introduce high bandwidth overhead and delays. These demanding performance and power requirements are not suitable for most IIoT devices. This problem has been solved by emerging computing paradigms like wireless sensor networks have been introduced to offload computation-intensive tasks from lowpower IIoT devices, many deep learning models still require to be executed in IIoT devices due to security and privacy concerns (i.e., keep data locally). Therefore, there are exemplary challenges and issues which are yet to be addressed by researchers in order to achieve sustainable computing solutions by the mean of different architectures, protocols, methods and technologies in IIoT and wireless networks i.e. edge computing, federated learning, deep learning, privacy/security, spectrum sensing, blockchain technology and many more which are crucial in success of modern IIoT and wireless network systems.

Federated learning enables the application of secure mechanisms enabled by data privacy to support IIoT. Many scholars and experts have done tremendous work in this area and many researchers are active in the research field. This topic is also propounded with the effect in the context of Industry 4.0. However, the topic is quite new and has not been investigated under its different profiles until now. There is a lack of literature from both a theoretical and an empirical point of view. Therefore, this book is dedicated to provide cutting-edge technologies and novel studies, which can realize and elevate the effectiveness and advantages of federated learning for advancing industrial IoT.

The book has a collection of solicit original research articles and review articles highlighting recent advanced security and privacy techniques relevant to the convergence of federated learning in IIoT-based systems based in blockchain. We are glad that this book also gathers submissions discussing arising new challenges and opportunities from traditional federated learning architectures.

Sandeep Kautish
Lord Buddha Education Foundation, Nepal

Gaurav Dhiman
Government Bikram College of Commerce, India

Acknowledgment

I am delighted to welcome the readers of my new book *Demystifying Federated Learning for Blockchain and Industrial Internet of Things*. I congratulate all chapter authors for their valuable submissions and keeping patience during critical review process. I wish to thank all reviewers as well who spared their precious time for the review process.

I am thankful to my wife Yogita and son Devansh and my parents for giving me eternal happiness and support during the entire process.

Last but not the least, I am thankful to almighty god for blessing me with wonderful life and showing me right paths in my all ups and downs during the so far journey of life.

Sandeep Kautish

Chapter 1

Integration of Blockchain and IoT (BIoT):
Applications, Security Issues, and Challenges

Sushma Malik
Institute of Innovation in Technology and Management, Janakpuri, India

Anamika Rana
iD https://orcid.org/0000-0002-6201-7831
Maharaja Surajmal Institute, Delhi, India

ABSTRACT

The internet of technology (IoT) refers to the connectivity of smart devices with the internet to accumulate data and transfer it to smart devices. But with the lack of built-in security measures, IoT is vulnerable to privacy and security threats. Blockchain technology assists in the security needs of IoT devices. The main characteristics of blockchain technology like immutability, transparency, auditability, and encryption of data sort out the inadequacy of IoT devices. This chapter represents an inclusive survey on blockchain and IoT technologies with the integration of these technologies to overcome the shortfall. This chapter includes an overview of both technologies with their advantages and disadvantages. It also highlights the domains of their applications and represents the advantages of integration of blockchain and IoT technology to develop BIoT (blockchain-based IoT). Also, it analyzes the main challenges faced during the smooth integration of blockchain and IoT technologies.

DOI: 10.4018/978-1-6684-3733-9.ch001

Figure 1. Structure of blocks

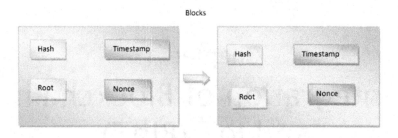

INTRODUCTION

Blockchain has a list of records which is called blocks. All the blocks are linked by using cryptographic techniques (Alphonse & Starvin, 2020). Blockchain can be defined as a transparent, trusted, and decentralized ledger on a peer-to-peer network and it is a virtual Bitcoin cryptocurrency invented by Satoshi Nakamoto in 2008. The transaction is the data unit on the Blockchain and certain numbers of transactions are bundled in a Block (N. Kumar & Aggarwal, 2020). The cryptographic hash value is calculated and placed in its next block along with the timestamp. Blockchain is a distributed and open ledger that records transactions very efficiently. The alteration of data in the blockchain is restricted (Bach et al., 2018). For all the participant's blockchain ledger is available to access but still not regulated by any network authorities and this can be possible by imposing strict rules and mutual agreement between the network nodes (Uddin et al., 2021). Each block in the blockchain has contained the hash value that stores the hash value of the previous block. Hash is a unique address of each block assigned during its creation and any modification in the block will lead to a change in its hash value. The root hash value for all the transactions is stored. The timestamp is stored as the creation time of the block and the Nonce value is ensuring that the present hash value is below the target shown in Figure 1.

Blockchain is the chain of blocks that enclose information. Digital documents are not possible to backdate or temper them because of this technology and double records problem are also sorted out since a central server is not required. Blockchain technology is used to transfer the items like money, property, contracts, and many more in a secure manner without the involvement of third parties like banks or the government. Data stored in blockchain are very hard to modify.

Blockchain is simply the correlation of three different technologies (Sharma et al., 2020):

Figure 2. Working of blocks

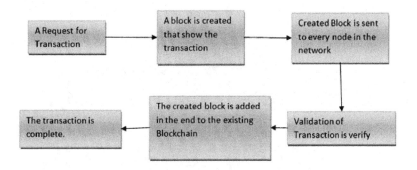

1. Internet,
2. Private key cryptography and
3. Protocol governing incentivization

This technology is distributed, decentralized, shared and immutable means stored data cannot be modified or wiped out from the database ledger were stored all the transaction records and the hash value of the previous block and also provide the global trust. Elliptic curve cryptography (ECC) and SHA 256 hashing algorithms are used to provide security by data authentication and integrity. Blockchain is a software protocol like SMTP which is used for email over the internet that's why blockchain cannot be run without the internet (Thompson, 2021).

Sometimes blockchain is replaced with bitcoin word but in reality, bitcoin is not the blockchain technology instead, blockchain technology is behind the bitcoin. Bitcoin is the digital token and blockchain is acts as the ledger used to store the information of bitcoins. Blockchain can be existing without bitcoin but the existence of bitcoin can be depending on the blockchain.

Working of Blockchain

A new block is created for any new record or transaction within the blockchain. After that created block is shared with each node of the block to verify the genuineness of the block. And after verifying the validity of the block, it is added at the end of the blockchain and it represents the completion of a transaction (Lastovetska, 2021). Figure 2 shows the working of blockchain.

Figure 3. Properties of blockchain

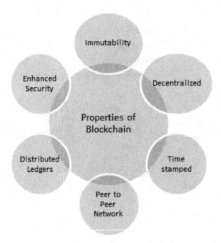

PROPERTIES OF BLOCKCHAIN

Blockchain is the technology that securely stores data. Figure 3 mainly highlight some properties of the blockchain (Alphonse & Starvin, 2020) (Zheng et al., 2017) like:

Immutability

Blockchain has a number of exciting features but among them, immutability is without any doubt is the key feature of blockchain technology. The meaning of immutability is something that cannot be modified or altered. Because of its feature, blockchain technology will remain as it is a permanent and unaltered network.

Decentralized

Another property of blockchain is decentralized as well as an open ledger which means that it has no single entity to control. In blockchain number of nodes work together to store the data and each and every node in the blockchain has the same copy of the ledger.

Time stamped

Blocks in the blockchain can store the timestamps like when it was created, updated and also store the information about who updated it.

Figure 4. Actors in blockchain

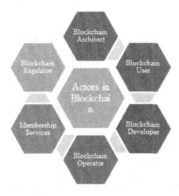

Peer to Peer Network

Blockchain technology provides the peer-to-peer network which means only two parties are involved in the transaction like the sender and the receiver by removing the third-party authorization. In peer to peer network, each node or block has able to authorize the transaction that's why no other party is required.

Enhanced Security

As per the decentralized property, blockchain has not any central authority to provide security. But to ensure the security of blockchain nodes is ensured by encryption methods like cryptography. This technique of encryption acts as the firewall for attacks. In simple terms, cryptography is a complex mathematical algorithm and hides the true nature of data on a network (Ferdous et al., 2020).

Distributed Ledgers

Blockchain is an open ledger which means every information of the user and transaction is available to all because the ledger is maintained by all users on the network which provides a better outcome.

Actors in a Blockchain

Actors are the main element of the blockchain and blockchain-based businesses are used these actors to provide the architecture and solutions. Now, most businesses are using blockchain technology to implement security and fast transactions in their

Figure 5. Functions of blockchain actors

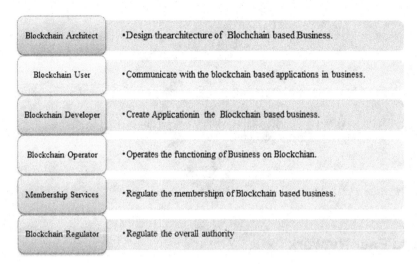

business (S. Aggarwal & Kumar, 2020). Actors of blockchain are listed in Figure 4 and their functions are highlighted in Figure 5.

Blockchain Architect: The responsibilities of a blockchain architect are to design the draft and provide the architecture of the blockchain-based business.

Blockchain User: The function can be done by the blockchain user in a business network and it interacts with the blockchain-based applications.

Blockchain Developer: After developing the architecture of the blockchain-based business; the blockchain developer will come to develop the applications based on the architecture.

Blockchain Operator: every blockchain-based business network has its blockchain operator whose main task is to manage, maintain, control, and monitor the blockchain network.

Blockchain Regulator: To regulate the overall authority in the blockchain-based business is done by the blockchain regulator.

Membership Services: Different kinds of certificates are required to run the blockchain-based business and it can be implemented by the membership services actors.

Components Used in a Blockchain

To accomplish the transactions in blockchain are required several components (S. Aggarwal & Kumar, 2020). The functionality and description of components are described in Figure 6 as:

Figure 6. Components in blockchain

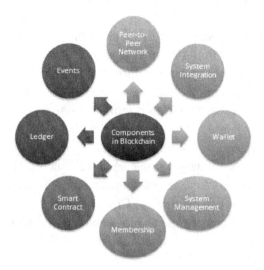

Ledger: It stores the data at each node on the network and contains the previous and current state of the data.

Smart Contract: It is the lines of codes that accumulate on the ledgers of the blockchain. These codes are executed automatically when predetermined terms and conditions are met up. People required these programs to run the applications on the network of blockchain.

Membership: To authenticate, authorize, and manage the identities on the blockchain network is required the permission of membership.

Peer-to-Peer Network: P2P network is the backbone of blockchain in which every node is connected to every other node and also shares the resources with other nodes of the network without the involvement of a third-party authenticator. In the network, all nodes are equally privileged in blockchain-based applications.

Events: In a blockchain network, create a notification of any operation like transaction execution, payment activation, etc is created by the event component. The internal processing of the organization controls the execution of the event.

System Management: This component of the blockchain has the potential to change, create, manage and also control the components of the blockchain.

Wallet: The wallet component is used to store the user's information securely and confidentially.

System Integration: System Integration is not part of blockchain but is used to integrate the blockchain with outside applications.

WHY BLOCKCHAIN TECHNOLOGY IS NEEDED?

There is any other way to accomplish the transactions without the involvement of online wallets, banks, and third-party applications? At that position, the answer is yes and it is possible only because of blockchain. Sometimes, transactions are failed in the traditional manner of banking because of many reasons like technical issues, account hacking, exceeding of daily transfer limit, transfer charges, and many more. Cryptocurrency is used to sort out these problems of the traditional mode of transactions. A cryptocurrency is a form of digital payment that can be used for products and services. Now many companies have issued their currencies which are called tokens and these tokens are used by the user to done the payment for the products and services for that companies. Cryptocurrency is the binary or virtual currencies that use a technology called a blockchain. Blockchain is a decentralized technology that spread across many nodes and these nodes are manage and record the transactions (Sharma et al., 2020).

The Layered Structure of Blockchain Technology

This section explains the layered structure of blockchain technology (Uddin et al., 2021). It consists of the five layers which are shown in Figure 9:

Application Layer

The application layer of blockchain technology contains smart contracts, chaincode, and dApps. The application layer includes the two sub-layers like

- **Presentation Layer:** This layer contains scripts, APIs, user interface, and these tools are used to connect both blockchain technology with the application layer.
- **Execution Layer:** This layer has smart contracts, chaincode, and underlying rules and gets the instructions from the presentation layer which runs transactions.

The main components of the application layer are:

1. **Smart Contract:** Smart contracts are simply program written in solidity language which executes o Ethereum runtime engine. It is simple lines of codes stored on a blockchain that execute when predetermined conditions are met. It automates the run of the program so that every user in the network get the result without the loss of time. It mechanizes a workflow and triggers the

next execution when the pre-set conditions are met. The transactions which are linked with smart contracts can affect the state change in the decentralized ledger (Uddin et al., 2021).

2. **Chaincode:** The lines of code that execute on the blockchain to apply the logic of business of how applications are interacting with the ledger is called the chain code. Each chain code has an isolated program that preserves its private state on the ledger. When a transaction is proposed, it triggers chain code to decide what change of state is applied to the ledger. The chain code can be accessed by REST APIs or SDK.

3. **dApps:** It means distributed web application. It executes on the technologies of blockchain like Ethereum and Bitcoin. Smart contracts and chain code are used by dApps to interact with the blockchain. It is not controlled by a single organization when ii is implemented on the network of blockchain.

The Data Layer

The data layer of blockchain has included transactions, blocks, hash functions, a Markle tree, and the digital signature for authentication. The main component of blockchain is blocked that are interlinked with each other. Block may consist of many transactions and a hash value of its immediately earlier block that helps to link the blocks. Blocks are can be traced with the help of this hash value and for that reason, alteration or modification in the blocks are not possible. A block can be portioned into two parts like transaction records and a header. Transaction records are maintained in a Merkle tree as shown in Figure 7. Merkle tree is a binary tree of data structure that sums up and helps to check the large data set efficiently and securely. Each node of the blockchain network is needed to maintain a complete copy of each transaction that takes place in the blockchain and help the user to check whether a transaction is included in a block or not. The header of the block may contain a hash value of the preceding block for authentication, a Merkle tree root, a Nonce that provides hash value, and a timestamp which refers to the created time of the block. The digital signature is used to authenticate the content on the digital platform. The digital signature is using the public key cryptography system which consists of the public and private keys for authentication of binary data.

The Consensus Layer

When a node in a blockchain network exchanges data no centralized body is present to monitor the transaction or prevent the alteration or modification of data on the block. The smooth sharing of information and avoiding fraud-related activities need a validation protocol which is known as a consensus algorithm. Several consensus algorithms that are implemented on this layer are listed in Figure 8.

Figure 7. Structure of Merkle Tree

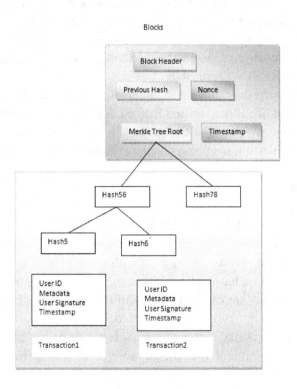

Figure 8. Consensus mechanism

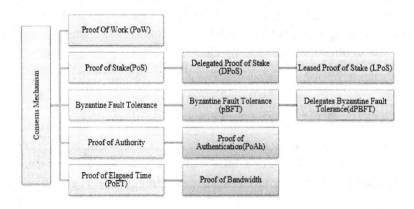

The Network Layer

The network layer is also called the peer-to-peer network which helps to communicate between nodes in the blockchain. With peer to peer network, all nodes in the blockchain network are easily tracked and help to connect each other blocks throughout the network. Peer to peer network is a network of computers which is called nodes that are distributed and network workload is also shared across the nodes. In peer to peer network of blockchain have two kinds of nodes:

The Full Node: It ensures the transactions and also checked and validated the blocks with rules set in the consensus mechanism. It stores the fully distributed ledger.

The Light Node: These nodes are making the transactions and after that send to the full node. It only stores the header of the blockchain. The sharding strategy is used to improve the performance of blockchain by partitioning a peer-to-peer network. Sharding is the splitting approach that is used to distribute computing and storage workloads on the network. Each node is not accountable for handling the whole network's transaction after implementing this approach but only handles the information related to its partition.

SECURITY FEATURES OF BLOCKCHAIN

A blockchain is a chain of blocks that have transactions records. Every block is connected which makes it difficult to alter or delete the single record. Some security features are highlighted as (Stephen & Alex, 2018) (Soni, 2019):

Ledger: Blockchain is using a ledger that stores every transaction. The ledger is immutable means data present in the ledger cannot be altered or deleted. Users can only able to read the data or information from the ledger.

Chain of Blocks: another main security feature of blockchain is a chain of blocks and each block should have a hash value. In blockchain technology, every block is connected by its preceding hash value. When any attacker modifies or deletes the data, at that time block hash value is also changed and it will affect the overall chain of blocks in the blockchain.

Decentralized: Blockchain technology is a decentralized application. Peer-to-peer communication between the nodes is done in blockchain technology. Each node in the network has a copy of the ledger and it authenticates the transaction. The transaction will be canceled if any of the nodes do not agree on a transaction.

Figure 9. Layered structure of blockchain

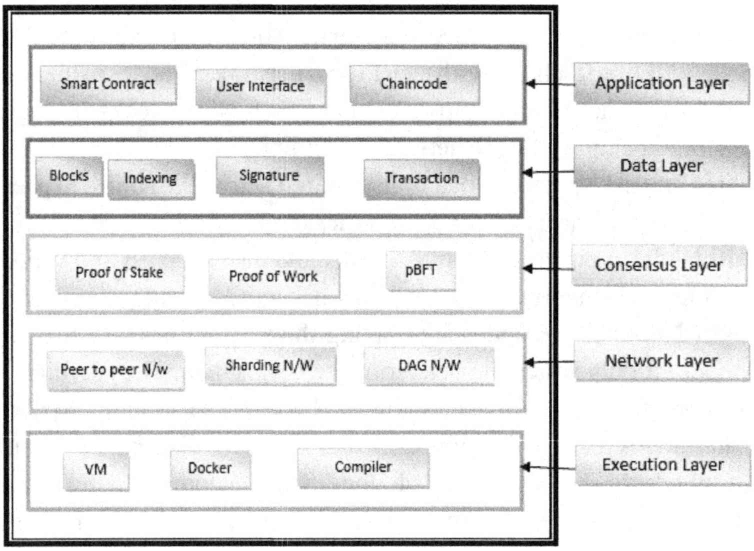

CHALLENGES

Blockchain technology come in 2009 and today it is one of the most revolutionizing technology. It is a distributed ledger that stores the transactions by nodes of the blockchain network. It is the most powerful technology of the 21st century but still adaptation of this technology is not easy. It faces a number of challenges during implementation, so it needs to overcome the challenges to accelerate its adoption. Some of the challenges are highlighted in Figure 10 and like (Chen, 2018):

Storage Capability: The storage capability of blocks in the blockchain has limited. It is not designed to store a large amount of data of transactions.

Low Scalability: The performance of the blockchain is affected and also increases the synchronization time as the size of the blockchain increase with the number of transactions. Blockchain technology works well for a limited number of users but does not give the best result when a mass integration will take place. As the number of user increase on the network, the transactions of blockchain consume large time to process and will also increase the transaction cost than usual. As blockchain is used because of its fast transaction process but it slows down when more users login to the system.

Security: Data is not secure in the blockchain network due to the decentralized structure of blockchain. And also third parties or Governments cannot regulate the functioning of blockchain.

Figure 10. Challenges of blockchain

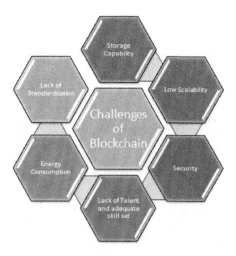

Lack of Talent and Adequate Skillset: To manage blockchain technology, adequate skilled persons are also required in addition to software and hardware. It is the emerging technology, that's why some people can support such kind of technology and handle it in very well manner.

Public Perception: The big challenge faced by blockchain technology is the lack of knowledge of technology by the public. A greater part of the public still does not have any knowledge of the existence and potential application of this emerging technology. The success of this technology is full depending on the acceptance of this technology by the users or public.

Lack of Standardization: No universal standard applies to blockchain technology as it uses a wide variety of networks. Due to lack of standardization, several issues like interoperability increased costs and impossible to adopt it on the mass level.

Energy Consumption: Blockchain technology required lots of computational power because it works on the Peer-to-Peer mechanism to validate the transactions and also add trust to the network.

APPLICATIONS OF BLOCKCHAIN

The application of blockchain is increasing day by day in every domain. Figure 11 highlights some domains or areas like healthcare, banking, real estate, social media, and many more where blockchain is implemented and worked properly (Sharma et al., 2020) (Al-saqqa & Almajali, 2020). Table 1 highlight the functions of blockchain technology in various domains.

Figure 11. Application domains of blockchain

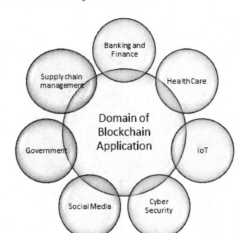

OVERVIEW OF INTERNET OF THINGS (IoT)

Internet of Things (IoT) comes into the picture when numerous devices integrate and initiate communication through the internet and become smart devices. The main point of IoT is the integration of the devices. These smart devices initially collect the data from the environment and after that share it on the network through the internet (Sharma et al., 2020). With the help of IoT technology, real-world objects are converted into an intelligent object of the virtual world (Bayani et al., 2018). This technology also helps in the control of the objects and updates the state of the objects and also provides the better accommodation of data. Internet of Things has a combination of two words: internet and things (Jalali et al., 2019).

Internet is the network of networks that help to communicate and sharing of information. Internet using the transmission control protocol (TCP). Internet protocol (IP) to connect the computers or devices. Many networks of private, public, and government organizations are connected with wired or wireless techniques. On the other hand, things are physically existing objects which present in the real world. These things are not only electronic gadgets but also the living and non-living objects of the real world (Alphonse & Starvin, 2020). The network will allow these things to collect data from the environment when these things are ingrained with software and sensors. The motive of IoT technology is the connectivity of the internet with electronic devices like smartphones, computers, tablets, smart TV to dumb devices like AC, microwave, fans, etc. IoT has the potential to make every object smart virtually and also high the standard of living of human beings by data collection,

Table 1. Application domains of blockchain

Domain	Application
Banking and Finance	• Digital Currency payment. • Core banking facilities like payment can be done with nominal or no fees. • Fast and secure transfer of payment among the clients. • Clearing and Trading • Bookkeeping
Health Care	• Maintain the database of the patients. • Help doctors and medical staff to retrieve the previous medical record of the patients. • Improve the functioning of the healthcare system. • Identification of disease is become fast and can be easily cured. • Digital health wallet.
IoT	• Data storage and trustworthy device connectivity. • Develop smart cities and smart homes. • Self Driving cars. • Drone and Personalized robots. • Digital Assistants. • Drone sensors networks in agriculture
Cyber Security	• Alteration of data is not possible. • Changes are reflected across all the nodes. • No one destroys the entire network.
Supply chain management	• Billing and data transfer. • Monitoring data. • Share Management. • Verify the chain of records.
Government	• Digitization of documents, contracts, and proof of ownership for transfers. • Launches welfare schemes. • Eliminate the middleman. • IP registration and exchange. • Registry and identification. • Prevent Tax fraud.
Social Media	• Identify and verify the source of data on the social platform. • Prevent the spread of fake information and news.

AI algorithms, and networks (Sharma et al., 2020). IoT platform using the number of elements to design it like (Sarmah et al., 2017):

Hardware: These are the collection of various kinds of sensors that are used to sense or collect the data from the external environment and also the communication hardware like modems for the internet and Wi-Fi.

Middleware: The middleware element has a collection of data analytical tools which analyze the collected data from the sensors and use the cloud for the storage of data.

Presentation: After the analysis of data, information can be delivered to the end-user by using this element. This element may conations the number of applications.

Characteristics of IoT

Internet of Things is the collection or integration of things/objected via the internet. IoT devices have numerous characteristics, some are listed here like (Sarmah et al., 2017):

Data: Data is the main characteristic of IoT that is shared among the objects or things in the IoT environment.

Connectivity: In the IoT environment, IoT devices and hardware with sensors are connected via a communication medium like the internet, Wi-Fi, or Bluetooth to share the data.

Things: Any physical world objects which become capable to share data via sensors have become things.

Heterogeneity: Due to different kinds of hardware platforms and networks, devices in IoT technology are heterogeneous.

Communication: In the IoT platform, things are connected for the communication motive. Things are sharing the data that can be analyzed. Communication may be for short distances via Bluetooth or for long-distance via internet or Wi-Fi.

Dynamic Changes: The things over the IoT platform have rapidly changed their states for example connected or disconnected as well as many devices are also changing dynamically.

ARCHITECTURE OF INTERNET OF THINGS

IoT is the combination of things over the network. With the help of IoT, the non-living things are also become active and help in the collection of data from the environment and become smart things. The IoT technology provides the potential to transform the functionality of the system and business by not only implementing the automation but also providing deep visibility driven by lots of data collection, analyzed that collected data, and acting on that basis without human interaction (S. Kumar et al., 2019). Four basic components govern the IoT system which are listed as and shown in Figure 12.

1. **Sensors or Devices:** The main components of IoT technology are sensors that help to collect data from the environment are sensors or devices. Sensors are taking inputs from the environment and transmitting the collected data for processing. Business owners make the right decision at the right time after analyzing the collected data from sensors that are implemented in the business and also help the clients to use the business products and services efficiently.

Figure 12. Architecture of IoT

A device can have many sensors like a smartphone has numerous sensors like GPS, camera, fingerprints, and many more (Sharma et al., 2020).

2. **Connectivity:** The collected data from the sensors of different devices are sent to the cloud infrastructure for storage and analysis. The connectivity between the smart devices and the cloud can be implemented in different communication of mediums like mobile phones, satellite networks, Bluetooth, Wi-Fi, WAN, and many more (Sharma et al., 2020).

3. **Cloud:** Cloud is the storage space of data collected through the sensors from the environment. It is a centralized system that assists to provide data to data centers through the internet. Processing of data is also implemented here. Cloud needs the software that helps to process the collected data. It can be simple as checking the temperature of the object after analyzing the collected data from the temperature sensor to the complex task of identifying objects and using computer vision on video (Sharma et al., 2020).

4. **User Interface:** The user interface is needed to provide the information to the end-user by sending a text message or email or activating an alarm. Ender users required an interface to communicate with the IoT systems. For example, let a user want to start the home AC and want to adjust the temperature of the AC on the way to home from the office and this can be easily implemented by using their mobile phone and chilling the room without the presence in the home (Sharma et al., 2020).

How Do Devices Act Like Smart Devices?

A normal device can be transformed into a smart device by interacting with the physical world by collecting the data with wireless communication technologies like RFID, Bluetooth, and Wi-Fi or with the implementation of sensors. For example, an ordinary mobile may become smart mobile via the internet and help to determine the path of destination by GPS, perform many functions with the help of applications, using touch sensors to provide input, voice sensors to detect and identify the voice with calling and messages. These smart devices are generating a huge amount of data and that data can be stored on the clouds and to provide the right decision at right time using the genetic algorithms, AI, and neural network for processing and analyzing. Reliable devices are required to make sure about the authentication of data and prevent unauthorized access.

APPLICATIONS OF INTERNET OF THINGS

Smart Home: A normal home is converted into a smart home by the implementation of internet and Wi-Fi connectivity. For example, the Google Home voice controller facilitates the user to control the lights of the home, TV, and speakers are controlled by the user's voice and many more. Same Amazon echo plus is also work on the voice instructions of the user like playing songs, making calls and messaging, providing information based on question, and many more. Another IoT application in a smart home is doorbell cams that constantly check the movement in the house from the door and the user can give the answer from anywhere (Sharma et al., 2020).

Wearable: Wearable industry is the first industry who adopt IoT technology at its services. Nowadays Fit Bits, Heart rate monitors, and smartwatches are used by many users.

Smart City: With the implementation of the internet in the city, the normal city can act as a smart city. Vital tasks like Traffic management, waste management, electricity management, and many more task are implemented easily by the deployment of IoT technology and also eliminating some day-to-day challenges faced by users (Atlam & Wills, 2018).

Telehealth: Telehealth and telemedicine become an essential need these days because of the corona pandemic after 2020. In this pandemic time, patients are not able to visit hospitals but this problem is solved by telehealth. With this technology, patients and doctors are easily communicating with each other.

Smart Grid: Smart grid is the best application of IoT technology. It enables the existing and new gridlines to reduce wastage of electricity and also minimize the cost.

Agriculture: Agriculture is also the one sector which not remain affected by IoT technology. IoT-enabled tools like Drip Irrigation; drones for farm surveillance are used by the farmers. With these tools, farmers have more production in the crops and also help in the care.

Connected Car: IoT technology is also playing a vital role in the automobile industry. The parking sensor is the best example. It basically identifies the real-time accessibility of parking places.

Figure 13. Advantages and disadvantages of IoT technology

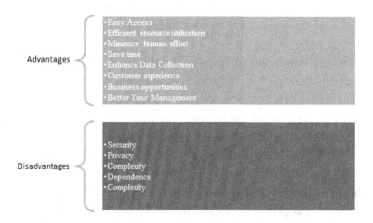

Advantages and Disadvantages of IoT

Today's available technologies are not touched their 100% capability. Each technology has faced some gaps to go. IoT technology has helped other technologies to reach its accurate and 100% capability. The present context elucidates the pros and cons of IoT technology in Figure 13.

IOT SECURITY, PRIVACY, THREATS AND CHALLENGES

Our lifestyles have transformed as a result of the Internet of Things age. Although the Internet of Things has many advantages, it is vulnerable to a variety of security dangers in our daily lives. The majority of security threats are related to data leaking and service disruption. The physical security risk is directly affected by security threats in IoT. The Internet of Things (IoT) is made up of a variety of devices and platforms, each with its own set of credentials, and each system has its own set of security requirements. Because a lot of personal information is transferred among various types of devices, the user's privacy is also very crucial. As a result, a secure technique is required to safeguard personal information.

Furthermore, for IoT services, there are a variety of devices that communicate across various networks. It implies that there are numerous security vulnerabilities relating to user privacy and the network layer. User privacy can also be discovered through a variety of methods. The following are some IoT security threats:

Data Protection from End-to-End (E2E): End-to-end data protection is offered throughout a comprehensive network to assure data security in an IoT environment.

Data is collected from various devices that are connected to one another and shared quickly with other devices. As a result, a framework is needed to safeguard data, maintain data confidentiality, and manage information privacy across the data life cycle.

Secure Thing Planning: The IoT's interconnection and communication among devices varies depending on the situation. As a result, the devices must be capable of maintaining a high level of security. When local devices and sensors in a home-based network communicate safely with one another, their communication with external devices should follow the same security rules.

Visible/Usable Security and Privacy: Misconfiguration of users causes the majority of security and privacy concerns. Users will find it extremely difficult and unreasonable to implement such privacy policies and extensive security mechanisms. Selecting security and privacy policies that may apply automatically is required.

IoT Challenges

The most significant difficulty with IoT is security. Industrial, commercial, consumer, or personal data could be used in IoT applications. This application's data must be kept secure and protected against theft and tampering. The Internet of Things improves device connection, but there are still challenges with scalability, availability, and reaction time. When data is securely transported over the internet, security is an issue. Government legislation may be used to apply safety measures while transporting data across international borders. The most essential security concerns pertinent to IoT are covered among various security challenges (Aldowah et al., 2019) are as listed if figure 14.

INTEGRATION OF BLOCKCHAIN AND IOT TECHNOLOGY

The motivation of this section is to explain the collaboration of two above-mentioned technologies like IoT and Blockchain which are referred to as Blockchain-based IoT (BIoT). Millions of heterogeneous IoT devices are generating a huge amount of data and need a technology that provides security to that data. This security problem of data is solved by the integration of IoT and blockchain technologies. Decentralized characteristics of blockchain technology help to eliminate the shortcoming linked with centralized architecture-based systems. IoT technology help to reduce the size of the objects and blockchain technology help to provide security to the data collected by IoT devices. Digital cameras, sensors, or smartphones are some IoT-based devices that provide gigantic large networks by device-to-device interactions. IoT technology has to face the challenge of trust where every device has access to data and will

Figure 14. IoT challenges

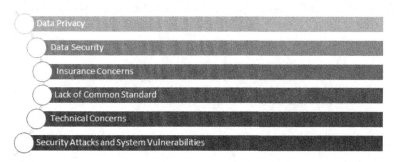

authenticate that the data is tamper by any device or node. BIoT integration can increase the data sharing between the IoT devices by providing security to data. IoT devices are required to share reliable data in the system and will ultimately improve performance. Integration of these two technologies allows users to get the benefit of both technologies more efficiently and powerfully (Sharma et al., 2020) (Reyna et al., 2018) shown in Figure 15. Blockchain technology improves the function of IoT technology by providing trustable services because blockchain data is reliable and also easy traceable. It increases security because data sources are recognized at any time and data remains immutable. In applications where the security of data is the main concern, the integration of technologies will provide a guaranty that the data will be shared between the trustworthy user (Tandon, 2019). So the integration of these two emerging technologies would represent a key revolution (Tandon, 2019). Some advantages of BIoT are listed in Figure 16. Table 2 listed some related work on the integration of IoT with the Blockchain technology.

Issues and Challenges Face During Integration of Blockchain and IoT Technologies

Integration of both emerging technologies like blockchain and IoT provides permission to users to take pleasure in both technologies more efficiently and powerfully. But some issues and challenges are faced during the integration of blockchain and IoT technology shown in Figure 17 like:

1. **Data concurrency and throughput issue:** IoT devices are constantly streaming data but blockchain throughput is limited because of its cryptographic security protocol. High bandwidth is needed to add a new block to the blockchain

network. That's why the challenge is faced to boost the throughput of blockchain to fulfill the need for frequent transactions in IoT systems (Panarello et al., 2018).

Figure 15. IoT-blockchain interaction

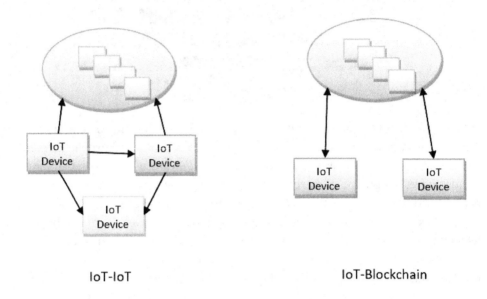

Figure 16. Advantages of BIoT

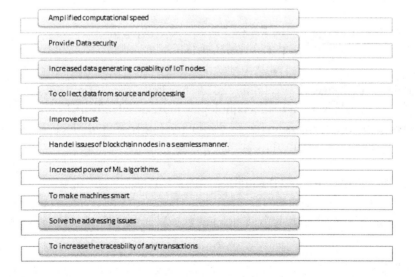

Table 2. Related work on integration of blockchain and IoT technologies

S.No	Reference	Description
1.	(Villegas-ch et al., 2020)	Integration of blockchain and IoT technologies are implemented on the campus to make the smart campus. During the COVID-19, all the education centers are closed, but with this BIoT technology, all the people on the campus are easily connected and also share their data in a secure manner.
2	(V. K. Aggarwal et al., 2021)	Services are easily shared between the users after the integration of blockchain and IoT.
3	(Porkodi & Kesavaraja, 2020) (Nehra et al., 2020)	IoT devices are integrated with blockchain technology to increase security and privacy. And also using less computation power with increasing the throughput.
4	(Puri et al., 2020)	Integration of IoT and blockchain technology has opened new prospects towards IoV development. This combination increases the IoV services like insurance of vehicles, road, and life safety.
5	(Banerjee, 2019)	In the supply chain and logistics domain, the integration of IoT and Blockchain technology has played a significant role. Problems like auto supply chain, product or order tracking, and traceability and distribution supply chain are easily sorted out by the combination of IoT and Blockchain technologies.
6	(Latif et al., 2021)	Blockchain technology plays a vital role in the Industrial Internet of Things (IIoT) by removing the centralized architecture and ensuring secure and trustworthy industrial operations.
7	(Panarello et al., 2018) (Atlam & Wills, 2018)	Integration of Blockchain and IoT technology sort out the inadequacy of IoT technology like immutability, transparency, auditability, and encryption of data.
8	(Hassan et al., 2019)	IoT technology plays a vital role in our daily life. Because of its centralized nature, some challenges like security, authentications have come into action but blockchain technology came to overcome these challenges.
9	(Hassan et al., 2019)	The fusion of blockchain and IoT technologies is named the blockchain of Things (BCoT). In which both technologies are getting the benefit from each other in a reciprocal manner.
10	(Hassan et al., 2019)	The security of IoT technology will integrate with blockchain technology to develop a system more reliable and stable.

2. **Handling Big data on the Blockchain:** Each block in the blockchain network maintains a local copy of the distributed ledger. When the new block is added to the network, then each node of the entire network needs to add the new block to their local ledger. IoT technology puts a burden on block storage space. Therefore, the integration of these technologies faces the challenge of more data storage space.

3. **Real-Time Data**: IoT devices are generating real-time data which can cause a limitation for BIoT.

4. **Transparency and Privacy:** Blockchain technology provides transparency and privacy to the data but in the IoT network, IoT devices can access the data and maybe modify it. So to implement transparency and privacy to the data in BIoT, need to design a cost-effective access control for IoT devices in BIoT.
5. **Connectivity challenge of IoT:** High computing storage and networking resources are needed to share IoT data. That's why IoT technology has limited capabilities to integrate with blockchain technology to provide new openings in the various domains (Tandon, 2019).
6. **Energy Efficiency:** Both blockchain and IoT technologies needs continuous power consumption to fulfill their work (V. K. Aggarwal et al., 2021).
7. **Lack of skills:** Both technologies are not well known by the user globally. Therefore it is also a challenge to find trained people who know both technologies (V. K. Aggarwal et al., 2021).

CONCLUSION

With the development of technologies, the Internet of Things (IoT) will progressively integrate with other technologies like AI, Big data, Cloud Computing, Deep Learning, Blockchain, and many more. IoT technology will integrate with Blockchain technology to implement more security and build systems and information more reliable. The decentralization features of both technologies help in the integration of these technologies. Blockchain technology provides reliable data interaction, complete data storage, authentication of nodes in the IoT technology which can help to access authentication, data protection on a large number of IoT devices. The consensus mechanism and decentralized nature of blockchain technology provide a secure and scalable atmosphere for IoT technology to implement distributed databases and consistent architecture. By the integration of IoT with Blockchain technology implement prevent security attacks and privacy breaches.

Figure 17. Issues and challenges face during integration of blockchain and IoT technologies

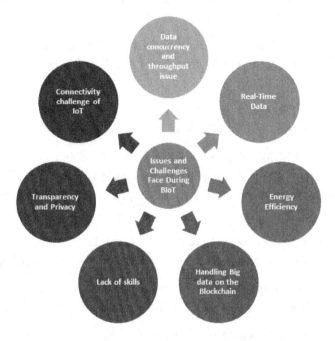

REFERENCES

Aggarwal, S., & Kumar, N. (2020). Blockchain components. In *The Blockchain Technology for Secure and Smart Applications across Industry Verticals* (1st ed.). Elsevier Inc. doi:10.1016/bs.adcom.2020.08.019

Aggarwal, V. K., Sharma, N., Kaushik, I., & Bhushan, B. (2021). *Integration of Blockchain and IoT (B-IoT): Architecture, Solutions, & Future Research Direction Integration of Blockchain and IoT (B-IoT)*. Architecture, Solutions, & Future Research Direction. doi:10.1088/1757-899X/1022/1/012103

Al-saqqa, S., & Almajali, S. (2020). *Blockchain Technology Consensus Algorithms and Applications: A Survey Types of Blockchain*. Academic Press.

Aldowah, H., Ul Rehman, S., & Umar, I. (2019). Security in internet of things: Issues, challenges and solutions. In Advances in Intelligent Systems and Computing (Vol. 843). Springer International Publishing. doi:10.1007/978-3-319-99007-1_38

Alphonse, A. S., & Starvin, M. S. (2020). Blockchain and Internet of Things: An Overview. In Handbook of Research on Blockchain Technology. Inc. doi:10.1016/B978-0-12-819816-2.00012-5

Atlam, H. F., & Wills, G. B. (2018). Technical aspects of blockchain and IoT. In *Role of Blockchain Technology in IoT Applications* (1st ed.). Elsevier Inc., doi:10.1016/bs.adcom.2018.10.006

Bach, L., Mihaljevic, B., & Zagar, M. (2018). Comparitive Analysis of Blockchain Consensus Algorithms. *MIPRO*, 1545–1550.

Banerjee, A. (2019). Blockchain with IOT: Applications and use cases for a new paradigm of supply chain driving efficiency and cost. In Role of Blockchain Technology in IoT Applications (1st ed., Vol. 115). Elsevier Inc. doi:10.1016/bs.adcom.2019.07.007

Bayani, M., Leiton, K., Loaiza, M., & Automation, I. L. (2018). *Internet of things (IoT) advantages on e-learning in the smart original research*. Academic Press.

Chen, X. (2018). *Blockchain challenges and opportunities : A survey Zibin Zheng and Shaoan Xie Hong-Ning Dai Huaimin Wang*. Academic Press.

Ferdous, S., Jabed, M., Chowdhury, M., Hoque, M. A., & Colman, A. (2020). Blockchain Consensus Algorithms. *Survey (London, England)*, 1–39.

Hassan, M. U., Rehmani, M. H., & Chen, J. (2019). Privacy preservation in blockchain based IoT systems: Integration issues, prospects, challenges, and future research directions. *Future Generation Computer Systems*, 97, 512–529. doi:10.1016/j.future.2019.02.060

Jalali, M. S., Kaiser, J. P., Siegel, M., & Madnick, S. (2019). The Internet of Things Promises New Bencfits and Risks A Systematic Analysis of Adoption Dynamics of IoT Products. *IEEE Security and Privacy*, 17(April), 39–48. doi:10.1109/MSEC.2018.2888780

Kumar, N., & Aggarwal, S. (2020). Architecture of blockchain. In *The Blockchain Technology for Secure and Smart Applications across Industry Verticals* (1st ed.). Elsevier Inc., doi:10.1016/bs.adcom.2020.08.009

Kumar, S., Tiwari, P., & Zymbler, M. (2019). Internet of Things is a revolutionary approach for future technology enhancement : A review. *Journal of Big Data*, 6(1), 111. Advance online publication. doi:10.118640537-019-0268-2

Lastovetska, A. (2021, August 25). *Blockchain Architecture Explained: How It Works & How to Build*. https://mlsdev.com/blog/156-how-to-build-your-own-blockchain-architecture

Latif, S., Idrees, Z., Ahmad, J., Zheng, L., & Zou, Z. (2021). Journal of Industrial Information Integration A blockchain-based architecture for secure and trustworthy operations in the industrial Internet of Things. *Journal of Industrial Information Integration, 21*(December), 100190. doi:10.1016/j.jii.2020.100190

Nehra, V., Sharma, A. K., & Tripathi, R. K. (2020). Blockchain Implementation for Internet of Things Applications. In *Handbook of Research on Blockchain Technology*. INC. doi:10.1016/B978-0-12-819816-2.00005-8

Panarello, A., Tapas, N., Merlino, G., Longo, F., & Puliafito, A. (2018). Blockchain and iot integration: A systematic survey. In Sensors (Switzerland) (Vol. 18, Issue 8). MDPI AG. doi:10.339018082575

Porkodi, S., & Kesavaraja, D. (2020). Integration of Blockchain and Internet of Things. In *Handbook of Research on Blockchain Technology*. INC. doi:10.1016/B978-0-12-819816-2.00003-4

Puri, V., Kumar, R., Van Le, C., Sharma, R., & Priyadarshini, I. (2020). A Vital Role of Blockchain Technology Toward Internet of Vehicles. In *Handbook of Research on Blockchain Technology*. INC. doi:10.1016/B978-0-12-819816-2.00016-2

Reyna, A., Martín, C., Chen, J., Soler, E., & Díaz, M. (2018). On blockchain and its integration with IoT. Challenges and opportunities. *Future Generation Computer Systems, 88*, 173–190. doi:10.1016/j.future.2018.05.046

Sarmah, A., Baruah, K. K., & Baruah, A. J. (2017). *A Brief Review on Internet of Things*. Academic Press.

Sharma, D. K., Kaushik, A. K., Goel, A., & Bhargava, S. (2020). Internet of Things and Blockchain: Integration, Need, Challenges, Applications, and Future Scope. In *Handbook of Research on Blockchain Technology*. INC. doi:10.1016/B978-0-12-819816-2.00011-3

Soni, S. (2019). *A Comprehensive survey on Blockchain : Working, security analysis, privacy threats and potential applications*. Academic Press.

Stephen, R., & Alex, A. (2018). A Review on BlockChain Security. *IOP Conference Series. Materials Science and Engineering, 396*(1), 012030. Advance online publication. doi:10.1088/1757-899X/396/1/012030

Tandon, A. (2019). Challenges of Integrating Blockchain with Internet of Things. *Challenges of Integrating Blockchain with Internet of Things.*, 9(9S3), 1476–1489. doi:10.35940/ijitee.I3311.0789S319

Thompson, B. (2021, August 28). *Blockchain Tutorial: Learn Blockchain Technology (Examples).* https://www.guru99.com/blockchain-tutorial.html

Uddin, M. A., Stranieri, A., Gondal, I., & Balasubramanian, V. (2021). A Survey on the Adoption of Blockchain in IoT: Challenges and Solutions. *Blockchain: Research and Applications*, 100006(2). Advance online publication. doi:10.1016/j.bcra.2021.100006

Villegas-ch, W., Palacios-pacheco, X., & Román-cañizares, M. (2020). *Integration of IoT and Blockchain to in the Processes of a University Campus.* doi:10.3390/su12124970

Zheng, Z., Xie, S., Dai, H., Chen, X., & Wang, H. (2017). *An Overview of Blockchain Technology : Architecture.* Consensus, and Future Trends. doi:10.1109/BigDataCongress.2017.85

ADDITIONAL READING

Fortino, G., Messina, F., Rosaci, D., & Sarné, G. M. L. (2020). Using Blockchain in a Reputation-Based Model for Grouping Agents in the Internet of Things. *IEEE Transactions on Engineering Management*, 67(4), 1231–1243. doi:10.1109/TEM.2019.2918162

Gharibi, M., Boutaba, R., & Waslander, S. L. (2016). Internet of Drones. *IEEE Access: Practical Innovations, Open Solutions*, 4, 1148–1162. doi:10.1109/ACCESS.2016.2537208

Goyal, S., Sharma, N., Kaushik, I., Bhushan, B., & Kumar, A. (2020). Precedence & issues of IoT based on edge computing. *Proceedings - 2020 IEEE 9th International Conference on Communication Systems and Network Technologies, CSNT 2020*, 72–77. 10.1109/CSNT48778.2020.9115789

Li, H., Lu, R., Misic, J., & Mahmoud, M. (2018). Security and Privacy of Connected Vehicular Cloud Computing. *IEEE Network*, 32(3), 4–6. doi:10.1109/MNET.2018.8370870

Misra, S., Deb, P. K., Pathak, N., & Mukherjee, A. (2020). Blockchain-enabled SDN for securing fog-based resource-constrained IoT. *IEEE INFOCOM 2020 - IEEE Conference on Computer Communications Workshops, INFOCOM WKSHPS 2020*, 490–495. 10.1109/INFOCOMWKSHPS50562.2020.9162706

Pedrosa, A. R., & Pau, G. (2018). ChargeItUp: On blockchain-based technologies for autonomous vehicles. *CRYBLOCK 2018 - Proceedings of the 1st Workshop on Cryptocurrencies and Blockchains for Distributed Systems, Part of MobiSys 2018*, 87–92. 10.1145/3211933.3211949

Rudra, B. (2020). Impact of Blockchain for Internet of Things Security. *Cryptocurrencies and Blockchain Technology Applications*, 99–127. doi:10.1002/9781119621201.ch6

Srivastava, G., Crichigno, J., & Dhar, S. (2019). A Light and Secure Healthcare Blockchain for IoT Medical Devices. *2019 IEEE Canadian Conference of Electrical and Computer Engineering, CCECE 2019*, 1–5. 10.1109/CCECE.2019.8861593

Uddin, M. A., Stranieri, A., Gondal, I., & Balasubramanian, V. (2021). A survey on the adoption of blockchain in IoT: Challenges and solutions. *Blockchain: Research and Applications*, *2*(2), 100006. doi:10.1016/j.bcra.2021.100006

Xie, L., Ding, Y., Yang, H., & Wang, X. (2019). Blockchain-based secure and trustworthy internet of things in SDN-enabled 5G-VANETs. *IEEE Access: Practical Innovations, Open Solutions*, *7*(c), 56656–56666. doi:10.1109/ACCESS.2019.2913682

Zhong, L., Wu, Q., Xie, J., Guan, Z., & Qin, B. (2019). A secure large-scale instant payment system based on blockchain. *Computers & Security*, *84*, 349–364. doi:10.1016/j.cose.2019.04.007

KEY TERMS AND DEFINITIONS

Big Data: Big data is a vast collection of information that continues to grow exponentially over time. It's a data set that's so large and complex that traditional data management tools can't store or analyze it efficiently. The difference between big data and regular data is that big data is substantially greater.

Bitcoin: Bitcoin is a cryptocurrency or virtual currency, that is supposed to operate as money and a form of payment while being independent of any single person, group, or entity, obviating the need for third-party involvement in financial transactions.

Blockchain: A blockchain is a distributed database that is shared across nodes in a computer network. A blockchain is a database that stores data in a digital manner. Blockchains are well-known for their role in maintaining a secure and decentralized record of transactions in cryptocurrency systems such as Bitcoin. The blockchain's unique feature is that it maintains data record integrity and security while also building confidence without the need for a trusted third party.

Cloud: The phrase "cloud" refers to servers that are accessible over the Internet, as well as the software and databases that run on them. Many data centers throughout the world host cloud servers.

Cryptocurrency: Any sort of digital or virtual currency that uses encryption to secure transactions is referred to as cryptocurrency. Cryptocurrencies work without a central authority issuing or controlling them, instead relying on a decentralised system to track transactions and create new units.

Internet of Things (IoT): The internet of things, or IoT, is a network of networked computers devices, mechanical and digital machinery, goods, animals, and people with unique identifiers (UIDs) and the ability to transfer data without human or computer contact.

Ledger: A ledger is a sort of record that is shared, copied, and synchronized across decentralised network members. The distributed ledger keeps track of transactions between network participants, such as the exchange of assets or data.

Peer-to-Peer Network: A peer-to-peer (P2P) network is a decentralised communication architecture in which two peers, referred to as nodes, can communicate with each other without the use of a central server.

Protocol: A protocol is a set of rules for formatting and processing data in networking. Computer protocols are similar to a common language. Although the software and hardware used by the computers in a network may differ greatly, protocols allow them to communicate with one another.

Sensors: A sensor is a device that detects physical input from its surroundings and transforms this into facts that can be evaluated by humans or machines.

Chapter 2
Application of Blockchain in Educational Big Data

S. B. Goyal

https://orcid.org/0000-0002-8411-7630
City University, Malaysia

Pradeep Bedi

https://orcid.org/0000-0003-1708-6237
Galgotias University, India

Jugnesh Kumar
St. Andrews Institute of Technology and Management, India

ABSTRACT

With the rapid development of big data technologies, their applications are growing rapidly. Conventional big data management is vulnerable. If any tampering occurs over stored database or sometimes untrusted data gathering occurs, then it causes serious issues with conventional data management. To resolve these problems, this chapter is focused on the development of blockchain technology for secure educational big data (EBD). Blockchain techniques divide the data blocks into secure data blocks using cryptography algorithms. The secure data blocks are connected in the chain with each other. This ensures security as well as flexibility. So, in this chapter, the proposed methodology had adopted blockchain technology and ensures its efficiency due to its decentralized and flexible approach.

INTRODUCTION

Growing demand and Internet development for things and big data encourage a

DOI: 10.4018/978-1-6684-3733-9.ch002

scientific measurement concept and discovery. Big data is a collection of strategies that could assist with the continuous assessment and transformation of the higher education system to meet the rapid speed of evolving developments in various sectors of the economy, which in turn generates a range of employee skills. Technology is an essential component that has radically altered how education is delivered. For example, mobile equipment, remote access systems and conference calling, academic platforms and services, etc. Teachers, students, academics evaluation experts, decision-makers interact, and researchers, including different types of technology used in education. These are aimed at affecting and enhancing learning and teaching and reflecting the use of modern technologies in real learning environments realistically. Large quantities of data are created through contact with these technologies, ranging from a single access log file to institutional-level operations. Educational systems, however, are not yet fully prepared to address them and use them to improve their continued quality (Qin, 2015). It is more pressing than ever that challenges be regulated within the education system. During the duration of the investigation and use of knowledge discovery, various options such as big data and analytics were indeed considered.

Big Data and Education

To explain and characterize the recent development and nature of massive data sets, Big Data (Bedi et al 2021) is now commonly used. In many sectors, it is found. There is constant receipt of large volumes of data from diverse sources and in different formats generated by the public, corporate, and social sectors. In certain situations, the information is exceptionally massive, such as petabytes that surpass the warehouse's structural or material capital, are handled and processed and are thus referred to as deep learning. Sector by sector or, in general, within the same sector, department by department (Qin, 2015). Because of its attribute of becoming huge, big data is referred to as such. Big data is therefore distinguished by additional features, including the various forms and ways and the distinct information streams, and the pace at which they are generated and, quite significantly, either by the intensity at which it is gathered. They are commonly extracted or often handled in actuality. They all have volume (size) and a wide range (sources, ways, and types) as well as pace (speed and frequency), illustrating and presenting challenges to data that would be another issue (Xuejuan, 2015).

When the number, diversity, and speed are high simultaneously, data in a particular system or domain is called big data, irrespective of whether all three of such features may be deemed 'tiny' for the text field. The data can vary between megabytes and petabytes, depending on the domain. Therefore, large data is context-specific and could refer to different types and sizes from one domain to the next. This is sufficient throughout this situation to question the limitations on how the information could be interpreted and evaluated so that it could be used only for multiple purposes. However, interpreting the data by analyzing it at a higher predictive rate and facilitating the development of data-driven systems and practices is the challenge common to all these areas (Abu et al., 2019).

Large amounts of data and analytics have brought benefits to results in various situations, thus providing an immensely helpful strategy in their possible impact on education, analysis methods in the area of business intelligence and analysis (Toivonen et al., 2019), or the field of professional data mining technologies (Miah et al., 2020). Due to the small analysis towards the use of Big Data and analysis in educational standards, we are looking to launch the user to the different territory of Big Data in academia where Data Analysis is integrated into technology, and also how information curriculum could be presented to different teams, such as politicians, assessment specialists, faculty, in different aspects and perspectives.

Educational Big Data (EBD)

Higher education is one area in which data contain volume, diversity, and speed. Massive volumes of educational data are gathered and generated daily in the higher learning environment from various sources and formats. Education data ranges from what comes through its use and engagement with learning analytics and networks by learners to active learning and course information that involves a curriculum such as learning materials, learning goals, test outcomes, activities, and a separate category of data related to processes and procedures for administrative, instructional, and quality improvement (Li, 2020).

Quite precisely, a few of the fields found wherein Large Knowledge management Systems are implemented adequately for higher education research and development are the program and its materials, as a major component of Global Academic Data (Li, 2020). In the context of teaching and learning, the restricted use of big data in academic achievement, as well as the scale and scope of such data, implies that particular strategies need to be applied to discover the valuable new information that is currently concealed in the data (Zhang et al., 2020). Such approaches could be extracted and modified from several other fields that are dominated by data analytics and used effectively to exploit big data in the curriculum. These methods will be used to allow us to experience student academic achievement strategies, and also, It can be dramatically influenced by explaining areas of large education data, such as children's real skills based on the curriculum taught (Yu et al., 2019). Together, Data technology has shown the ability to facilitate different higher education activities at this time. These activities include "administrative decision-making and institutional distribution of resources," preventing individuals at risk through failing to recognize them early, developing successful teaching strategies, and transforming the conventional view of the program to rethink it as a pattern of interactions and links between various data individuals collected and frequently generated from LMS.

Objectives of EBD

- Prediction and identification of student learning behavior.
- We are improving the learning experience.
- Identification of student progress and teaching pattern of faculty.
- To design and develop a course structure and its impact on learning.
- Development of a learning model by application of data mining or machine learning.
- It helps to improve the administrative structure, and organize resources.
- It helps to improve curricular effectiveness.

Blockchain in Educational Big Data

Blockchain was introduced in 2008 as an emerging technology. It was initially used in the registry of Bitcoin cryptocurrency transactions as a peer-to-peer ledger (Memon et al., 2019). The goal is to eliminate any third-party agents and to encourage people to monitor their financial affairs. Cryptocurrency has been established as a distributed network of peer nodes. The transaction replica in each of the nodes on the Network is provided by (1) the entrance in its booklet is written when it is supported from either device in the System, (2) the activity by its users is simulcast to several other nodes within the Network, and (3) the booklet is verified regularly to be the same as the booklet held on the Network. Researchers and practitioners are realizing the enormous significance of its underlying technology as Bitcoin continues to grow in popularity (Gatteschi et al., 2018). In cryptocurrencies, as well as in many other fields, Block chain's unique capacity, including immutability, transparency, and confidence, is useful. The number of cryptocurrency technologies has, however, become built-in in different fields (Chen et al., 2018), (Nwosu et. al 2021).

The main purpose of this paper is to examine blockchain technologies and their impact on the analysis of large educational data. It cannot be completed with a fork, and developers nearby the world remain to enlarge their functions. Many Blockchain-based data systems have previously been developed by many researchers (Li, 2020). Though many studies are proposed to use Blockchain to accomplish academic records, it is still essential to improve the usage of Blockchain technology in the education system to offer secure record management, validation, authorization, and integrity of educational data.

This paper provides the following main contributions:

- In this paper, a state-of-the-art application of Blockchain and its associated challenges are presented.
- Related works of researchers are also focused on in this paper to explore their advantages and limitations for further improvement.
- A blockchain-based trust model is proposed with educational big data.

The remaining section of this paper are illustrated to be as follows: Section 2 describes related works about the different contributions of researchers for integrating Blockchain in the field of education. Section 3 paper illustrates the challenges summarized from the existing blockchain educational model. Section 4 gives a descriptive overview of the proposed model. Finally, in section 5 conclusion and future research scope are discussed.

LITERATURE REVIEW

According to Gatteschi et al. (2018), the growth of crypto-currency implementation may be broken into three key phases: 1.0, 2.0, and 3.0. It was used to promote cryptocurrency and basic cash trading. Block-chain 1. Blockchain 2.0 for properties and intelligent contracts was then introduced. Such intelligent agreements impose additional requirements and criteria which must be met before they can be registered within the Blockchain. Registration occurs without a third party's intervention. Several applications in different sectors, such as education, health, and science, the government, were developed in Blockchain 3.0. Blockchain persists in the primary level of education. Only a smaller number of education institutions used blockchain technology. It is used by most of these organizations to justify and exchange educational credentials and/or learning results attained by their students (Chen et al., 2018). Field experts suggest that cryptocurrency technology can bring much more and greatly improve the ground. Nespor (2018) reports that cryptocurrency could weaken schools' central position as certifying officers and provide students with more educational experiences. While the volume of literature on the application of Blockchain to education has increased in recent years, it is still fragmented, and no systematic review on the subject has yet been carried out. This analysis is of considerable value to include a state-of-the-art overview and advice-proof practice. This article, however, contributes in an actual and reasonable manner to the research of teaching methods by examining the use of cryptocurrency technologies in schools. The main target audience of these companies is managers, policymakers, academics, and researchers who want to secure knowledge of this emerging technology (Okoli et al., 2010).

Trainee powered by blockchain education has recently become the subject of interest, and relevant system architectures and intelligent systems are discussed. However, in the education blockchain, difficult to experiment and optimize need to be further solved, and problems of difficult to model, and further research is required for driving mechanisms, application scenarios, and other issues. Gong et al. (2019) presented an overview of education blockchain, including problems and concerns, before incorporating a parallel analytical approach and blockchain technology. The author also suggested blockchain parallel education and its guided process, delivery of functions, application scenarios, data transfer, and related issues; Eventually, many questions are posed for debate. Naumova et al. (2019) described the major attributes of Blockchain emerging technologies, which have produced many valuable responses among professional and academic groups. The prospects for evaluating the possibility of its successful application in other areas were evident following its success in the financial market, where the block chained contains iced blocks the chain which describes all transactions with virtual coins, like Bitcoin, Litecoin, Ethereum, and others. Since education in Russia is undergoing a duration of initiatives, the possibilities and issues of implementation in this sphere are given special attention. The article explores the feasibility of implementing blockchain technology in the field of education for distributed registries and mass applications. And the probability that the teaching material can be improved is also assessed. Liu et al. (2019) used the blockchain system's openness and – anti properties to achieve a collaborative system for education and industry based on the Hyperledger blockchain framework. The System replicates the positions of universities and businesses in the System using the Certificate Authority service and transactions in the Hyperledger network. It allows institutions and businesses to access ideas in a clear manner that achieves information symmetry between participant knowledge and skills information business selection requirements, and competitive analysis. The above represents a tremendous endeavor to apply blockchain technology as a pilot for new technologies in academic achievement and industrial cooperation.

EduBloud, the interdependent Blockchain facilitated education cloud, was proposed by Wang et al. (2019). This framework demonstrated increased reliability, lower latency, better data performance, and improved economic productivity than the configuration options of the Blockchain. Zaiarnyi et al. (2019) have mentioned the advantages and inconveniences of implementing in higher education of distributed information systems using blockchain technology. The report also describes the requirements for introducing institutions of higher education of shared information management based on blockchains. The main guidelines of this technology application in the higher education system are devoted to particular attention. The findings also highlight the kinds of quality education that can be integrated using blockchains. Examples of institutions of higher education utilizing hedging strategies in their operations are listed in the report. A few standards for creating blockchain-based shared information security are drawn up.

CHALLENGES OF ADOPTING BLOCKCHAIN TECHNOLOGY IN EDUCATION

There have been eight different challenges described below in figure 1.

Figure 1. Challenges of adoption of blockchain in processing EBD

- Scalability of Blockchain: The rise in blockchain network transactions causes bigger blocks. It will greatly affect the redundancy of exchanges.
- Privacy and Security: Several types of security and privacy issues can be encountered when using blockchain technology, such as targeted activity or information theft.
- Adoption costs: power cost, infrastructure change costs, timescale cost because of slow transactions, costs for managing large-scale data.
- Trust: The schools were also afraid to disclose their information on a public blockchain.
- Technology adoption: It could be difficult for public universities to decide which information and services are to be awarded via the blockchain network.

- Immutability: It presents a risk in education to adopt blockchain technology. Many investigators have stated that utilizing new storage media laws or right flawed information can be difficult for educational institutions.
- Immaturity: Some immaturity problems, such as bad utilization and complicated settings, continue to affect the Blockchain.
- Data unavailability: Putting information systems throughout the hands of consumers might render this rejection region and significantly impact requests that rely heavily on just this information.

PROPOSED METHODOLOGY

Remote data access, such as in educational big data (EBD), is based on two pillars: data integrity and data privacy. If any unauthorized modification is performed, the application developed over these malicious data is dangerous. If such tampering occurs in big data applications, it is quite difficult to identify easily. So, there is a need to develop an efficient trust management application to ensure privacy over big data. Another requirement of security is during data processing. There is a need for secure and flexible usage control of EBD. This paper intends to improve understanding of Blockchain as a secure data store to improve the usage of large software systems and the proper use of Blockchain. Data processing problems that are crucial in developing and managing blockchain-based applications must be defined and analyzed. This section proposes the model to deploy Blockchain in educational big data (EBD).

There are some sectors in EBD that can implement Blockchain:

- Securing student/faculty account management
- Key agreement and management
- Secure data management

The best way to implement blockchain-based data trust management is to create metadata and store its hash value in the chain that acts as a link between data and metadata. If there is tampering with the data, then the hash value of metadata will not match. Fig 2 illustrates the Blockchain-based EBD (BlockEBD). The following steps are performed to ensure secure data storage and management.

- Step 1: In this approach, the user information or data are packed into blocks by a smart contract.
- Step 2: The smart contract checks the user's authentication and their information and then checks for their personal information in the chain.

- Step 3: If it is not present, then hashing of their data is performed and added with the key field in the chain. And finally, update the blockchain server.
- Step 4: If any of the users want to query someone's data, he has to enter their entity key ID and track the data history. Before checking the entity ID, the legality of the incoming request has to be verified.
- If the hash result is equal, the central database will be accessed.

Figure 2. Proposed blockchain based EBD

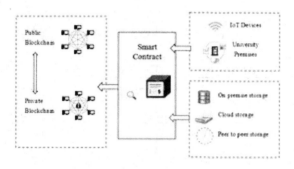

DISCUSSIONS

In this section, various blockchain based educational big data security system is discussed and their performance is discussed in table 1. These models were presented with limitation of centralized architecture with global security system using blockchain. Therefore, the proposed model will ensure the following features as compared to existing works:

- Non-token based (decentralized architecture)
- The proposed model ensures local as well as global secure storage systems.
- Secure user control of EBD to avoid misuse or copyright infringement.

CONCLUSION

This paper proposed the blockchain model in a decentralized architecture to reduce the trust and privacy issues that arise in educational big data (EBD) management. A blockchain model is proposed to ensure secure data usage of EBD and its user access control. Several data operations such as data capturing, data processing, and its storage or transfer are processed over a blockchain server, a smart contract. In the future, the proposed model will be implemented for large-scale evaluation and scalable decentralized trust management using Blockchain.

Table 1. Result comparison on blockchain technology

Ref	Technique used	Result	Limitation
Gong et al. (2019)	Spectral clustering, Fuzzy clustering	82.5% of accuracy	Very sensitive to parameter adjustment
Ji et al. (2020)	Hyper ledger fabric CA server, hyper ledger fabric ordered	87.29 of accuracy	The system consumes high energy
Liu et al. (2018)	Apriori algorithm	91.96 of accuracy	Low Scalability
Li et al. (2020)	Blockchain	-	Not make use of a personal e-learning platform to evaluate the performance
Toivonen et al. (2019)	Augmented Intelligence method and a cluster analysis algorithm Neural N-Tree	88.9 of accuracy	Limited to small sample sizes.
Okoli and K. Schabra (2010)	K-means clustering	29.3% cost saved overall	The system consumes high energy

REFERENCES

Abu Saa, A., Al-Emran, M., & Shaalan, K. (2019). Factors Affecting Students' Performance in Higher Education: A Systematic Review of Predictive Data Mining Techniques. *Technology. Knowledge and Learning*, 24(4), 567–598. doi:10.100710758-019-09408-7

Bedi, P., Goyal, S. B., Sharma, R., Yadav, D. K., & Sharma, M. (2021). Smart Model for Big Data Classification Using Deep Learning in Wireless Body Area Networks. In D. K. Sharma, L. H. Son, R. Sharma, & K. Cengiz (Eds.), *Micro-Electronics and Telecommunication Engineering. Lecture Notes in Networks and Systems* (Vol. 179). Springer. doi:10.1007/978-981-33-4687-1_21

Chen, G., Xu, B., Lu, M., & Chen, N.-S. (2018). Exploring blockchain technology and its potential applications for education. *Smart Learning Environments, 5*(1), 1–10. doi:10.1186/s40561-017-0050-x

Gatteschi, V., Lamberti, F., Demartini, C., Pranteda, C., & Santamaría, V. (2018). Blockchain and Smart Contracts for Insurance: Is the Technology Mature Enough? *Future Internet, 10*(2), 20. doi:10.3390/fi10020020

Gong, X., Liu, X., Jing, S., Xiong, G., & Zhou, J. (2019). Parallel-Education-Blockchain Driven Smart Education: Challenges and Issues. *Chinese Automation Congress*, 2390–2395. 10.1109/CAC.2018.8623198

Ji, L., Zhang, X., & Zhang, L. (2020). Research on the algorithm of education data mining based on big data. *Proceedings of 2nd International Conference on Computer Science and Educational Informatization*, 344–350. 10.1109/CSEI50228.2020.9142529

Liu, Q., Guan, Q., Yang, X., Zhu, H., Green, G., & Yin, S. (2019). Education-Industry Cooperative System Based on Blockchain. *Proceedings of 2018 1st IEEE International Conference on Hot Information-Centric Networking*, 207–211. 10.1109/HOTICN.2018.8606036

Li, Z. (2020). New employee student repast big data analysis research application. *Proceedings - 2020 International Conference on Intelligent Transportation, Big Data and Smart City*, 583–586. 10.1109/ICITBS49701.2020.00128

Memon, M., Bajwa, U. A., Ikhlas, A., Memon, Y., Memon, S., & Malani, M. (2019). Blockchain beyond Bitcoin: Block Maturity Level Consensus Protocol. *International Conference on Engineering Technologies and Applied Sciences*. 10.1109/ICETAS.2018.8629232

Miah, S. J., Miah, M., & Shen, J. (2020). Editorial note: Learning management systems and big data technologies for higher education. *Education and Information Technologies, 25*(2), 725–730. doi:10.100710639-020-10129-z

Naumova, O. A., Svetkina, I. A., & Naumov, D. V. (2019). *The Main Limitations of Applying Blockchain Technology in the Field of Education*. Advance online publication. doi:10.1109/EastConf.2019.8725411

Nespor, J. (2018). *Cyber schooling and the accumulation of school time*. doi:10.1080/14681366.2018.1489888

Nwosu, A. U., Goyal, S. B., & Bedi, P. (2021). Blockchain Transforming Cyber-Attacks: Healthcare Industry. In A. Abraham, H. Sasaki, R. Rios, N. Gandhi, U. Singh, & K. Ma (Eds.), *Innovations in Bio-Inspired Computing and Applications. IBICA 2020. Advances in Intelligent Systems and Computing* (Vol. 1372). Springer. doi:10.1007/978-3-030-73603-3_24

Okoli, C., & Schabram, K. (2010). *A Guide to Conducting a Systematic Literature Review of Information Systems Research. SSRN.* Electronic Journal., doi:10.2139/SSRN.1954824

Qin, Z. (2015). Research Progress on Educational Data Mining:A Survey. *Journal of Software, 26,* 3026–3042.

Sun, X. (2019). Application of data mining technology in teaching information. *J. Information Communication,* 277-278.

Toivonen, T., Jormanainen, I., & Tukiainen, M. (2019). Augmented intelligence in educational data mining. *Smart Learning Environments.*, *6*(1), 1–25. doi:10.118640561-019-0086-1

Wang, G., Zhang, H., Xiao, B., Chung, Y. C., & Cai, W. (2019). EduBloud: A Blockchain-based Education Cloud. *Computing, Communications and IoT Applications,* 352–357. doi:10.1109/ComComAp46287.2019.9018818

Yu, L., Wu, X., & Yang, Y. (2019). An Online Education Data Classification Model Based on Tr_MAdaBoost Algorithm. *Chinese Journal of Electronics, 28*(1), 21–28. doi:10.1049/cje.2018.06.006

Zaiarnyi, O. A., & Zaiarna, I. S. (2019). The Application of Distributed Information Systems Based on Blockchain Technologies in Higher Education: Benefits and Challenges for Ukraine. *IEEE International Conference on Advanced Trends in Information Theory,* 340–343. 10.1109/ATIT49449.2019.9030456

Chapter 3
Task Offloading Using Deep Reinforcement Learning for Edge IoT Networks

Pradeep Bedi
 https://orcid.org/0000-0003-1708-6237
Galgotias University, India

S. B. Goyal
 https://orcid.org/0000-0002-8411-7630
City University, Malaysia

Jugnesh Kumar
St. Andrews Institute of Technology and Management, India

ABSTRACT

Edge computing is a type of distributed computing that was designed especially for internet of things (IoT) users to provide computational resources and data management nearby to users' devices. By introducing edge computing for IoT, networks have reduced the bandwidth and latency issue while handling real-time applications. The major benefit of edge computing is that it reduces the communication overhead between IoT user and server. With integration of IoT in our daily lives, it has attracted researchers towards its performance management such as complexity minimization, latency minimization, memory management, energy consumption minimization, etc. In this chapter, deep reinforcement learning is focused to minimize the computational complexity at IoT user end. The task offloading decision process is designed using Q-Learning, which minimizes the system cost and curse of high dimensional data. In addition, the proposed methodology will perform better as compared to existing algorithms with respect to system costs.

DOI: 10.4018/978-1-6684-3733-9.ch003

INTRODUCTION

The term Internet of Things (IoT), clearly refers to the objects, things and things in an Internet structure which can be easily identified, was first proposed in 1998 (Liu et al., 2020). In recent years, due to some representative application (for example, intelligent monitoring of greenhouses, while reading electricity meters, monitoring of telemedicine and intelligent transport) the IoT concept has become popular. Typically, the IoT has four main components- sensors, data processing, applications and services. The new era applications such as smart city, smart educational system, smart industries, etc are integrated with Internet of Things (IoT) (Anand et al, 2021). The IoT architecture is composed of IoT devices such as sensors, actuators and gateways that are used to collect and perform computation over these generated and collected data (Liu et al. 2020).

With advancement of technologies, every day new innovations in hardware as well as software are being made which had contributed in increase of IoT networks and their applications. With usage of IoT devices on large scale, there is increase in data processing and storage requirements (Alfakih et al., 2020). For instance, for adopting smart farming, there is requirement of many sensors, computational devices to monitor temperature, humidity, pH, light, nutrition level, etc required for proper growth and developments of plants. In IoT network scenario, these data are generated by deployed sensors and collected the gateway devices and further sent to the cloud server end where processing over collected data is performed (Wang et al., 2019).

While processing such large amount of data in dynamic and real channel environment, there arise some challenges that are needed to be addressed. In case of smart farming, first issue is that where to locate sensors so that they can cover maximum area. Another issue is that most of the farms are located mostly outside the city where internet services are limited and are not capable to connect to the remote servers all the time. This issue can be addressed by integrating IoT-cloud architecture with edge computing that can provide promising solution to such issues (Wang et al., 2019) (Alelaiwi, 2019). Another issue that arise in IoT network is that there is requirement of large processing services to edge server by these deployed IoT sensors that burdens on the radio services and the storage services. So, the IoT devices required to be developed such that they can process some simple data processing tasks locally. Therefore, for fast and optimal processing of large amount of data in Edge-IoT network, there is requirement to design an optimal computation task offloading scheme (Chen et al., 2020).

User equipment processing some computationally expensive programmes and uploading the data processing these applications to the edge server through wireless transmission on the condition of weighing continuous or other indicators is referred to as task offloading. The processing programme assigns certain computational resources to the edge server for these uploads in order to receive ongoing or progressive replacements, leading to a positive user engagement. A fundamental aspect of selecting whether to offload, that is, the offloading choice, is usually an initial part of computer offloading and resource allocation. End devices are viewed as agents in this article, making judgments on whether or not the network should offload compute chores to edge devices. The computing resource allocation problems were framed as a sum cost delay of this framework to address resource allocation and task offloading. In this paper, an optimal computational offloading choice is presented, and reinforcement learning is used to fix the issues.

Reinforcement learning is a branch of artificial intelligence. The main distinction between unsupervised and supervised learning is that unsupervised learning does not involve artificial labelling. The exploration of an unknown area and the application of previously acquired knowledge are at the heart of the game. Reinforcement learning is achieved through constant trial and error, continual interaction with the environment, and receiving rewards or punishment from the environment, followed by the acquisition of acquiring knowledge to upgrade its very own paradigm. It picks up a new behavior strategy. It may make judgments to maximise long-term profits based on environmental variables after a specific period of training. Reinforcement learning can now handle high-dimensional actions and states, learning efficiency has increased dramatically, and the constraints of reinforcement learning have been broken to some extent. Deep reinforcement learning techniques will be utilized to solve the task offloading problem in edge computing in order to make the model adaptively learn to offload decisions.

But still there are some issues that has been identified in existing deep learning models are such as:

Compatibility with IoT/Edge: A new edge paradigm has emerged as a result of the spread of edge computing and IoT, with artificial intelligence being integrated into edge. Three-tier design for IoT-edge AI integration uses a DNN with numerous levels utilized on both the edge server and cloud servers. The DNN's front layers are located on the edge server, while its backend layers are located on the cloud. How to deploy a deep neural network (DNN) on an IoT-edge is an important consideration when it comes to offloading the AI-integrated IoT-output edges into the cloud.

Offloading Compatibility with heterogeneity: For the most part, earlier research on the topic of offloading models has assumed that the computations are all of a similar type. Because of this, offloading modelling is made easier. Modeling becomes more difficult due to the wide range of responsibilities. The computing units themselves may be a source of variability (hardware).

Offloading Compatibility with Mobility: To ensure service continuity and quality of service (QoS) criteria, nodes must undertake a handover to another edge/fog domain. If the jobs are being offloaded to a VM container, the question is whether this VM should be moved to the new server. This problem derives from the fact that migration costs are offset by the benefits of reduced delays and communication costs. Furthermore, dynamic VM migration and optimal offloading decisions necessitate a prediction technology. In a mobility context, offloading modelling is more difficult because of these features.

EDGE COMPUTING

Edge computing is a distributed approach that was designed for task processing and data management of IoT networks' tasks. These computing resources are deployed nearby to IoT devices with an aim to reduce response time and to reduce overall bandwidth requirements to handle real-time applications over internet. Its main benefit is that it reduces the communication gaps between the IoT users and cloud server (Wei et al., 2018). Task offloading by using edge servers have attracted researchers to explore new scope for performance enhancement IoT network to handle computational complexities. For this there is requirement of latency minimization, task offloading, storage management, power consumption and so on. With implementation of Edge computing these objectives can be achieved. But still there is requirement of more advancement as everyday size of data is increasing which require more processing speed. As local computing is not possible all the time because IoT devices have limited battery power and computation resources (Higuchi et al., 2019).

So, to support real time high latency consuming IoT applications, it is needed to reduce the offloading complexities at edge servers. Offloading algorithm are concerned to meet Quality-of-Service (QoS) requirements for different resource-demanding applications (Khayyat et al., 2020). Due to limited spectrum allocated to gateway devices, they cannot handle large set of computation tasks (Li et al., 2020). Hence, some researchers implemented the clustering concept to group the IoT devices to handle their demand according to their clusters. These clusters are made according to their computational demand (Guo et al., 2019).

Subsequently, there is need of optimal offloading of task that can handle the major issues and challenge of the IoT edge computing networks. Traditional offloading schemes are not much efficient to give optimal decisions for dynamic environment (Zhang et al., 2018) (Wang et al., 2019). Many researchers proposed dynamic task offloading algorithms, such as Markov decision process (MDP), by interaction with environment parameters. But MDP can handle single task at same time. Further, reinforcement learning showed its effectiveness to resolve the issues of MDP but still it needs to be make the learning process more adaptable to channel environment (Zhang et al., 2019) (Chen et al., 2019).

COMPUTATIONAL OFFLOADING USING REINFORCEMENT LEARNING

Reinforcement learning is an optimal learning process that learns the channel state by interacting with environment. In Edge-IoT network, each IoT user is considered to be as agent and their requirements are considered as environment. As shown in Figure 1, three-layer architecture is given for designing Cloud-Edge-IoT computing network. There are many IoT networks connected with Edge server. Each IoT network composed of large number of IoT users, gateway devices (or edge devices) that can collect data from IoT users. These gateway devices collect data from IoT users in particular coverage area and process them at edge server equipped with finite storage capacity and computational resources. So, these devices, either gateway or edge server can allow limited processing simultaneously as each IoT user have different type of task of different size. These computing resources are equipped with limited resources and battery power as well, so, there is need of optimal task offloading to improve the performance and lifetime of the entire network.

In Figure 2, Edge-IoT task offloading scheme is illustrated with reinforcement learning. In this architecture, each agent, IoT user (u_i), having state (S_k), at time instance (k) with action (A_k) to determine the computing mode based on the decision policy given by environmental parameters. Therefore, if there is change in environment new state (S_{k+1}) is observed with new reward R_k.

A reinforcement learning consists of following elements:

- Agent: These are the end users, IoT devices, that can perform some actions.
- Environment: These are the determining parameters that decides the reward of agents.
- State: The states explores the environment status such as channel gain, queue status, computation capacity, etc.
- Policy: A policy defines the way the agent behaves in a given time or it can be said that a policy is a mapping from the states of the environment to actions to the actions the agent takes in the environment.
- Reward: A reward can determine whether an agent can offload the task or not. For this, reinforcement learning is implemented. For task offloading each agent maximizes the rewards during learning. In Edge computing, to minimize the system computation cost with respect to power, time and space, negative reward is adopted make right decisions.
- Action: The action is performed by each IoT users for choosing local computing or offloading.

Figure 1. IoT network with edge computing with offloading scheme

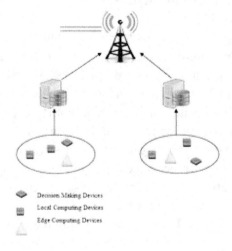

Figure 2. Reinforcement learning for IoT users

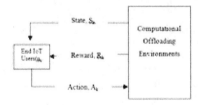

RELATED WORK

Liu et al. (2020) investigated the machine learning approach for resource allocation with edge computing in Internet-of-Things (IoT) networks. In this work, centralized clustering of IoT users is proposed is by assigning user's priorities. The highest priority cluster is selected and assigned to offload their task at the edge server whereas the task having lowest priority is can compute their task locally. The distributed task offloading is performed by Markov decision process which consider all the IoT user as agent and makes a series of task offloading decision. This policy is designed with respect to cost effectiveness based on channel dynamics. In this approach, deep Q-network was used for high dimensional tasks to learn the optimal policy.

Alfakih et al. (2020) proposed an algorithm using deep reinforcement learning approach for designing state-action-reward policy for task offloading from IoT users to edge server. The optimal offloading decision was performed to minimize system cost in respect to time delay and energy.

Wang et al. (2019) proposed task offloading algorithm for fog-cloud network design of Internet of Vehicles (IoV). The objective was to minimize the power consumption and computational resources of the vehicles.NP-hard problem was formulated as optimization of offloading issues.

Alelaiwi et al. (2019) proposed a structure for forecast of reaction time utilizing deep learning and studying how to off the utilization of a deep learning-based reaction time-prediction system to make the decision of whether to offload in the cloud hub, to close by haze/edge hub or neighbor haze/edge hub, nearby fog/edge node or neighbor fog/edge node. Besides, a limited Boltzmann machines learning is applied to handle the irregularity in the accessibility of assets.

Chen et al. (2020) proposed an algorithm for offloading task between IoT and edge server and termed it as intelligent Task Offloading Algorithm (iTOA). As compared to existing algorithms, iTOA decides the offloading activities on current state of network by using Monte Carlo Tree Search (MCTS). To provide quick search facilities, the MCTS algorithm was merged with Deep Neural Network (DNN).

Wei et al. (2018) analyzed a system comprising of multiple mobiles which are intended to carry out uploading tasks to a MEC server and in a single cell, hence the proper allocation to limited server with wireless channels emerge out as a problem. The author has hence designed an optimization problem for energy and tasks on the mobile so that they are efficiently divided. A Select Maximum Saved Energy First (SMSEF) algorithm being the key algorithm utilized.

Higuchi et al. (2019) investigated a type of virtual edge server and its compatibility of dealing it with the multiple vehicles, however he concluded that the during its early development stage, its feasibility requires more concern. The concluding simulations of the paper suggested that for vehicles the horizontal form of offloading can bring about reduction in the peak load on edge computing structure nearly by 53%. The penetration rate of V2V communication technology was kept low during this study.

Khayyat et al. (2020) focused on multilevel vehicular edge cloud networks and presented an advanced deep learning-based algorithm for it. The main focus is on achieving energy conservation and an effective utilization of the resources shared by the vehicles which is achieve by achieving an integration model for computational constrained offloading. The reduction in the time and energy consumption is attained by achieving the binary formulation for the resource allocation. However, it was found that due to problem of dimensionality, this type of solution is NP difficult and is thus very complex/prohibited to solve them. Thus, the authors have developed a similar reinforcement learning method and proposed a distributed deep learning algorithm along with neural network-based learning so as to finally achieve an optimum solution for taking offloading decision.

Li et al. (2020) proposed a deep reinforcement learning calculation to take care of the intricate calculation offloading issue for the Edge Computing Server (ECS) that is heterogeneous in nature with combined computing resources. The main concern in this work that was focused are such as network condition as well as task characteristics. The actor gradient policy was designed to settle on enhanced choices of offloading of tasks. Considering performing multiple tasks, the heterogeneity of edge subnet and versatility of edge tasks, the proposed calculation can get familiar with the network and create the calculation offloading choice to limit the allotment delay.

Guo et al. (2019) & Bedi et al (2021) focused on improving the operation earning by dropping the charge of the MDs. As the computation demands vary according to regions and there is difference in the availability of the computational edge servers, the traditional method to achieve the objective cannot be chosen. To solve this, the paper concluded that we can develop an efficient computing resource strategy and offloading task profile in UDN scenarios with time variation. The author concluded a deep Q-network based scheme for solving the problem.

In IoT networks, with the emergence of edge computing has resulted in many challenges for the researchers and developers, which include dynamic computation offloading scheme designing, resources such as computing resource, spectrum useful resource and their allocation, and transmit electricity controlling. It has been found that these are very difficult to solve independent as the designing of and computational offloading scheme for the edge server has to learn about the resource of the gateway as well as the transmit power capability of the end user. There has been focused study on computational offloading schemes that are capable of handling multiple resources in the edge servers, more specifically in the MEC frameworks. Power consumption and latency are the two main area of concern while working in IoT network with offloading scheme of task. So, many researchers have proposed an optimized task offloading scheme that can handle energy requirement as well as latency such as MEC system. But MEC based task offloading can handle single user at a time. Then, multi-user framework was implanted using deep reinforcement learning using MEC framework. However, these algorithms are not much efficient to handle multi-user multi-task at same time optimally.

Along with this in order to achieve threshold structure of the system, an optimal task offloading policy is validated. The clustering of the IOT users into various groups has been proposed by making use of clustering optimizing algorithm which is framed as initial step for the task offloading scheme designing. The reduction in the power utilization, time and system cost along with considerable decrement in the execution latency is achieved by making use of distribution computation task offloading algorithm. Diverse contributions from various authors towards the work have been described in the table I.

In view of the previous studies, following main issues were being listed:

- One of the main issues of Markov Decision Problem (MDP) is that it can be only utilized with single user with task scheduling.
- MDP can lead to most effective values however creates time-constraint troubles.
- Q-learning is a method that can be utilized for resolving the MDP issue however it may face huddles such as overestimated function. For some stochastic environments the famous reinforcement studying algorithm Q-getting is known to perform very poorly. This poor performance is resulting from massive overestimations of action values. These overestimations due to a positive bias that is added due to the fact Q-learning uses the maximum action value as an approximation for the most predicted action value.

PROPOSED WORK

In the world moving towards digitalization the small all mobile devices are able to perform small and medium level computation problems with no ability to deal with high computation processes. However, offloading the computation processes at the Gateway can emerge as one of the key solutions for this problem. While it is considered that x IoT devices are capable of performing T_x task while they offload the task at the edge, the entire computational model can be summarized in the following three steps (figure 3):

- All the x IoT devices around to carry and deliver sufficient input information at the gateway by making use of various sensors and accomplish the task at the edge.
- Edge shall allocate some portion from its computational resource to enable the computation of task for the x IoT devices.
- Results are then sent to IoT, end device, after the computation via edge server.

To deal with the sequential learning and achieving the decision making, machine learning such as Reinforcement learning (RL) can serve as an agent in making decisions and help in attaining the objective of cumulative rewards (Liu et al., 2019). The process has many key advantages such as energy sparing, quick offloading, low inertness, and ideal load distribution, so it is a critical contender for the future of the digitalization that is yet to come of remote correspondence. The ongoing research and examination depend on proper and effective offloading and

Table 1. Gives the comparative study of various methods for task offloading in iot network

Author	Description	Results	Drawbacks
Liu et al. (2020)	Deep reinforcement learning approach with markov decision process	Optimal clustering of IoT users and results in optimal energy cost.	Not adaptable to multiple users processing simultaneously.
Li et al. (2020)	Deep Deterministic Policy Gradient	minimize the task delay	Energy cost consumption was not considered.
Alelaiwi et al. (2019)	Deep learning for prediction of response time	Improves the offloading computational performance	Time-constraint issues
Xiaolan et al. (2019)	Greedy Q learning algorithm for optimal offloading t=of task	Achieved better performance of task offloading with respect to energy consumption and latency requirement of the entire network.	Not adaptable to multiple users processing simultaneously.
Chen et al. (2019)	Deep Reinforcement Learning Approach	Improved service latency performance	There is no predictive model as well not adaptable to massive IoT scenario
Min et al. (2019)	Fast deep Q-network (DQN) based offloading scheme	Optimal offloading policy after sufficiently long learning time	Local power control and offloading decision-making problem
Zhang et al. (2018)	Cost as well as energy aware offloading task is proposed using deep reinforcement learning.	Energy and cost were estimated	Multiple users cannot be served optimally

Figure 3. IoT task offloading

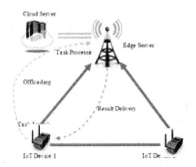

Figure 4. Proposed task offloading flow chart

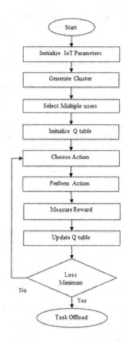

task allocation for MEC frameworks. The resource allocation scheme is considered as partial offloading schemes.

The proposed work is performed in following steps (figure 4):

- Step 1: Proving input as tasks and with respective IOT user.
- Step 2: IOT user cluster generation.
- Step 3: Priority level determination of IOT users (multiple) in each cluster.
- Step 4: Q learning algorithm utilization for training deep reinforcement network.
- Step 5: Following above steps, next step is to offload tasks.
- Step 6: Performance parameters valuation and determination.

DISCUSSIONS

In this section, the paper presents some comparative analysis of existing research works are presented which shows efficiency of deep reinforcement learning for task offloading in edge computing. Table II to shows the comparative analysis of existing techniques and average miili second. Ali et al. (2021) proposes deep learning

Table 2. Comparative analysis

Ref	Techniques	Optimization	Average Delay (in ms)
Ali et al. (2021)	DL	MCC	100
Li et al. (2020)	DDPG	DRL	6
Chen et al. (2019)	Deep-SARL	DRL	3
Chen et al. (2019)	iRAF	DRL	20
Liu et al. (2019)	DRL	DRL	25
Hussain and Mausa (2020)	DL	ACO	85
Hussain and Mausa (2020)	DL	PSO	90

techniques and have maximum average delay i.e.100 millisecond. Liet al. (2020) proposes ddpg technique having average delay of 6 ms. Another techniques proposed in Chen etl al. (2019) has minimum average delay of 3ms. Chen et al. (2019) with iRAF has average delay of 20sec. Liu et al. (2019) proses DRL based method with an average delay of 25sec. Hussain and Mausa (2020) Also proposes Deep learning techniqus having and average dealt of 85 and 90ms. Several fundamental concerns connected with fog computing, including structure, interface, and programming, offloading processing, efficient resource provisioning, and security aspects are discussed in this paper. Various optimization approaches have been developed in previous publications to solve such processing and transmission latency constraints. With delay as a limitation, a Q-learning priority-based task offloading strategy is presented to minimize the energy consumption in communications systems and computing.

CONCLUSION

Edge computing is well known for providing computational capabilities to IoT consumers, as IoT computing necessitates a vast resource spectrum. Furthermore, sending computational activities to an edge server uses more energy. As a result, conserving energy locally at the IoT user end is a difficult challenge. This can be accomplished through the optimization of network design or routing policies. The purpose of this paper is to summaries the research that has been done in the subject of edge computing for job offloading. To overcome the issue of offloading and to deploy an intelligent decision-making system that can accomplish the aforementioned duty while reducing human efforts, a variety of algorithms, frameworks, and predictive models have been proposed so far. A brief examination of several task offloading schemes is covered in this paper, along with their limitations. Based on a review of

Figure 5. Comparative analysis

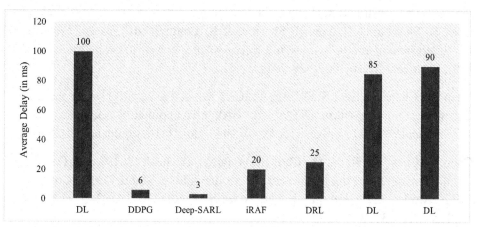

the literature, it has been determined that deep reinforcement techniques outperform standard approaches in terms of lowering computational effort. Furthermore, a method based on a modified Q-learning-based deep reinforcement technique is proposed to manage multiple users and tasks at the same time with little computing cost. The proposed methodology, which may be used with most types of offloading, such as vehicular and mobile offloading, will be implemented in the future. It can also be enhanced by using it in multi-agent networks.

REFERENCES

Alelaiwi, A. (2019). An efficient method of computation offloading in an edge cloud platform. *Journal of Parallel and Distributed Computing*, *127*, 58–64. doi:10.1016/j.jpdc.2019.01.003

Alfakih, T., Hassan, M. M., Gumaei, A., Savaglio, C., & Fortino, G. (2020). Task offloading and resource allocation for mobile edge computing by deep reinforcement learning based on SARSA. *IEEE Access: Practical Innovations, Open Solutions*, *8*, 54074–54084. doi:10.1109/ACCESS.2020.2981434

Ali, A., Iqbal, M. M., Jamil, H., Qayyum, F., Jabbar, S., Cheikhrouhou, O., Baz, M., & Jamil, F. (2021). An Efficient Dynamic-Decision Based Task Scheduler for Task Offloading Optimization and Energy Management in Mobile Cloud Computing. *Sensors, 21*(13), 4527. doi:10.3390/s21134527

Bedi, P., Goyal, S. B., Sharma, R., Yadav, D. K., & Sharma, M. (2021). Smart Model for Big Data Classification Using Deep Learning in Wireless Body Area Networks. In D. K. Sharma, L. H. Son, R. Sharma, & K. Cengiz (Eds.), *Micro-Electronics and Telecommunication Engineering. Lecture Notes in Networks and Systems* (Vol. 179). Springer. doi:10.1007/978-981-33-4687-1_21

Chen, J., Chen, S., Luo, S., Wang, Q., Cao, B., & Li, X. (2020). An intelligent task offloading algorithm (iTOA) for UAV edge computing network. *Digital Communications and Networks*, 6(4), 433–443. doi:10.1016/j.dcan.2020.04.008

Chen, J., Chen, S., Wang, Q., Cao, B., Feng, G., & Hu, J. (2019). IRAF: A Deep Reinforcement Learning Approach for Collaborative Mobile Edge Computing IoT Networks. *IEEE Internet of Things Journal*, 6(4), 7011–7024. doi:10.1109/JIOT.2019.2913162

Chen, X., Zhang, H., Wu, C., Mao, S., Ji, Y., & Bennis, M. (2019). Optimized computation offloading performance in virtual edge computing systems via deep reinforcement learning. *IEEE Internet of Things Journal*, 6(3), 4005–4018. doi:10.1109/JIOT.2018.2876279

Guo, H., Lv, J., & Liu, J. (2019). Smart Resource Configuration and Task Offloading with Ultra-Dense Edge Computing. *International Conference on Wireless and Mobile Computing, Networking and Communications*. 10.1109/WiMOB.2019.8923227

Higuchi, T., Ucar, S., & Altintas, O. (2019). Offloading Tasks to Vehicular Virtual Edge Servers. *Proceedings - 2019 IEEE 16th International Conference on Mobile Ad Hoc and Smart Systems Workshops, MASSW 2019*, 162–163. 10.1109/MASSW.2019.00040

Hussein, M. K., & Mousa, M. H. (2020). Efficient task offloading for IoT-Based applications in fog computing using ant colony optimization. *IEEE Access: Practical Innovations, Open Solutions*, 8, 37191–37201. doi:10.1109/ACCESS.2020.2975741

Khayyat, M., Elgendy, I. A., Muthanna, A., Alshahrani, A. S., Alharbi, S., & Koucheryavy, A. (2020). Advanced Deep Learning-Based Computational Offloading for Multilevel Vehicular Edge-Cloud Computing Networks. *IEEE Access: Practical Innovations, Open Solutions*, 8, 137052–137062. doi:10.1109/ACCESS.2020.3011705

Li, Y., Qi, F., Wang, Z., Yu, X., & Shao, S. (2020). Distributed Edge Computing Offloading Algorithm Based on Deep Reinforcement Learning. *IEEE Access: Practical Innovations, Open Solutions*, 8, 85204–85215. doi:10.1109/ACCESS.2020.2991773

Liu, X., Qin, Z., & Gao, Y. (2019). Resource Allocation for Edge Computing in IoT Networks via Reinforcement Learning. *IEEE International Conference on Communications*, 1-6. 10.1109/ICC.2019.8761385

Liu, X., Yu, J., Wang, J., & Gao, Y. (2020). Resource Allocation With Edge Computing in IoT Networks via Machine Learning. *IEEE Internet of Things Journal, 7*(4), 3415–3426. doi:10.1109/JIOT.2020.2970110

Min, M., Xiao, L., Chen, Y., Cheng, P., Wu, D., & Zhuang, W. (2019). Learning-Based Computation Offloading for IoT Devices with Energy Harvesting. *IEEE Transactions on Vehicular Technology, 68*(2), 1930–1941. doi:10.1109/TVT.2018.2890685

Rajawat, Bedi, Goyal, Alharbi, Aljaedi, Jamal, & Shukla. (2021). Fog Big Data Analysis for IoT Sensor Application Using Fusion Deep Learning. Mathematical Problems in Engineering. doi:10.1155/2021/6876688

Wang, X., Han, Y., Wang, C., Zhao, Q., Chen, X., & Chen, M. (2019). In-edge AI: Intelligentizing mobile edge computing, caching and communication by federated learning. *IEEE Network, 33*(5), 156–165. doi:10.1109/MNET.2019.1800286

Wang, X., Wei, X., & Wang, L. (2019). A deep learning based energy-efficient computational offloading method in Internet of vehicles. *China Communications, 16*(3), 81–91. doi:10.12676/J.CC.2019.03.008

Wei, F., Chen, S., & Zou, W. (2018). A greedy algorithm for task offloading in mobile edge computing system. *China Communications, 15*(11), 158–170. doi:10.1109/CC.2018.8543056

Zhang, C., Liu, Z., Gu, B., Yamori, K., & Tanaka, Y. (2018). A Deep Reinforcement Learning Based Approach for Cost-and Energy-Aware Multi-Flow Mobile Data Offloading. *IEICE Transactions on Communications, 101*(7), 1625–1634. doi:10.1587/transcom.2017CQP0014

Chapter 4

Object Identification in Remotely–Assisted Robotic Surgery Using Fuzzy Inference System

Meghana P. Lokhande
Pimpri Chinchwad College of Engineering, India

Dipti Durgesh Patil
(iD) https://orcid.org/0000-0001-7379-863X
MKSSS's Cummins College of Engineering for Women, Pune, India

ABSTRACT

Although telemedicine is still practiced today, high-speed connections and improved organizational capability have enabled remote operation of medical equipment, known as telerobotic surgery. The technologies have a number of benefits, including enhanced performance and the ability to reach complex operations to geographically isolated places where trained surgeons are unavailable. This study proposed an early robotic solution for limited teleoperation tasks in a complex and unpredictable environment. So, the research is inspired by future human-robot collaboration. It focuses on limiting or preventing accidents between the robot and its environment. In order to enable access to robotic surgery equipment in a confined area, a fuzzy control method is used. We may infer that an adaptive robotic system capable of accomplishing limited tasks while also responding to external factors in an unpredictable and dynamic environment is potentially feasible.

DOI: 10.4018/978-1-6684-3733-9.ch004

INTRODUCTION

Teleoperated robotic systems have attracted the attention of many people during the last two decades due to their numerous medical and non-medical uses. The emergence of robots in medicine has opened new opportunities for advancement, not just in terms of surgeon precision and comfort, but also in terms of patient benefits. In terms of health applications, two major groups may be distinguished: remote - controlled surgery and teleoperated recovery robotic systems, both of which have shown significant potential in terms of improving healthcare delivery. Teleoperated surgery has been extensively researched and marketed in this line. The sensory-motor capabilities of humans have been significantly enhanced by telerobotic systems. The capacity of humans to attain increased sensorimotor abilities, allowing them to connect with things and places from a distance (Mehrdad et al., 2021). Authors in the domains of image analysis, machine learning, and automation have moved to geometric technologies for collecting and analysing images as a result of recent developments in technology in terms of memory and processing capability. In automation and immersive virtual reality research, information technology is employed to give efficient solutions in clinical imaging, practical surveillance, automation, and computer aided manufacturing (Thilahar & Thilahar, 2019).

Traditional robot assisted systems are made up of a master module and a slave module. The human operator will control the master unit, and the slave system will follow the master robot's actions for interaction with the environment. During surgery, the operative region is frequently the patient's body portion on which the procedure is being conducted. The operator will get sensory information from the operating area in feedback loop. The sensory information repeated by the leader robot for the operator allows her/him to complete the operation. In reality, the most serious worry with human-robot collaboration is safety (Haddadin & Hirzinger, 2010; Haddadin et al., 2009).

The key motivations for telerobotic surgery were the necessity to provide remote medical surgery. Remotely placed hospitals usually have limited resources and skilled physicians on a worldwide scale. This successful study demonstrates the feasibility and possibility of using telerobotic devices for telesurgery in rural and underserved locations. The fundamental issue in this scenario was a large delay. Despite these enlightening tests, current standard practice demands that the patient and the surgeon be at the same hospital. Robots solved the majority of the tasks that could not previously be completed due to security concerns (Bauer et al., 2008; Hägele et al., 2002). Researchers addressed the difficulty of safe human-robot interaction in 2017 while designing architecture for operating a teleoperated industrial manipulator used in surgical applications (Capolei et al., 2017). The investigation's goal was to insert and position a long and light surgical instrument, the laparoscope, properly and safely through a small incision in the patient's skin, which serves as the fulcrum point for tool motions. This eventually brought into question the idea of human interaction, as well as the design of a system that was reactive and safe enough while dealing with several constraints in such a sensitive and unpredictable situation. This challenging issue needs a well-organized architectural design capable of managing several events in real time. Telesurgery offers the ability to enable the "global exchange of medical expertise without the need for specialists to visit." Another reason surgical telerobots are appealing is their ability to aid surgeons in their training. In addition to that it was found that the human collaboration might result in a significant decrease in workplace accidents as well as the optimization of production processes in a variety of economic industries (Bauer et al., 2008; Kaplan et al., 2016).

The requirement for a minimal time lag between issuing commands, executing surgery, and obtaining visual confirmation on the screen has been one of the most difficult issues in producing clinically effective telerobotic surgery. Multiple variables influence this latency, including the time necessary to translate video and motions into suitable signals and delay in the communication network itself. This work proposes an initial secured robotic solution for limited teleoperation tasks in a dynamic and unpredictable environment. The study explains the developed control architecture, which incorporates expertise from several disciplines such as control theory, computer vision and decision-making theory in its modular structure. The experiments are run on simulated systems. A rule-based attribute governs all of the system's components.

In section II, the study is dedicated to related work. This part describes the background study for decision making process in robot assisted surgery. Section III depicts system architecture for object identification. The third half of the article focuses on the results and discussion in section IV. We finish with conclusion of article in section V.

RELATED WORK

Advanced analytics, pattern recognition, smart systems and the Internet of Things are just a few of the modern approaches that can help improve healthcare applications (Abdelaziz et al., 2018; Ali et al., 2018; Gao et al., 2018). Artificial intelligence techniques such as machine learning have also aided healthcare specialists' tasks by analyzing massive amounts of healthcare data accessible. Data analytics has showed the potential to find pattern and hidden aspects in health data, hence enhancing healthcare quality through efficient decision-making (Mehta & Pandit, 2018). The usage of cloud in medical applications gives a way for processing and sharing medical reports, as well as delivering new healthcare services with more adaptability (Casola et al., 2016). The integration of robot assisted system is intended to provide some level of user flexibility while reducing manual interference. This unified system employs data mining methods to construct and develop computers capable of operating in a medical setting. IoT and robots have been widely used for solving a variety of healthcare challenges, ranging from remotely supporting physicians during surgery (Akkas et al., 2020; Joseph et al., 2017; Postolache et al., 2020).

Furthermore, it reduces stress on medical personnel by releasing them of a routine duty and making proper procedures better and less expensive than before. The benefit of using robots increases accuracy by reducing human error. A constant movement of the robot is required in several healthcare applications. In this case, the robot must discover an ideal path to the target while avoiding obstacles in congested locations. As a result, ensuring effective navigation is the primary focus of numerous studies (Hou et al., 2020). This is due to the typical robot's incapacity to handle a dynamic environment with stochastic mobility of people. Furthermore, due to people's unpredictable mobility, avoiding collisions in robotic environment is challenging, especially when operating at confined location. Many researches in the study have recently found the subject of robotic system obstacle detection (Ahn et al., 2018; Fraga-Lamas et al., 2019). IoT is employed in this case to do this without any physical interaction (Safeea et al., 2019). The device employs a map-based navigation system that generates a map of its surroundings while simultaneously tracking its position. When numerous robots are involved in the healthcare setting, it is critical to have an additional way of connectivity among them (Rodriguez-Losada et al., 2005). Its purpose is to prevent misinformation in robotic environment following the weak Internet access. IoT-enabled robotics serves as a companion to the handicapped and elderly who require particular care (Aly & Tapus, 2014). Although device to device interface is widely used in robotic systems, the incorporation of smart system can improve the efficiency of human-robot interaction. In (Sharif & Alsibai, 2017), researcher proposed a "Nao Robot" that can evaluate clinical data and communicate with patients. Patients would be able to interpret their body's vital indicators and draw assumptions about their health state after interacting with the robot. Furthermore, it can estimate the risk of heart disease in the future and prescribe lifestyle modifications to reduce medical hazards.

Numerous studies have employed a Smart robotic system in a range of applications, including endoscopic procedures (Akimana et al., 2016; Guntur et al., 2019; Lehman et al., 2008). Researchers in (Ishak & Kit, 2017) created robotic arm that can help a physician at the time of surgery and care for patients. Gesture and posture information might be used to operate the robotic arm. Researchers in (Su et al., 2020) describe the creation of an Internet of Things-based collaborative control technique for robot-assisted microsurgery. The proposed methodology may handle multiple jobs in a scheduled manner and also regulating mobility limitations and collisions during surgery. Recently, the IoT enabled system has begun to use haptic technology (Sreelakshmi & Subash, 2017) to allow surgeons to work on patients from an isolated section via the robotic interface (Kim et al., 2018). Furthermore, the use of the Network to connect numerous robots and doctors may be impeded by network connectivity issues and quality of service (Guntur et al., 2019). This can have a significant impact on the precision and success of a surgical treatment.

Many researchers have already created a work in the fields of identification of feature, segmentation, and virtual region (Ganapathy et al., 2016; Kanimozhi et al., 2018; Sarakoglou & Tsagarakis, 2012). Researchers in (Ramesh et al., 2015) altered the fuzzy membership function, which was utilized to focus the fusion over the detection system over fuzzy set. In (Banga et al., 2011) devised a fuzzy rule based for providing optimal routing over wireless communication. They have increased their network longevity and transmission performance. This is because of the application of fuzzy logic and intelligence principles. In (Kumar & Dhiman, 2021), studies investigate a rule-based approach for predicting relevant information, as well as mathematical equations for fuzzy sets, which are used to determine the robustness of the system. The researcher in (Chatterjee, 2021) emphasized the importance of intellectual patent protection in the artificial intelligence field. The model for COVID 19 analytical analysis is described in (Vaishnav et al., 2021) utilizing machine learning methodologies. Researchers in (Mule et al., 2021) provide a brief overview of exhaled breath in the human body. The study of telerobotic surgery in a 5G network was presented by the researchers in (Lokhande & Patil, 2020; Meshram & Patil, 2020).

SYSTEM ARCHITECTURE

In the health sector, robots can be employed to either monitor patients' health or identify health issues. In all circumstances, the robot must first gather health data from several sensors. Before giving relevant information, this information goes through a number of processing processes.

Denoising, preprocessing, and thresholding are all steps in the extraction process. Again, it broadens the capability of a robotic platform by incorporating more senses into the system. This increases the amount of information accessible to the forecasting model, boosting the rate of precise estimate. Adaptability is the ability to prepare a system for unexpected occurrences, defects, changes in environmental circumstances, activities, or human behaviour. Adaptability may be attained by the use of the previously described abilities of perception, intelligence, and decision-making.

Decision Making in Robotic System

Robot mobility is critical to human collaboration because, in such an uncertain environment, the robot must reason not just about itself but also about its surroundings in carryout appropriate actions. In the problem under consideration, the robot gets instructions that must cover a variety of scenarios and whose execution is affected by a number of context-sensitive decisions. What if, for example, the robot is awaiting the next order and an issue arises? Assume the robot is waiting for the next user's instruction while performing a restricted function, such as situating a tool; it is critical that the robot does not collide with any external rigid body due to the fragility or harmfulness of the handled object. As a result, the robot should be able to avoid any accidents. If the robot encounters a barrier while moving, it will halt and decide its next move.

Decision making helps in deciding the next move. System architecture as shown in figure 1 for object identification is made up of seven primary components: the Image Dataset, the User Interface Module, the Object Identification System, the Fuzzy Inference system, the Multiple Rule-Based Decision Manager that helps in taking decision during surgeries.

Image Dataset: For analyzing the proposed system, a common benchmark data set with millions of images is utilized.

User Interface Module: This module receives required data from the dataset and also chooses which data must be gathered in order to evaluate the proposed solution. The acquired data is given to the identification system for further processing of the data, and the multiple rule based system for the suggested outcome.

Object Identification System: It is made up of four subsystems: selection of feature, segmentation, and device identification system, and the classification subsystem, which includes an existing classification technique known as Convolutional Neural Network (CNN). Furthermore, an existing classification technique known as Convolutional Neural Network is applied in this article to accomplish successful classification of the image dataset. There is a genetic algorithm process in this classification technique that employs temporal restrictions and temporal fuzzy rules.

A fuzzy Inference system (FIS) is made up of a series of linguistic conditional statements obtained by human operators that convey information about the system under control. These statements define a series of control actions based on if-then logic (Passino & Yurkovich, 1998).

The initial step is to fuzzify each input, which is accomplished by associating each input with a collection of fuzzy variables. A membership function is applied to each variable in order to give the semantics of a fuzzy variable a numerical sense. Triangle and exponential forms are two types of continuous membership functions that are often used in fuzzy logic control. The fuzzy inputs are then paired with the fuzzy

Figure 1. System architecture

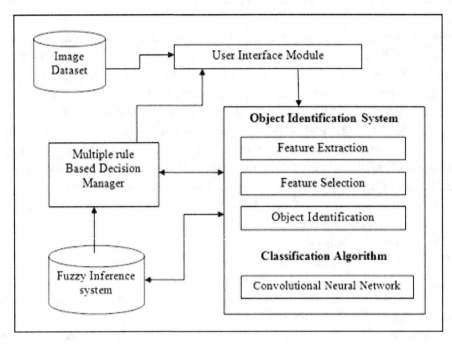

controller's knowledge base, which contains a set of control rules. Defuzzification is necessary to convert the fuzzy control actions into an accurate output value.

Figure 2 shows is a block diagram of a fuzzy system applied to an extending manipulator. The conversation environments are separated into fuzzy sets for inputs and fuzzy sets for outputs, with values ranging from [-1, +1]. As a result, scaling gains are used to normalize the control system. The output is mapped with the access permission wherein the access for the medical instruments is decided and the instrument operates accordingly in surgical environment.

Multiple Rule-Based Decision Manager: This is definitely not a standard procedural or object-oriented control issue in which the robot understands what to do, how to do it, and in what sequence. Furthermore, the system must be able to respond quickly to changing conditions or malfunctions. As a result, researchers turned to a rule-based technique, which use rules to generate conclusions from facts. A rule is a command that only applies to a subset of issues, and a rule engine determines which rules to use at any particular time and executes them. The rule-based method addressed the requirement for a rapid and constantly reactive system suitable for dynamic contexts; such a system is capable of changing intents based on the scenario and dynamic situations. This decision manager assists in making final decisions on image data supplied from the object recognition system using a fuzzy rule base.

Figure 2. Block diagram of Fuzzy Inference system

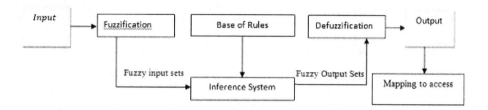

RESULTS AND DISCUSSION

Models of master-slave surgical robots are placed in a simulation. The corresponding signals are chosen to place the end-point at the desired location (Boucetta, 2015). The simulation results are shown in figures 3 and 4.

The master and slave robots' first Z-angle theta1 are stable and achieve consignment steadily and without overshoots. The master robot's second X-angle theta 2 is faster, whereas the slave robot's is slower with occasional variations.

These systems need to deal with a vast number of data collected from numerous sensors throughout the network. Patients have been observed to be accepting modern technologies, although they are concerned with safety of the data. This section describes the findings of running the performance metrics. The NS-2 parameter is

Figure 3. Responses and first angle Theta 1(Boucetta, 2015)

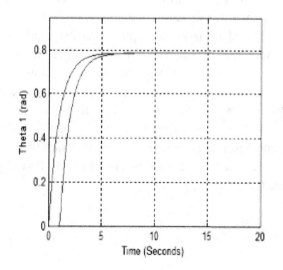

Figure 4. Responses and first angle Theta 2(Boucetta, 2015)

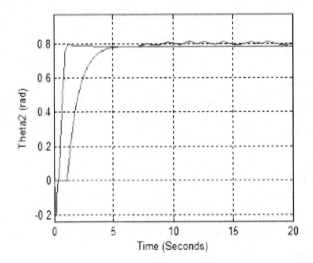

used to design the system. Nodes are medical equipment that are used in the operating room. Simulation of nodes such as cameras, health check-up equipment, and other medical sensors is used in the investigation. Article uses sensory channels such as haptic input, visual data, and auditory data.

The sensor network is a concept that has received a lot of attention and investigation. It continues to extend beyond its horizon, presenting several opportunities and difficulties. Concerns about security are always at the forefront. The fast growth of network also provides attackers with a potential to investigate this technology as a new attack vector. One of the most significant forms of attacks is distributed denial of service (DoS). The system in this work was built to employ the Low Energy Adaptive Clustering Hierarchy (LEACH) protocol, with the cluster head making decisions depending on remaining energy (Lokhande & Patil, 2021; Passino & Yurkovich, 1998). This protocol reduces power consumption while increasing network longevity.

LEACH protocol was developed further to increase network lifespan and minimizes packet loss. Here 10% of nodes behave as attacking nodes. Packet Delievry Ratio (PDR), throughput and delay in presence of attacking node using LEACH model is shown in figure 3,4 and 5 respectively. The blue line indicates the LEACH protocol in the absence of an attack, whereas the red line reflects the LEACH protocol in the presence of an attack (LEACH-A).

Figure 5. Avg. Packet delivery ratio

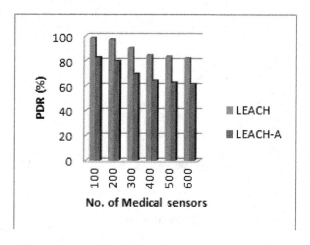

CONCLUSION

The study describes an intelligent and autonomous robotic system that can move smoothly in an environment with dynamic external inflexible bodies. The created system solves generic teleoperation problems as well as limited activities. The management system, in particular, responds efficiently to external disturbances while adhering to the constraints specified. The fundamental benefit of a rule-based decision system is its ability to respond quickly to changing situations or failures. The entire vision system is capable of obtaining useful information from the field in real time, filtering out the robot and quickly notifying the higher level

Figure 6. Average throughput

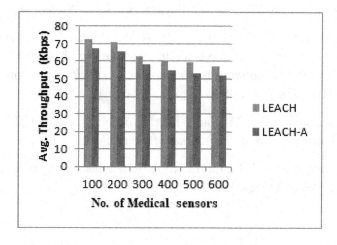

Figure 7. Average delay

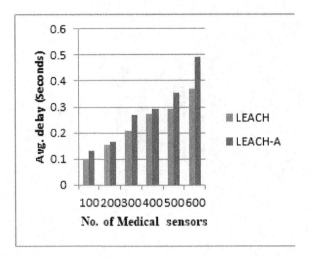

structure in the event of a probable incident. The suggested study aims to improve the network's efficiency in the medical area. Medical research is heavily focused on reducing energy use and improving node lifespan. Due to the dynamic nature of IoT networks, the study indicates that energy minimization is a critical issue. However, the performance might be enhanced by improving noise reduction or deploying more object recognition cameras to provide multiple viewpoints.

REFERENCES

Abdelaziz, A., Elhoseny, M., Salama, A. S., & Riad, A. M. (2018). A machine learning model for improving healthcare services on cloud computing environment. *Measurement, 119*, 117–128. doi:10.1016/j.measurement.2018.01.022

Ahn, H. S., Zhang, S., Lee, M. H., Lim, J. Y., & MacDonald, B. A. (2018). Robotic healthcare service system to serve multiple patients with multiple robots. In *Proceedings of the International Conference on Social Robotics* (pp. 493–502). Springer. 10.1007/978-3-030-05204-1_48

Akimana, B.T., Bonnaerens, M., Van Wilder, J., & Vuylsteker, B. (2016). *A survey of human-robot interaction in the internet of things*. Academic Press.

Akkas, M.A., Sokullu, R., & Çetin, H.E. (2020). Healthcare and patient monitoring using IoT. Internet of Things, 11.

Ali, O., Shrestha, A., Soar, J., & Wamba, S. F. (2018). Cloud computing-enabled healthcare opportunities, issues, and applications: A systematic review. *International Journal of Information Management, 43*, 146–158. doi:10.1016/j.ijinfomgt.2018.07.009

Aly, A., & Tapus, A. (2014). Towards enhancing human-robot relationship: customized robot's behavior to human's profile. *Proceedings of the AAAI Fall Symposium Series (AIHRI)*.

Banga, V. K., & Kaur, JKumar, RSingh, Y. (2011). Modeling and Simulation of Robotics Arm Movement using Soft Computing. *World Academy of Science, 75*, 614–620.

Bauer, A., Wollherr, D., & Buss, M. (2008). Human–robot collaboration: A survey. *International Journal of HR; Humanoid Robotics, 5*(1), 47–66. doi:10.1142/S0219843608001303

Boucetta, R. (2015). *Telerobotic Surgery: Fuzzy Path Planning Control for a Telerobotic Assistant Surgery. 14th Computer Information Systems and Industrial Management*. CISIM.

Capolei, M. C., Wu, H., Andersen, N. A., & Ravn, O. (2017). Positioning the laparoscopic camera with industrial robot arm. In *Proc. 2017 3rd International Conference on Control, Automation and Robotics (ICCAR)* (pp. 138–143). IEEE.

Casola, V., Castiglione, A., Choo, K. K. R., & Esposito, C. (2016). Healthcare-related data in the cloud: Challenges and opportunities. *IEEE Cloud Computing, 3*(6), 10–14. doi:10.1109/MCC.2016.139

Chatterjee, I. (2021). Artificial Intelligence and Patentability: Review and Discussions. *International Journal of Modern Research, 1*(1), 15–21. https://ijmore.co.in/index.php/ijmore/article/view/2

Fraga-Lamas, P., Ramos, L., Mond'ejar-Guerra, V., & Fern'andez-Caram'es, T. M. (2019). A review on IoT deep learning UAV systems for autonomous obstacle detection and collision avoidance. *Remote Sensing, 11*(18), 2144. doi:10.3390/rs11182144

Ganapathy, S., Vijayakumar, P., Yogesh, P., & Kannan, A. (2016). An Intelligent CRF Based Feature Selection for Effective Intrusion Detection. *The International Arab Journal of Information Technology, 13*(1), 64–74.

Gao, J., Yang, Y., Lin, P., & Park, D. S. (2018). Computer vision in healthcare applications. *Journal of Healthcare Engineering*, 1–4.

Guntur, S. R., Gorrepati, R. R., & Dirisala, V. R. (2019). Robotics in healthcare: an internet of medical robotic things (IoMRT) perspective. In *Machine Learning in Bio-Signal Analysis and Diagnostic Imaging* (pp. 293–318). Elsevier. doi:10.1016/B978-0-12-816086-2.00012-6

Haddadin, A. A.-S., & Hirzinger, G. (2010). Safety analysis for a human-friendly manipulator. *International Journal of Social Robotics*, 2(3), 235–252. doi:10.100712369-010-0053-z

Haddadin, S., Albu-Schäffer, A., & Hirzinger, G. (2009). Requirements for safe robots: Measurements, analysis and new insights. *The International Journal of Robotics Research*, 28(11-12), 1507–1527. doi:10.1177/0278364909343970

Hägele, M., Schaaf, W., & Helms, E. (2002). Robot assistants at manual workplaces: Effective co-operation and safety aspects. *Proc. the 33rd ISR (International Symposium on Robotics)*, 7–11.

Hou, Y. C., Mohamed Sahari, K. S., & Yeng Weng, L. (2020). Development of collision avoidance system for multiple autonomous mobile robots. *International Journal of Advanced Robotic Systems*, 17(4). doi:10.1177/1729881420923967

Ishak, M. K., & Kit, N. M. (2017). Design and implementation of robot assisted surgery based on Internet of Things (IoT). In *Proceedings of the 2017 International Conference on Advanced Computing and Applications (ACOMP)* (pp. 65–70). IEEE. 10.1109/ACOMP.2017.20

Joseph, A., Christian, A., Abiodun, A. A., & Oyawale, F. A. (2017). A review on humanoid robotics in healthcare. *Proceedings of the International Conference on Mathematics and Mathematics Education (ICMME-2017)*.

Kanimozhi, U., Ganapathy, S., Manjula, D., & Kannan, A. (2018). An Intelligent Risk Prediction System for Breast Cancer Using Fuzzy Temporal Rules. National Academy Science Letters. *Online (Bergheim)*. Advance online publication. doi:10.100740009-018-0732-0

Kaplan, K. E., Nichols, K. A., & Okamura, A. M. (2016). Toward human-robot collaboration in surgery: performance assessment of human and robotic agents in an inclusion segmentation task. *Proc. 2016 IEEE International Conference on Robotics and Automation (ICRA)*, 723–729. 10.1109/ICRA.2016.7487199

Kim, S. S. Y., Dohler, M., & Dasgupta, P. (2018). Internet of skills: Use of fifth-generation telecommunications, haptics and artificial intelligence in robotic surgery. *BJU International*, 122(3), 356–358. doi:10.1111/bju.14388 PMID:29750403

Kumar, R., & Dhiman, G. (2021). A Comparative Study of Fuzzy Optimization through Fuzzy Number. *International Journal of Modern Research*, *1*(1), 1–14. https://ijmore.co.in/index.php/ijmore/article/view/1

Lehman, A., Berg, K., Dumpert, J., Wood, N. A., Visty, A. Q., Rentschler, M. E., Platt, S. R., Farritor, S. M., & Oleynikov, D. (2008). Surgery with cooperative robots. *Computer Aided Surgery*, *13*(2), 95–105. doi:10.3109/10929080801956706 PMID:18317958

Lokhande, M. P., & Patil, D. D. (2020). *Network Performance Measurement through Machine to Machine Communication in Tele-Robotics System*. Academic Press.

Lokhande, M. P., & Patil, D. D. (2021). Secured energy efficient machine -to-machine communication for telerobotic system. *Informatics in Medicine Unlocked*, *26*, 100731. doi:10.1016/j.imu.2021.100731

Mehrdad, S., Liu, F., Pham, M. T., Lelevé, A., & Atashzar, S. F. (2021). Review of Advanced Medical Telerobots. *Applied Sciences (Basel, Switzerland)*, *11*(1), 209. doi:10.3390/app11010209

Mehta, N., & Pandit, A. (2018). Concurrence of big data analytics and healthcare: A systematic review. *International Journal of Medical Informatics*, *114*, 57–65. doi:10.1016/j.ijmedinf.2018.03.013 PMID:29673604

Meshram, D., & Patil, D. (2020). 5G Enabled Tactile Internet for Tele-Robotic surgery. Third International Conference on Computing and Network Communications. *Procedia Computer Science, 171*, 2618–2625.

Mule, N. M., Patil, D. D., & Kaur, M. (2021). A comprehensive survey on investigation techniques of exhaled breath (EB) for diagnosis of diseases in human body. *Informatics in Medicine Unlocked*, *26*, 100715. doi:10.1016/j.imu.2021.100715

Passino, K. M., & Yurkovich, S. (1998). *Fuzzy Control*. Addison-Wesley, Longman.

Postolache, O., Hemanth, D. J., Alexandre, R., Gupta, D., Geman, O., & Khanna, A. (2020). Remote monitoring of physical rehabilitation of stroke patients using IoT and virtual reality. *IEEE Journal on Selected Areas in Communications*, *39*(2), 562–573. doi:10.1109/JSAC.2020.3020600

Ramesh, L. S., Ganapathy, S., Bhuvaneshwari, R., Kulothungan, K., Pandiyaraju, V., & Kannan, A. (2015). Prediction of user interests for providing relevant information using relevance feedback and re-ranking. *International Journal of Intelligent Information Technologies*, *11*(4), 2. doi:10.4018/IJIIT.2015100104

Rodriguez-Losada, D., Matia, F., Jimenez, A., & Lacey, G. (2005). Guido, the robotic SmartWalker for the frail visually impaired. *Proceedings of the First International Conference on Domotics, Robotics and Remote Assitence for All-DRT4all*, 153–167.

Safeea, M., Neto, P., & Bearee, R. (2019). On-line collision avoidance for collaborative robot manipulators by adjusting off-line generated paths: An industrial use case. *Robotics and Autonomous Systems*, *119*, 278–288. doi:10.1016/j.robot.2019.07.013

Sarakoglou, I., & Tsagarakis, N. G. (2012). A High Performance Tactile Feedback Display and its Integration in Teleoperation. *IEEE Transactions on Haptics*, *5*(3), 252–263. doi:10.1109/TOH.2012.20 PMID:26964111

Sharif, M. S., & Alsibai, M. H. (2017). Medical data analysis based on nao robot: an automated approach towards robotic realtime interaction with human body. In *Proceedings of the 2017 7th IEEE International Conference on Control System, Computing and Engineering (ICCSCE)* (pp. 91–96). IEEE.

Sreelakshmi, M., & Subash, T. D. (2017). Haptic technology: A comprehensive review on its applications and future prospects. *Materials Today: Proceedings*, *4*(2), 4182–4187. doi:10.1016/j.matpr.2017.02.120

Su, H., Ertug Ovur, S., & Li, Z. (2020). Internet of things (IoT)- based collaborative control of a redundant manipulator for teleoperated minimally invasive surgeries. In *Proceedings of the 2020 IEEE International Conference on Robotics and Automation (ICRA)* (pp. 9737–9742). IEEE. 10.1109/ICRA40945.2020.9197321

Thilahar, R., & Thilahar, C. R. (2019). Fuzzy neuro-genetic approach for feature selection and image classification in augmented reality systems. *International Journal of Robotics and Automation*, *8*(3), 194–204. doi:10.11591/ijra.v8i3.pp194-204

Vaishnav, P. K., Sharma, S., & Sharma, P. (2021). Analytical Review Analysis for Screening COVID-19 Disease. *International Journal of Modern Research*, *1*(1), 22–29.

ADDITIONAL READING

Lokhande, M. P., & Patil, D. D. (2019). Access Control Approaches in Internet of Things. *International Journal on Computer Science and Engineering*, *7*. Advance online publication. doi:10.26438/ijcse/v7i5.11581161

Lokhande, M. P., & Patil, D. D. (2020). Security Threats In M2M Framework Of Iot. *IJAST*, *29*(8), 1809–1823.

Lokhande, M. P., & Patil, D. D. (2021). Device Classification for Machine to Machine Communication in Internet of Things for Tele-Robotic Surgery: A Review. *Indian Journal of Computer Science and Engineering.*, *12*(3), 618–628. doi:10.21817/ indjcse/2021/v12i3/211203102

Lokhande, M. P., & Patil, D. D. (2022). Enhancing the Energy Efficiency by LEACH Protocol in the Internet of Thing. *International Journal on Computer Science and Engineering*, *25*(1), 1–10.

KEY TERMS AND DEFINITIONS

Adaptability: A system is able to configure by itself in open environment.
Decision Manager: It gives the decision based on object properties.
Denoising: Removing the unwanted signals from original signal.
Dynamic Context: A system works in changing node behavioral properties.
Semantic: Provide meaning to fuzzy variables.
Unpredictated: A network wherein the devices are continuously works in open environment.

74

Chapter 5
Fog-IoT-Assisted-Based Smart Agriculture Application

Pawan Whig
Vivekananda Institute of Professional Studies, India

Shama Kouser
Jazan University, Saudi Arabia

Arun Velu
Equifax, USA

Rahul Reddy Nadikattu
University of Cumbersome, USA

ABSTRACT

Increased agricultural activity is intended as intelligent agriculture or precision agriculture to be of critical importance. The fast growth of networking has resulted in IoT-based farm management systems. Increased agricultural activity is intended as intelligent agriculture or precision agriculture to be of critical importance. The established cloud-based platforms cannot cope with the huge quotas and diverse data provided by the connected IoT devices, which are based on conventional cloud models. It is important to get data processing closer to the origins of their output to reduce lag in aiding real-time decision-making based on the data generated. The adoption of fog-based models will solve this and will be discussed in this chapter. To ensure optimum bandwidth usage and low latency for real-time decision-making, an IoT-Fog farm management system may be more capable.

DOI: 10.4018/978-1-6684-3733-9.ch005

INTRODUCTION

In Fog Computing, the data, computer, store, and applications are situated anywhere between the data source and the cloud, which is a decentralized computing infrastructure (Whig et al., 2022). Fog computing, like edge computing, brings the cloud's benefits and power closer to where data is produced and acted upon. Because both entail moving intelligence and processing closer to where the data is produced, the phrases fog computing and edge computing are sometimes used interchangeably. This is frequently done to increase productivity, but it might also be done for security or compliance concerns (Anand et al., 2022).

Fog computing extends the cloud's power closer to where information is generated and used. In other words, more people may remain on the internet simultaneously (Alkali et al., 2022). It provides the same networking and cloud services, but with additional safety and compliance.

[1] Dean Research, Vivekananda Institute of Professional Studies
[2] Assistant Professor, Jazan University Saudi Arabia
[3] Researcher Director Equifax, Atlanta USA
[4] Research Scholar, University of Cumbersome, USA

Characteristics of FOG Computing

According to IDC, by 2025, 45 percent of all data will be created at the network edge, with 10 percent of that data coming from edge devices like phones, smartwatches, connected cars, and so on (Chopra & WHIG, 2022). The only technology that can survive the test of time is considered to be Fog Computing and it will even trump Artificial Intelligence, IoT App, and 5G in the next five years.

It delivers highly virtualized storage, computing, and networking services from traditional data centers and end devices in the cloud. Low latency, location awareness, edge location, interoperability, real-time data-cloud connection, and support for online cloud interaction are all characteristics of fog computing (Chopra & Whig, 2022b).

Instead of batch processing, fog apps require real-time interactions and typically interface directly with mobile devices (Chopra & Whig, 2022a). Fog nodes have also been used in diverse contexts with different form factors. The Basic of Fog Computing is shown in Figure 1.

Although a lot has been published and investigated on fog-computing, how various fog actors will align in the future is not simple to say. Based on the nature of major services and applications, it is nonetheless clear to conclude: subscriber models will have an extensive role in fog computing [smart grid, clever cities, linked cars, etc.] (George et al., 2021).

Figure 1. Basic of fog computing

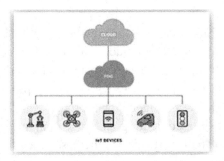

Suppliers of worldwide services are expected to collaborate. New holders, including transport providers, vehicle manufacturers, government authorities, etc., will enter the fog domain. Some recognized Fog Players are cloud-based providers like Apache CloudStack7, OpenStack6, and OpenNebula8 (Mamza, 2021).

FOG VS. EDGE COMPUTING

The cloud allows consumers to quickly and easily access computer, networking, and storage options, but it is a centralized resource (Bhargav & Whig, 2021). This can lead to performance problems and delays for data and devices situated distant from the cloud.

The objective of cutting-edge computing is to bring data sources and equipment closer together, eliminating processing time and distance. In principle, this, in turn, enhances application and device performance and speed (Khera et al., 2021).

Fog computing, a Cisco phrase, also brings the computer to the edge of the network. It also refers to the criteria for the optimum functioning of this procedure. The pyramidal representation of Fog, cloud, and Edge computing is shown in Figure 2.

Figure 2. Pyramidal representation of Fog, Cloud, and Edge

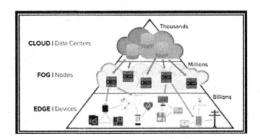

Processing latency is eliminated or significantly reduced by bringing storage and computing systems as close as feasible to the applications, components, and devices that require them. This is especially essential for devices connected to the Internet of Things, which create huge volumes of data. Because they are closer to the data source, these devices have much lower latency in fog computing (Velu & Whig, 2021).

The fog is the standard that allows repetitive, well-structured, scalable performance inside the editing framework to conceive about the distinction between edge computing and fog computing (Whig, 2019a). Data is created, processed, and

stored close together in edge computing, which a kind of fog is computing. Edge processing, as well as the requisite infrastructure and network connections for data transmission, are all part of fog computing (Whig, 2019c).

That is because the objective is to minimize latency and increase efficiency, both in fog and mobile edge computing, while processing data in somewhat different places. Cutting edges generally occur when sensors are connected to equipment and where data collection takes place—there is a physical link between data source and place of processing. Fog computing closes the distance between the processing site and the data source, but does so by carrying out edge computing activity with, or within, the LAN processors linked to, an IoT or fog node (Whig & Ahmad, 2019). This results in a physically more distant processing distance from the sensors, but no further delay (verma, 2019).

Advantages of Fog Computing

Some Advantages of fog Computing is described below

Minimum Latency

Keep analysis closer to the data source, particularly in vertical systems that count every second, prevents system failures, line shutdowns, and other severe difficulties. Faster alarms and less danger for users and loss of time mean the opportunity to do data analysis in real-time.

Good Bandwidth

Keep good bandwidth in the network. Many activities in data analysis, even important analyses, do not require the size of cloud-based storage and processing. Connected gadgets generate additional data for analyses continuously. Most of this large number of data is transported by fog computers to save bandwidth for other vital activities (Reddy, 2019).

Figure 3. Advantage of fog computing

Operational Cost

Operational costs are reduced. The local processing and retention of network bandwidth mean that operational expenses are reduced. Improve safety. It is important to safeguard IoT data, whether during transmission or storage [17]. Users can monitor, defend, and enable fog nodes using the same controls, policies, and processes over the whole IT system.

Confidence

As IoT devices are usually used under severe environmental and emergencies, conditions might be severe. Under these circumstances, fog computing can improve dependability and reduce the load of data transfer. Deepen insights without compromising confidentiality (chouhan, 2019). Your team may locally examine it to the devices that collect, analyze and store the data instead of risking a data breach by transferring sensitive data to the cloud for analysis. This is why fog computing provides wiser choices for more sensitive data in terms of data security and confidentiality.

Agility

Enhance the agility of the business. Only by recognizing the resources consumers require, where these resources are needed, and where help is needed can companies respond swiftly to consumer demand. Fog computing enables developers to quickly create and deploy fog applications as required (Ahmed & Chaudhari, 2022). Fog Computing technology also allows users, based on current capabilities and infrastructure, to give their clients more specialized services and solutions and find data and data tools in which they are best handled.

High dependence on the transportation of data includes fog computing problems. The deployment of the 5G network has addressed this problem, however, there are restricted availability, reduced speeds, and high-frequency congestion. Special care is needed for speed and safety near fog nodes as well (H. Sharma et al., 2016).

Limitations of Fog Computing

Since fog computing is linked to a physical position, some of them anytime/anywhere' advantages of cloud computing are undermined.

Security

Fog computing may, in the appropriate situation, be vulnerable to security challenges, such as Internet Protocol (IP) spoofing or middle man attacks (MitM).

Costs

Fog computing is a system that uses edge and cloud resources, which means that the hardware is expensive.

Ambiguous

While there is some ambiguity in the concept of fog computing among different providers that define fog computing differently, even though fog computer has been present for some years.

RELATIONSHIP OF FOG COMPUTING WITH IOT

IoT and end-users are growing stronger. There is now a great deal of data immediately handled on the cloud. Figure 4 shows IoT devices with Fog Computing (Whig & Ahmad, 2011). In addition to this, there are many advantages to the IoT app development process from fog computing:

Greater Agility for Business

You can create and deploy fog apps with the appropriate tools. The gadget can work like these applications in the user's manner (Whig & Naseem Ahmad, 2012).

Figure 4. Fog computing with IoT

Improved Safety

Fog computing works as a proxy for devices that restrict their resources and upgrade their security software and credentials. It employs fog nodes in different sections of the IT infrastructure utilizing the same policies, procedures, and controls.

Data processing is a sophisticated distributed system via a large number of nodes that makes it easier to check the security status of the nearly linked devices (Whig & Ahmad, 2014b).

Low Delay

Have you noticed just how fast Alexa is asking? This is because fog computing causes minimal latency. As the fog is closer to all users (and devices) geographically, it provides immediate answers. This technology is excellent for all time-sensitive activities.

The Efficiency of Network Bandwidth

Fog computing allows quick and efficient data processing dependent on applications, computer resources, and networking available. Instead of transmitting them over a single route, pieces of information are mixed at several places.

This minimizes the amount of data to be transmitted to the cloud, conserving bandwidth on the network and thus cutting expenses (Bhatia et al., 2015).

Services Continuous

Even if network access to the cloud hinders, Fog Computing can function on its own and provide continuous services. In addition, loss of connection is practically impossible due to many linked channels.

User Experience Enhanced

Edge nodes run stronger protocols such as Zigbee, Z-Wave, or Bluetooth. Instant communication between devices and end-users, independently of networking, is enabled by fog computing which enhances user experience (Whig & Ahmad, 2015).

AGRICULTURE AND FARMING FOG COMPUTING

With the aid of Fog Computing, the agricultural business has profited and revolutionized. The SWAMP project stands for Smart Water Management Platform is a highly notable example in this context (Verma et al., 2015).

Water, which utilizes 70% of freshwater, is a vital component of the agricultural business, making it the most important consumer. Often, leakages in distribution and irrigation systems in-field application methods lead to a waste of resources.

Standard approaches such as surface irrigation waste have a high water content by only watering regions where plants are not advantageous. Local irrigation here allows for more efficient and efficient use of water, which prevents irrigation or irrigation. The main problem is that farmers give extra water to prevent under-irrigation. It not only causes a loss of production but increases the waste of a crucial resource (Shridhar et al., 2014).

Therefore, farmers needed a method to tackle these circumstances and give an adequate answer. And this is when the SWAMP project discovers and addresses IoT, data analysis, stand-alone devices, etc. With the assistance of Fog Computing, SWAMP creates a smart water system idea for agriculture that ensures that water wastes are kept to a minimum (Whig & Ahmad, 2014c). Fog Computing also enables the system to gather and then analyze a sensor analysis from the field to enhance the distribution of water.

The SWAMP project has released an article on the notion of a smart farming environment, in which data are gathered and stored for analysis in real-time. Two various ways of employing fog to filter the data are discussed in the approach (Whig & Ahmad, 2014a). The experiment filters the techniques and uses a real-time data package containing measurements such as temperature and moisture. Agrifog, smart agriculture or precision agriculture which has allowed IoT-based farming systems, is another use of Fog computing in agriculture (Whig & Ahmad, 2013). The software is created with iFogSim.

It seeks to minimize latency in decision-making in real-time cases through data processing. IoT-Fog is a cost-effective and comparative analysis of data collected from the cloud and fog-based systems.

Fog Computing has revolutionized the agricultural and agricultural industries as a platform, enabling farmers to decrease waste and comprehend and analyze processed information to identify ways to benefit from it.

HEALTHCARE COMPUTING AND FOG

In the medical sector, new technologies are regularly used to enhance services and solutions. In addition, Fog Computing was also used to its advantage, similar to previous technical developments (Whig, 2016).

eHealth is one of fog computing's most important uses for healthcare. eHealth is an online and print platform that leads health workers elegantly over the health care trajectory, which regularly sees exciting changes owing to rising technical and other structural changes (Sinha et al., 2015).

They use a network mix in which medical equipment is connected to cloud platforms. The application organizes, transmits, saves, and records information that is important to the process of treatment, payment, and recording. Fog computing facilitates diagnostic and assessment procedures since professionals have access to electro-medical records (EMR), which include documents such as X-rays, ultrasounds, CT scans, or MRIs. It also maintains data in a private cloud secure (Bhatia & Whig, 2013).

The program may save private data on several networks with fog computing and track this information instead of retaining a physical copy. The recorded information allows a physician to access and diagnose the state of the patient and obtain its medical records fast. Fog Computing also enables eHealth to offer rapid answers for essential medical needs (Collings & Shen, 2014).

Likewise, wall, a different health solution, delivers a clever home environment with a fog computer, by building an advanced sensor-based customized context-conscious program.

SMART CITIES AND FOG COMPUTING

Intelligent cities are urban groups using electronic devices and collecting data from populations that are able or unable to live there. Then the data contributes to the quality of life in this town.

People choose to stay and make those clever cities their home with employment possibilities and increased living conditions. To safeguard citizens' and visitors' privacy, Fog Computing creates cost-effective, real-time, and latency-sensitive surveillance systems (A. Sharma et al., 2015).

For several places, Fog computing already made marvels, improving traffic problems. People are located and GPS technology forecasts traffic and offers other routes and arrivals.

Another interesting use of fog computing is autonomous cars, where many data sets need processing. Fog computing plays a major role in connecting low-level sensors and allowing high bandwidth for real-time processing.

Intelligent waste management solutions need to be addressed in intelligent cities that are safe and mindful of the needs of their inhabitants. The municipal council can use sensor data and improvise trash management techniques here. Intelligent waste management solutions are implemented.

Smart cities are evolving more rapidly every day with new technology solutions accessible. With a fog computing platform, the quantity of data being gathered and processed is permitted

EDUCATIONAL FOG COMPUTING

Progress in technology, especially in the light of Covid 19, has changed the education business (Rupani et al., 2017). The whole sector depended significantly on electronic devices and many experts who needed to further their careers were trained via online programs.

The Fog Computing Platform allows simple communication and ensures that networks retain data storage and management. To protect privacy and safety, it enhances scalability, flexibility, and redundancy for education systems.

Computers and Entertainment for Fog

In recent decades, the entertainment business has gone a long way. Both the customers and the producers have enjoyed substantial demand.

Figure 5. Model of smart agriculture

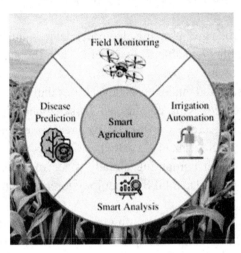

Take Sports into account, all live broadcasts of contests that span wide fields, such as ESPN, NBA TV, NBC Sports Network, etc, and Sports fans want high-quality and accurate coverage of each game minute.

CASE STUDY: AGRICULTURE WITH FOG COMPUTING/ IOT

With 10% of all data from companies created outside the cloud or centralized data centers generated and processed the edge computing gains pace slowly in many sectors (Nadikattu et al., 2020). However, given that the percentage will reach 75% by 2025, we can see an exponential increase in edge computing use shortly. The model of Smart Agriculture is shown in Figure 5.

Edge computing in agriculture has, for a good reason, already been a key IoT trend. Edge computing is gaining strength from the cloud infrastructure as regards speed and efficiency.

While the advantages of IoT applications cannot be overestimated in agriculture, smart farming technologies can nevertheless offer some problems, particularly when they rely on the cloud.

There are some key obstacles to IoT cloud computing. Intelligent and intelligent farming

Case 1

Security Problem: When data is transmitted from one device in the field to the cloud, the likelihood of a breach is quite high. Moreover, a possible vulnerability point may be every device or sensor in the IoT network.

Possible Answer: Continuous computing allows you to limit the danger of data infringement or theft while your data is gathered — inside the device.

Case 2

Concern: Data collection, transmission, and analysis is a time-intensive job. This is why certain companies may confront the problem of choosing between the depth and processing speed of insight derived from the information. This applies in particular to distant farming instruments in the field.

Simple Answer: Edge computing removes this problem through enhanced network efficiency and data processing efficiency. In each network device, the data collected and feedback may be analyzed and processing speeds increased and the depth of insight increased.

Case 3

Cost difficulty: cloud computing costs created by the items and sent through the network usually rely on the volume of data generated by these. The cost of cloud computing may rapidly skyrocket considering the number of devices utilized by a single smart farming system and the amount of data it delivers.

Possible answer: You don't need to crowd or move your warehouse with unnecessary and worthless data by employing cutting-edge computers in agriculture. Solution: As a consequence, both storage and bandwidth costs may simply be reduced in your cloud.

There are many instances of intelligent farming, from monitoring climate change and the monitoring of crop/cattle conditions to automatic greenhouse processing and even end-to-end agricultural management solutions that are IoT-enabled.

The major possibility comes within the so-called "precision agriculture" for the application of edge calculations for smart agriculture. With this strategy, farmers depend on information to better oversee the enterprise, enhance their operational efficiency and thus decrease operating expenditures.

Figure 6.

SOME POSSIBILITIES FOR THE USAGE OF EDGE COMPUTING

Bots

Availability of autopilots autonomous tractors and robotic machines may communicate with adjacent sensors to get the required environmental information as shown in Figure 6.

The most efficient pathways for the area to be covered, taking account of the type of work done, the number of vehicles already in the field, tool dimensions, etc, are calculated with the use of computer vision and pre-loaded field data (Lahade & Hirekhan, 2015). Moreover, if there is an unforeseen barrier or if, for example, a person is on the road, it can re-route automatically or stop entirely.

In this way, the intelligent equipment may carry out several duties, for example, irrigating and weeing fields as necessary or even harvesting crops independently.

Automation

A greenhouse, or even entire farms, may be set on autopilot using IoT edge computing, just like ag robots. To process the collections and decider regular activities, e.g., watering plants, feeding cattle, temperature management, lights, humidity in a room, etc., the closed ecosystem can therefore handle itself without relying on a remote server Figure 7 shows automation in agriculture.

Edge computing, as with robots, enables the farms or greenhouses to function independent of the main server link and take local choices based on local sensor data. This has the potential to increase the dependability of the operations and minimize the waste production processes of agriculture (Arun Velu, 2021; Whig, 2019b).

Figure 7. Agriculture automation

Protection from Natural Disasters

Agriculture IoT systems can make educated choices regarding potential environmental risks or natural catastrophes by utilizing edge computing (Kautish et al. 2022).

Figure 8. Protection using bots

Remote sensors, for example, can gather and analyze data on changes in the weather or the environment to forecast future disasters and, if specific indicators of danger are detected, instantly inform the general control center. As a result, farmers will be able to take early precautions to safeguard their crops, at least partially, in the event of a wildfire, Figure 8 shows protecting crops using Bots (Sharma et al. 2022; Rajawat et al. 2022).

CONCLUSION

This chapter includes various aspects in which Fog computing is connected with IoT and helps in the various sectors particularly in Agricultural Sector. This chapter is very useful for researchers working in the same field. With the advancement in technology soon we have a new revolution in the agriculture sector which is known to be agriculture 4. O.

REFERENCES

Ahmed, S. V., & Chaudhari, A. L. (n.d.). *Development of Microcontroller Based Tool for Effective Learning of Concepts in Control System*. Academic Press.

AlkaliY.RoutrayI.WhigP. (2022). Study of various methods for reliable, efficient and Secured IoT using Artificial Intelligence. *Available at* SSRN 4020364. doi:10.2139/ssrn.4020364

Anand, M., Velu, A., & Whig, P. (2022). Prediction of Loan Behaviour with Machine Learning Models for Secure Banking. *Journal of Computing Science and Engineering: JCSE, 3*(1), 1–13.

Arun Velu, P. W. (2021). Impact of Covid Vaccination on the Globe using data analytics. *International Journal of Sustainable Development in Computing Science, 3*(2).

Bhargav, R., & Whig, P. (2021). More Insight on Data Analysis of Titanic Data Set. *International Journal of Sustainable Development in Computing Science, 3*(4), 1–10.

Bhatia, V., & Whig, P. (2013). Secure d Dual Tone Mul Mu l ti Frequency based Smart Elevator. *Control Systems (Tonbridge), 1*(4), 1–5.

Bhatia, V., Whig, P., & Ahmad, S. N. (2015). Smart PCS Based System for Oxygen Content Measurement. *International Journal of Information Technology and Computer Science, 7*(6), 45–51. doi:10.5815/ijitcs.2015.06.06

Chopra, G., & Whig, P. (2022). A clustering approach based on support vectors. *International Journal of Machine Learning for Sustainable Development, 4*(1), 21–30.

Chopra, G., & Whig, P. (2022a). Energy Efficient Scheduling for Internet of Vehicles. *International Journal of Sustainable Development in Computing Science, 4*(1).

Chopra, G., & Whig, P. (2022b). Smart Agriculture System Using AI. *International Journal of Sustainable Development in Computing Science, 1*(1).

Chouhan, S. (2019). Using an Arduino and a temperature, humidity sensor, Automate the fan speed. *International Journal of Sustainable Development in Computing Science*, *1*(2).

Collings, N., & Shen, Y. (2014). Development of low power Dynamic threshold PCS System. *Journal of Electrical & Electronic Systems*, *03*(03). Advance online publication. doi:10.4172/2332-0796.1000131

George, N., Muiz, K., Whig, P., & Velu, A. (2021). Framework of Perceptive Artificial Intelligence using Natural Language Processing (PAIN). *Artificial & Computational Intelligence*.

Khera, Y., Whig, P., & Velu, A. (2021). efficient effective and secured electronic billing system using AI. *Vivekananda Journal of Research*, *10*, 53–60.

Lahade, S. V., & Hirekhan, S. R. (2015). Intelligent and adaptive traffic light controller (IA-TLC) using FPGA. *2015 International Conference on Industrial Instrumentation and Control (ICIC)*, 618–623. 10.1109/IIC.2015.7150816

Mamza, E. S. (2021). Use of AIOT in Health System. *International Journal of Sustainable Development in Computing Science*, *3*(4), 21–30.

Nadikattu, R. R., Mohammad, S. M., & Whig, P. (2020). *Novel economical social distancing smart device for covid-19. International Journal of Electrical Engineering and Technology*.

Reddy, R. (2019). Purification of indoor air using a novel pseudo PMOS ultraviolet photocatalytic oxidation (PP-UVPCO) sensor. *International Journal of Sustainable Development in Computing Science*, *1*(3).

Rupani, A., Whig, P., Sujediya, G., & Vyas, P. (2017). A robust technique for image processing based on interfacing of Raspberry-Pi and FPGA using IoT. *2017 International Conference on Computer, Communications and Electronics (Comptelix)*, 350–353. 10.1109/COMPTELIX.2017.8003992

Sharma, A., Kumar, A., & Whig, P. (2015). On the performance of CDTA based novel analog inverse low pass filter using 0.35 µm CMOS parameter. *International Journal of Science, Technology & Management*, *4*(1), 594–601.

Sharma, H., Rao, N., & Sharma, M. (2016). Analysis of astrology and scientific calculation through orbital period. *2016 3rd International Conference on Computing for Sustainable Global Development (INDIACom)*, 236–239.

Shridhar, J., Ruchin, & Whig, P. (2014). Design and simulation of power efficient traffic light controller (PTLC). *2014 International Conference on Computing for Sustainable Global Development, INDIACom 2014.* 10.1109/IndiaCom.2014.6828157

Sinha, R., Whig, P., & Ranjan, A. (2015). Effect of Variable Damping Ratio on design of PID Controller. *2015 4th International Conference on Reliability, Infocom Technologies and Optimization: Trends and Future Directions, ICRITO 2015*, 4–7. 10.1109/ICRITO.2015.7359340

Velu, A., & Whig, P. (2021). Protect Personal Privacy And Wasting Time Using Nlp: A Comparative Approach Using Ai. *Vivekananda Journal of Research*, *10*, 42–52.

Verma, T. (2019). A comparison of different R2R D/A converters. *International Journal of Sustainable Development in Computing Science, 1*(2).

Verma, T., Gupta, P., & Whig, P. (2015). Sensor controlled sanitizer door knob with scan technique. *Advances in Intelligent Systems and Computing.* doi:10.1007/978-3-319-13731-5_29

Whig, P. (2016). Modelling and Simulation of Economical Water Quality Monitoring Device. *Journal of Aquaculture & Marine Biology, 4*(6). https://doi.org/10.15406/jamb.2016.04.00103

Whig, P. (2019a). A Novel Multi-Center and Threshold Ternary Pattern. *International Journal of Machine Learning for Sustainable Development, 1*(2), 1–10.

Whig, P. (2019b). Exploration of Viral Diseases mortality risk using machine learning. *International Journal of Machine Learning for Sustainable Development*, *1*(1), 11–20.

Whig, P. (2019c). Machine Learning Based Techniques for Communication and Signal Processing Problem. *International Journal of Machine Learning for Sustainable Development, 1*(3), 1–10.

Whig, P., & Ahmad, S. N. (2011). On the Performance of ISFET-based Device for Water Quality Monitoring. *Int'l J. of Communications, Network and System Sciences, 4*(11), 709–719. doi:10.4236/ijcns.2011.411087

Whig, P., & Ahmad, S. N. (2013). A novel pseudo NMOS integrated CC-ISFET device for water quality monitoring. *Journal of Integrated Circuits and Systems.* https://www.scopus.com/inward/record.url?eid=2-s2.0-84885357423&partnerID=MN8TOARS

Whig, P., & Ahmad, S. N. (2014a). CMOS integrated VDBA-ISFET device for water quality monitoring. *International Journal of Intelligent Engineering and Systems*. https://www.scopus.com/inward/record.url?eid=2-s2.0-84901490722&partnerID=MN8TOARS

Whig, P., & Ahmad, S. N. (2014b). Simulation of linear dynamic macro model of photo catalytic sensor in SPICE. In *COMPEL - The International Journal for Computation and Mathematics in Electrical and Electronic Engineering* (Vol. 33, Issues 1–2). doi:10.1108/COMPEL-09-2012-0160

Whig, P., & Ahmad, S. N. (2014c). Simulation of linear dynamic macro model of photo catalytic sensor in SPICE. *COMPEL - The International Journal for Computation and Mathematics in Electrical and Electronic Engineering*. doi:10.1108/COMPEL-09-2012-0160

Whig, P., & Ahmad, S. N. (2015). Novel FGMOS based PCS device for low power applications. *Photonic Sensors*. doi:10.1007/s13320-015-0224-5

Whig, P., & Ahmad, S. N. (2019). Methodology for Calibrating Photocatalytic Sensor Output. *International Journal of Sustainable Development in Computing Science*, *1*(1), 1–10.

Whig, P., Nadikattu, R. R., & Velu, A. (2022). COVID-19 pandemic analysis using application of AI. *Healthcare Monitoring and Data Analysis Using IoT: Technologies and Applications*, 1.

Whig, P., & Naseem Ahmad, S. (2012). DVCC based Readout Circuitry for Water Quality Monitoring System. *International Journal of Computers and Applications*, 49(22), 1–7 https://doi.org/10.5120/7900 1162

Kautish, S., Reyana, A., & Vidyarthi, A. (2022). SDMTA: Attack Detection and Mitigation Mechanism for DDoS Vulnerabilities in Hybrid Cloud Environment. *IEEE Transactions on Industrial Informatics*.

Rajawat, A. S., Bedi, P., Goyal, S. B., Kautish, S., Xihua, Z., Aljuaid, H., & Mohamed, A. W. (2022). Dark Web Data Classification Using Neural Network. *Computational Intelligence and Neuroscience*.

Sharma, C., Sharma, S., Kautish, S., Alsallami, S. A., Khalil, E. M., & Mohamed, A. W. (2022). A new median-average round Robin scheduling algorithm: An optimal approach for reducing turnaround and waiting time. *Alexandria Engineering Journal*, *61*(12), 10527–10538.

ADDITIONAL READING

Raman, A. (2019). Potentials of fog computing in higher education. *Int J Emerg Technol Learn*, *14*(18), 194–202. doi:10.3991/ijet.v14i18.10765

Ray, P. P., Adhikary, P., lana, S., Mitra, S., Halder, T., Paul, M., Mukherjee, A., Koshika, De, A., Chakravorty, N., Goswami, R., Kundu, V., & Sarkar, D. (2018). A survey on internet of things architectures. *J King Saud Univ Comput Inf Sci.*, *30*(3), 291–319. doi:10.1109/IEMCON.2018.8614931

Bhatia, V., & Whig, P. (2013). A secured dual tune multi frequency based smart elevator control system. *International Journal of Research in Engineering and Advanced Technology*, *4*(1), 1163–2319.

Pervan, G. P. (1998). A review of research in Group Support Systems: Leaders, approaches and directions. *Decision Support Systems*, *23*(2), 149–159. doi:10.1016/S0167-9236(98)00041-4

Rupani, A., Whig, P., Sujediya, G., & Vyas, P. (2017). A robust technique for image processing based on interfacing of Raspberry-Pi and FPGA using IoT. *2017 International Conference on Computer, Communications and Electronics (Comptelix)*, 350–353. 10.1109/COMPTELIX.2017.8003992

Sharma, A., Kumar, A., & Whig, P. (2015). On the performance of CDTA based novel analog inverse low pass filter using 0.35 μm CMOS parameter. International Journal of Science. *Technology & Management*, *4*(1), 594–601.

Singh, A. K., Gupta, A., & Senani, R. (2018). OTRA-based multi-function inverse filter configuration. *Advances in Electrical and Electronic Engineering*, *15*(5), 846–856. doi:10.15598/aeee.v15i5.2572

Whig, P., & Ahmad, S. N. (2012). Performance analysis of various readout circuits for monitoring quality of water using analog integrated circuits. *International Journal of Intelligent Systems and Applications*, *4*(11), 103. doi:10.5815/ijisa.2012.11.11

Whig, P., & Ahmad, S. N. (2014). Simulation of linear dynamic macro model of photo catalytic sensor in SPICE. *COMPEL: The International Journal for Computation and Mathematics in Electrical and Electronic Engineering*.

Jeschke, S., Brecher, C., Meisen, T., Özdemir, D., & Eschert, T. (2017). Industrial internet of things and cyber manufacturing systems. In *Industrial internet of things* (pp. 3–19). Springer. doi:10.1007/978-3-319-42559-7_1

McRae, L., Ellis, K., & Kent, M. (2018). *Internet of things (IoT): education and technology. Relatsh. between Educ. Technol. students with Disabil.* Leanne, Res.

KEY TERMS AND DEFINITIONS

Agriculture Sector: The Agriculture sectors comprise establishments primarily engaged in growing crops, raising animals, and harvesting fish and other animals from a farm, ranch, or their natural habitats.

AI: Artificial intelligence (AI) is the ability of a computer or a robot controlled by a computer to do tasks that are usually done by humans because they require human intelligence and discernment.

Big Data: Big data is a combination of structured, semi structured and unstructured data collected by organizations that can be mined for information and used in machine learning projects, predictive modeling and other advanced analytics applications.

Cloud Computing: Cloud computing is a general term for anything that involves delivering hosted services over the internet.

Fog Computing: Fog computing is a decentralized computing infrastructure in which data, compute, storage, and applications are located somewhere between the data source and the cloud.

IoT: The term IoT, or Internet of Things, refers to the collective network of connected devices and the technology that facilitates communication between devices and the cloud, as well as between the devices themselves.

Machine Learning: Machine learning is a branch of artificial intelligence (AI) and computer science which focuses on the use of data and algorithms to imitate the way that humans learn, gradually improving its accuracy.

Smart Cities: A smart city is a municipality that uses information and communication technologies (ICT) to increase operational efficiency, share information with the public and improve both the quality of government services and citizen welfare.

Chapter 6
Demystifying Federated Learning in Artificial Intelligence With Human–Computer Interaction

Pawan Whig
Vivekanada Institute of Professional Studies, India

Arun Velu
Equifax, USA

Rahul Ready
University of Cumbersome, USA

ABSTRACT

Today, attempts have been made to overcome entertainment objectives in the production of video games. In reality, much work has gone into seeking tools in computer science using AI and advanced technologies to develop games so that they can be used in educational, industry, or political processes. For these goods to be successfully introduced into society, they must be crafted to be as available as possible to all people, including those who belong to minorities with special needs. Adaptability and compatibility need to ensure better quality and adoption of goods to meet accessibility requirements. With demystifying federated learning in artificial intelligence, the possibilities of combining human-computer interaction with artificial intelligence to enhance usability in games, and thus to make them more democratic and useful to society, especially for those who rely on assistive technology services, are discussed in this chapter.

DOI: 10.4018/978-1-6684-3733-9.ch006

INTRODUCTION

Human-computer interaction is the study of the design and use of computer technology, with an emphasis on the interfaces between humans and computers (Whig et al., 2022). HCI researchers study how people interact with processors and create knowledge that allows humans to connect with computers in innovative ways.

Human-computer interaction is a research subject that combines computer science, behavioral sciences, design, media studies, and numerous other disciplines. Stuart K. Card, Allen Newell, and Thomas P. Moran popularized the phrase in their landmark 1983 book, The Thinking of Human with Computer Interaction, while the authors originally used the word in 1980 and the earliest documented usage was in 1975. The phrase implies that, in contrast to other instruments with restricted applications, a computer has numerous uses, which occur as an open-ended conversation between the user and the computer. The concept of dialogue compares human-computer interaction to human with the human conversation, which is important for theoretical concerns in the subject (Anand et al., 2022).

Previously, Human-Computer Interface (HCI) was known as man-machine research or man-machine interaction. It is worried about the design, implementation, and evaluation of computer systems and associated phenomena for human use.

HCI may be applied in any discipline where computer installation is possible (Alkali et al., 2022). Some of the areas where HCI may be applied with particular significance are listed below in Figure 1.

Humans engage with computers in a variety of ways, and the edge that exists between humans and the computers they use is critical to allow this connection. Desktop programs, web browsers, portable computers, and computer kiosks all make use of today's popular graphical user interfaces (GUI) (Chopra & Whig, 2022). Voice user interfaces (VUI) are utilized in voice recognition and synthesis systems and developing multi-modal and gestalt User Interfaces (GUI) enable people to interact with embodied character agents in ways that conventional interface paradigms cannot. In its history, the HCI field has grown in terms of interaction quality and branching (George et al., 2021). Rather than building traditional interfaces, several study disciplines have focused on concepts like multimodality versus mono modality, intelligent adaptive interfaces against command/action based interfaces, and active versus passive interfaces. (Mamza, 2021).

Human-computer interaction is defined by the Association for Computing Machinery (ACM) as "a field concerned with the design, development, and implementation of interactive computing systems for human use, as well as the study of key phenomena surrounding them." Securing user happiness is an essential aspect of HCI (Sinha & Ranjan, 2015). "Because human-computer interaction investigates the interaction of a human and a machine, it depends on supporting information

Figure 1. Areas associated with HCI

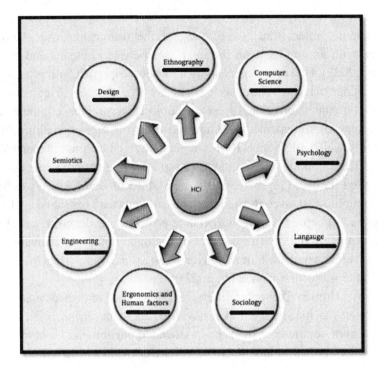

from both the machine and the human side. On the machine side, techniques in computer graphics, operating systems, programming languages, and development environments are important. (Parihar & Yadav, 2022.).

On the human side, communication theory, visual and industrial design disciplines, linguistics, social sciences, cognitive psychology, social psychology, and human factors like computer user satisfaction are all vital. Of course, engineering and design approaches are important (Bhargav & Whig, 2021). People from many backgrounds contribute to the success of HCI due to its interdisciplinary character. Human-machine interaction (HCI) is also known as HMI, man-machine interaction (MMI), and computer-human interaction (CHI) (Khera et al., 2021).

The Framework of how the human-computer interface work is shown in Fig. 2. The Framework shows the complete flow of the information in human-computer interactions D1-D4 shows the development process starts from Design approaches, Implementation techniques and tools, evaluation techniques, and case studies. U1-U3 indicates Social Organization and work Human-machine Fit and adaptation, and Application areas as described in the figure 2.

Figure 2. Framework of human-computer interface

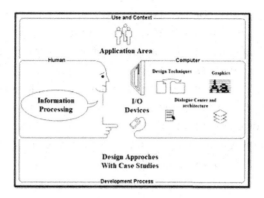

Various Goals of HCI

Human-computer interaction is the study of how people utilize or do not use computing products, systems, and infrastructures. As a result, most of the research in the subject aims to improve human-computer interaction by making computer interfaces more usable (Velu & Whig, 2021). There are rising disagreements on how usability should be defined, how it relates to other social and cultural standards, and when it is and when it is not a desirable quality of computer interfaces

Component of HCI

HCI, as a field, focuses on establishing a "natural" conversation between the user and the computer. The engagement with a computer in such a conversation does not necessitate a great deal of cognitive work on the part of the user. We assist our consumers in using machines to solve their issues when we invest a lot of work into creating effective human-computer interfaces (verma, 2019; Whig, 2019c; Whig & Ahmad, 2019). In contrast, failure to pay attention to human-computer interaction nearly invariably leads to the creation of poor user interfaces. Poor HCI leads to poor usability, which raises the likelihood of product failure.

Human-computer interaction is made up of four major components. Let's take a closer look at each of them:

USER

The term "user" can refer to either an individual or a group of users who collaborate. HCI examines how people behave, interact with technology, and what their wants and aspirations are. Consider their talents and cognitive processes, as well as their personality, experience, motivation, and emotions (Arun Velu, 2021). It is critical in today's modern, highly competitive industry to provide the greatest possible customer experience. Not unexpectedly, user-centered design (a method in which designers focus on users and their requirements at every stage of the design process) is critical in the design process.

Product teams that practice user-centered design include people in the design process from the start, and important design decisions are assessed based on how well they perform for users. Product teams also strive to strike a balance between user and business requirements (chouhan, 2019; Reddy, 2019; Whig, 2019b; Whig & Ahmad, 2019). The Major Component of Human-computer interactions is shown in Figure 3.

Figure 3. Component of HCI

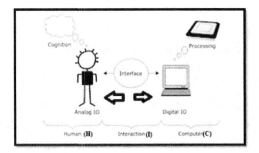

Goal

When a user interacts with a computer, they usually have a purpose in mind - often, it is a task that they wish to complete (Nadikattu et al., 2021). A digital product is just a tool that enables consumers to complete this activity more efficiently. In an e-commerce setting, for example, a job may be to add an item to the shopping basket and then purchase it.

When considering goal-driven experience, consider the following factors:

How difficult or simple it is for the user to complete a task

The abilities necessary to interact with a product

The amount of time needed to operate.

Medium

Designers must focus on developing a suitable design hierarchy while creating graphical user interfaces. Users can explore and absorb material more easily when there is a clear structure. The medium, device, or interface is an essential component in human-computer interaction.

For example, while designing a visual user interface, you must consider the following factors: display size, resolution, and principal mode of interaction (Aparicio et al., 2022). To improve the user experience, you must change the hierarchy based on these characteristics. When people visit your website from their mobile devices, for example, you may want to present only the most important information and size the text for pleasant engagement by making content simpler to read on tiny screens.

Context

The term "human-computer interface" refers to the interaction between a human user and a computer system. Interactions are an important element of this communication. Human-computer interaction is influenced not just by the tasks that users do with gadgets, but also by the context in which such actions occur. The context specifies the real circumstances in which the computer system is employed. For example, when designing a mobile app, you must consider how the visual design will seem in both dim lighting and sun glare, as well as whether the app will function properly in the event of a bad internet connection. These are only two of the numerous factors that may influence user experience (Sharma et al., 2016).

Good interaction design is always the product of thorough user testing and ongoing refining of specific design features, particularly those that may be impacted by the context of usage. As a result, the human-computer interface should always be tested with real users who are representative of the intended population (Kumavat et al.,2022).

RESEARCH IN THE FIELD OF HCI

Some of the research areas of HCI is mentioned below

- Methods for creating innovative computer interfaces, to optimize a design for the desired attribute such as learnability or usability
- Methods for implementing interfaces, such as through software libraries
- Methods for assessing and comparing interfaces in terms of usability and other desired qualities

- Methods for researching human-computer usage and its broader societal consequences
- The use of cognitivist user models and Activity Theory descriptions of human-computer use, as well as conceptual frameworks for computer interface design
- Considerations of computational design, computer use, and HCI research.

Researchers in the field have different ideas of what they want to accomplish. As part of a cognitivist approach, HCI researchers may seek to align computer interfaces with the mental picture that humans have of their activities A post-cognitivist perspective may be taken by HCI researchers to integrate computer interfaces with contemporary social behaviors or conventions. (Mathurkar et al., 2021).

New design approaches, gadgets, software and hardware prototypes, interaction paradigms, and interaction models and theories are all of interest to HCI researchers (Srivastava et al., 2020).

Human-computer interaction research focuses on the user, their purpose and task, the medium and the human-computer interface, as well as the context in which the interaction occurs. As technology advances and influences every aspect of our life, it is critical to continue to investigate and advance the subject of HCI.

Adobe, Microsoft, and Facebook research are regularly translated into technological innovations that aid in the creation of intuitive and usable interfaces for a wide range of industries. Voice is just the beginning of how user interfaces will evolve (Sowmya et al., 2020).

RESEARCH CHALLENGES IN AI WITH HCI

Various research challenges in the field of AI with HCI are described in this section

1. **Significant human control**

Intelligent autonomous systems should be overseen and managed by humans, despite their "intelligence" and capacity to make automated judgments and conclusions, according to a major concern. Pilots, who have supervisory control over systems and the flight deck, are a good example of human control over automated systems (Nadikattu et al., 2020b). Outer-loop control rather than inner-loop control is used by the pilots as shown in Figure. 4. As a result, the nature of the pilot's control duties on the flight deck has changed dramatically. A comparable design problem arises with the introduction and diffusion of semi-automated driving, which is

Figure 4. Significant human control

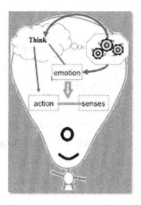

relevant to a considerably larger number of users. There are trade-offs to be made between human control and automation when shifting control from driver to vehicle.

As part of the short-term research goals for robust and useful AI, meaningful human control has been described as human in the loop and human on the loop, when human intervention directly impacts the acting entity, it is referred to as "human in the loop", whereas when it influences the activities or community of the active entity, it is referred to "human on the loop".

People, not computers or algorithms, should ultimately be in command of autonomous systems' behaviors - and hence ethically responsible for them. (Ruchin & Whig, 2015).

Transparent, understandable, and accountable aspects of intelligent systems are key to achieving human control. They also contribute to creating a relationship of trust between users and systems, as well as boosting the performance of both teams.

Furthermore, transparent user interfaces allow users to see and understand their actions and results. A machine learning system's capacity to explain and display information in an intelligible manner is directly connected to transparency. As well as the capacity to verify and enhance a system, explainable AI has the potential to learn from humans and acquire new insights (Shrivastav et al., n.d.).

As an alternative, the idea of transparency in complex systems suffers from technological and temporal restrictions, in addition to severe flaws. Because of this lack of impact on the world, transparency might lose its strength, while simultaneously posing privacy risks. Even more significantly, just because something is visible, it doesn't imply it's comprehensible, which is a difficult undertaking when dealing with complicated systems. When it comes to accessibility, transparency means offering clear and concise explanations that are easy to understand (Bhatia & Bhatia, 2013).

2.   Intelligence

What we've just discussed points to a more holistic view of digital intelligence, which emphasizes people and their experience with technology rather than 'intelligent functioning' or 'intuitive usability' When it comes to adopting new technologies, the focus will shift from technical concerns to how well the skill is linked with the values of humans (Ahmad, 2012).

"Clever" means "smart but only if cooperative and compassionate" as a result This means that humans will be supported in their activities, their privacy will be respected, and they will be enabled to maximize their own personal creative, social and economic potential as well as live a self-determined existence (Nadikattu, 2020a).

3.   Variation of needs

It is also important that these intelligent environments support humans by providing personalized, adaptive, and proactive services in a variety of settings: homes, offices, public spaces, as well as on the road. They were first introduced in 2001 and are expected to be fully developed by 2010 according to the IST Advisory Group Ambient Intelligence scenarios (Nadikattu, 2014). When the API method was developed, it already had an orientation towards the aims and values that are currently being addressed and expressed in the scientific community.

AI and big data must be incorporated into adaptation and personalization techniques to achieve the vision of personalized, adaptive, responsive services. As deep learning algorithms require a large amount of data to learn from and refine their decision-making, these technologies are predicted to operate in concert in intelligent settings in the meantime, AI has already been utilized in a variety of ways to ease the capture and arranging of big data, as well as to analyze big data for critical insights. There are several situations where it is reasonably straightforward to identify a user's present behavior, such as in smart and ambient assisted living settings (AAL). Users' mobility patterns are being tracked using a rising number of sensors and sensing devices. In addition to individual preferences, variation should take into account organizational and social factors, such as organizational culture and degree of competence in leveraging technology to gather huge data, such as corporate culture (Bhatia & Gupta, 2015).

4.   Skill

People's expectations of what they need to learn to live and work effectively might shift fundamentally when robots gain the ability to learn profoundly and actively from data. A symbiotic method, for example, would have humans handle qualitative subjective judgments while machines handle quantitative components, a strategy that relies on tools to assist human talent and inventiveness rather than robots that would objectively measure knowledge. In instances when a human has to digest a large quantity of complicated data or make a vital choice quickly or under high stress, advanced technology, like AI, can be utilized to enhance human memory and problem-solving (Nadikattu, 2020b). PA, notices, memory, and cognitive aids as well as a decision aid and recommender schemes are all examples of technology that compensates for human functional limits. Using artificial intelligence (AI) is being used to aid people in managing daily chores such as shopping and managing finances.

By giving the capacity to capture events holistically, technology will be able to transcend human perception and overcome human sense limits in the future. Additionally, it can enhance human memory by providing access to networked cognitive intelligence technologies that can aid people in completing ordinary daily tasks. A convergence of ICT and the biological brain might ultimately be utilized to improve human perception and cognition through technology According to this idea, human judgment and tacit knowledge, as well as intuition and intuition should be combined with the potential of machine intelligence.

However, such development is presently only an idea and research goal, not a concrete reality. So that we may better understand human cognition and the brain, cognitive sciences will be required to enhance our efforts here. Recent advances in ICT, such as big data derived from human activity, can aid cognitive science research by providing hints towards understanding underlying principles of cognition.

5. Simulation of Emotion

As emotional and empathic beings, humans exhibit their emotions via relationships with other humans and computers. A significant problem in improving the human-technology relationship is how ICT can record and correlate emotional signals, as well as how technology can convey emotions and demonstrate empathetic behavior (Bhateja et al., 2018). Human-technology connection and cooperation are facilitated by simulated effects; nevertheless, people may be deceived into thinking that computers don't truly have these affective states and may become emotionally over-attached as a result. The Flow Chart Representation of the simulation of Emotions is shown in figure 5.

It's also possible for individuals to be deceived deliberately by an emotional computing system, such as by convincing them to make a purchase. In this regard, a new code of ethics is essential. If such a code of ethics is to be reinforced, a multi-level strategy must be taken, starting with the training of software engineers, followed by rigorous difficult and new benchmarking processes (Whig, 2021).

Figure 5. Flow chart representation of simulation of Emotions

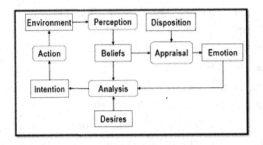

6.   Safety

Human safety is important in this new context and should be taken into account throughout design and implementation, as well as through unique testing techniques **(Chopra & Whig, 2021)**. Development and usage of self-evolving intelligent systems, in particular, carries significant dangers owing to technological misuse or bad design. So, sophisticated intelligent systems should be "safe by design," which means that they should be designed utilizing safe and safer technology paradigms as early as feasible in the lifespan **(Velu & Whig, n.d.)**.

When it comes to autonomous systems, conventional software testing techniques can't keep up since systems' behavior depends not just on project and execution, but also on the gained information of the system. It will also become increasingly important to study the impact of AI on humans and society, both in the short- and long term, as AI develops (Asopa et al., 2021). This will require collaboration with a variety of interdisciplinary groups that include computer scientists as well as social scientists and psychologists, economists as well as lawyers.

7.   Ethnic shift

Intelligent environments and artificial intelligence (AI) require a cultural transformation in addition to technological hurdles and shifts. The technical change must thus progress in tandem with the cultural change Social-systems analysis is needed to have a better understanding of the implications of smart ecosystems (Whig, 2019a). Most people believe that increasingly clever computers will eventually surpass human capabilities, making us ineffective and taking our jobs, and even killing us. For smart ecosystems to become widely trusted and used, present ideas and attitudes must be changed. This may be accomplished through reevaluating the field's purpose, aims, and possibilities. Detailed assessments of ethical and confidentiality problems, as well as design methods with their underlying ideas around the character of individuals, are required to be persuasive to both the public and the scientific community (Ajay Rupani, 2019). The Ethnic Composition as an example is shown in figure 6

Figure 6. The ethnic composition as an example

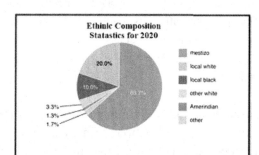

Research Issues

In smart settings and ecosystems, communication will become more implied hidden in the continuity between the corporeal and numerical worlds, and more subtle. Virtual/digital things in the physical/architectural realm are only two examples of 'hybrid worlds' that must be taken into consideration. Although all objects are represented in both domains, there isn't a one-to-one mapping between the two, which has a significant impact on interaction design (Rupani & Kumar, 2020).

There's no need for computers to stand out in the surroundings, and soon there won't be a need for them at all. for example, the company's culture. There are two ways to do this: physically, by integrating with the surroundings, or intellectually, by changing our perceptions. Computers become part of the décor in such situations. Embedding a computer in the environment makes it "disappear," raising the question of how people perceive an object's interactivity and how they view it as a partner in interaction (Ahmad, 2019).

It's important to remember that 'users' are often unaware of the engagement choices accessible in their present smart surroundings since traditional 'affordances' are no longer available in these situations. Like the method described in Interactive Maps, where users may transfer their present knowledge and engagement patterns from a digital to a real-world context. Interactions in settings with many interacting items and systems provide additional problems, such as how users may properly address a specific system.

It has also been possible to integrate interactivity in jewelry and haute couture due to the shrinking of computers even though smart gadgets such as glasses, wristwatches, and wristbands are currently commercially accessible, they yet to become popular and have a slower diffusion rate than other portable technology such as smartphones. When it comes to wearable gadgets, aesthetic aspects such as captivating design and originality play a role in their adoption (Purva Agarwal1, 2016). They are hence "technology" objects, which combine fashion and technology. A growing society of information overload, information exploitation, and information inequity might result despite the enthusiasm and promises of concealing computers in ordinary things such as furniture and accessories.

1.   Hidden interactions

In addition to conscious and deliberate interactions, we expect subconscious and even unintentional/incidental interactions or interactions that are subconscious yet intentional, with direct but imperfect control, in the periphery of attention. A significant challenge when designing for such settings is how to build experiences that are interaction-intensive yet not overly intrusive.

The best way to deal with the inevitable fluctuations in attention between the core and the peripheral is to plan. Users should not be put under undue cognitive and perceptual strain, nor should they experience confusion or dissatisfaction as a result of the interactive environment. Intelligent settings may create privacy problems because of implicit interactions. Technically speaking, to enable such interactions, the environment must capture contextual and user data, and do the necessary analysis to reply properly and effectively (Nadikattu et al., 2020a).

2.   Heightened interactions

New types of interaction might emerge shortly that make the use of sensors and mimic human senses. Most people engage with technology through their eyesight, hearing, and touch, but taste and smell are still mostly unknown. Multisensory interactions in future settings might include digitalized chemical senses such as taste and smell and perhaps physical haptics For intelligent settings, various types of natural interaction are essential (Whig & Ahmad, 2018).

As a result, the level of engagement will skyrocket in terms of possibilities, combinations, and technological needs. Aside from that, the focus of design will shift away from a single user-artifact interaction. He or she will have to take into consideration whole ecosystems, ecologies, and data sets as well as huge user groups dispersed in a variety of physical places and contexts of usage Instead of just adding more people, data, or artifacts to the design process, this wider context calls for new design techniques

Intelligent settings will require a design approach that puts the human being at the forefront, such as user-centered design (UCD) or human-centered design (HCD). Since their major purpose is to guarantee that technology meets users' requirements in the best possible way, this is especially true, since it is stated that this is the ultimate goal of this new technical domain. To meet the new obstacles in terms of obtaining and structuring the prospective use contexts, extracting user needs, generating designs, and conducting evaluations, such design techniques must continue to evolve (Chouhan et al., 2017).

3. Public spaces Interaction

Public areas with a large number of people make all of the aforementioned problems and challenges much more complex. Ongoing research explores different user roles and interaction styles, as well as recommends frameworks for the design of public space interaction. According to how they engage with a public system, users can be classified as onlookers, spectators, etc. It's important to think about how interactive systems may capture passersby's attention and inspire them to participate with the system Challenge, curiosity, and a sense of responsibility have been identified as factors that encourage participation in public systems.

In addition, the proliferation of technology in public contexts that blur the lines between private and public contact is a source of worry for interface designers For example, how should a third party perceive a user's engagement. Interactive experiences in public areas must give clear and timely feedback on who is in charge of the interaction, define what both users are in switch of, and support the different user roles in terms of (social) interaction and content. Privacy and public contact have "blurred" borders (Whig & Ahmad, 2017).

As a result, the encounters that take place in public places tend to be fleeting. There are many "transient places" such as cities and airports, which are being changed into smart cities and smart airports as a result of multi-user as well as multi-device activities. Additionally, public places must accommodate a wide range of user characteristics because of the transitory nature of interactions Among them include calming aesthetics, assistance for short-term fluid interactions, and quick usability In addition, new ways of user engagement in the design process are needed.

4. Interactions in VR and AR

One of the "scientific, philosophical, and technological frontiers of our time," virtual reality (VR) poses unprecedented challenges because Navigation and interaction with virtual items and characters, who may represent actual individuals anywhere in the globe, are possible. VR has been made possible by recent technical

Figure 7. Human-object interaction in AR/VR

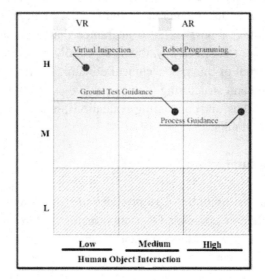

developments, and most industry projections indicate that VR will soon have a big influence (Ahmad & Whig, 2011).

Immersion, presence, and interaction are key aspects of the VR experience, as well as the virtual environment, the producers, and the players. There has been a focus in recent years on improving hardware systems. Following significant technological advancements, the goal now is to create realistic experiences that improve the sense of immersion and presence in the virtual worlds. Advances in the sense of embodiment are required in AR/VR, which encompasses the self-location and body ownership aspects as shown in Figure 7. User cyber-sickness and the absence of accurate replication of location are obstacles that need to be solved in offering realistic experiences.

New potential for social encounters in VR is revealed by recent trends towards networked VR, which encourages researchers to address innovative UI and interaction design needs and assessment methodologies, as well as privacy and ethical considerations. Meanwhile, it is necessary to further develop and broaden the relevant design principles to incorporate features of social interactions in virtual worlds. Currently, user experience evaluation depends on subjective user judgments of occurrence and engagement, but forthcoming wits should concentrate on integrating such valuations with detached measurements also observations.

Augmented Reality may become more popular as technology develops and user acceptance grows (AR). The user interacts with a digital overlay placed on their actual real environment using AR (Augmented Reality). Even though technology is still in its infancy, it is predicted to change the way we communicate, work and interact with our world when it achieves its full potential in the future. According to some, voice commands, artificial intelligence and augmented reality (AR) will eventually render displays useless. Geographic AR experiences, messaging, and narrative have enormous potential. Current and upcoming information technologies that are connected to "reality" have the potential to change society (Pawan Whig 2 Anupam Priyam3, 2018).

5.   Estimation calculation

It's necessary to move beyond performance-based approaches when evaluating the entire user experience in intelligent settings. Traditional assessment practices have been judged unsuitable for innovative interactive systems that include new sensing capabilities, shifts in the initiative, diversifications in the physical interface, and variances in application purpose. Interpreting signals from multiple communication channels in a realistic interaction environment, contextual awareness, and the unsuitability of task-specific metrics in systems that are often purposeless, are a few examples.

When it comes to such situations, it's apparent that new assessment methodologies and tools are needed, which augment self-reported or observed metrics with automatically collected user experience indicators. As a result, a new set of frameworks and models is required to give holistic and systematic means of evaluating UX in intelligent settings, taking into account a wide range of characteristics and qualities.

Intelligence might become a service in the future and new design material. Even Artificial Intelligence (AI)-based services are now accessible to help developers create AI-based apps without having any technical expertise. Also, AI as a design material might help designers throughout iterative design and assessment by plugging into apps or objects Using intelligence as a tool to genuinely empower professionals, such a mindset suggests that technology will become even more valuable. However, it also highlights the necessity for specific guidelines to be put in place in the future (Rupani et al., 2018).

Research Issues

HCI-related research is pushed to transcend outside lab studies and enlarge to new domains and settings, resonant out investigation "in the wild" as interactive technology permeates every life sphere. Particularly in public places, researchers confront the issue of following standard protocols to educate participants and obtain their agreement vs investigating real user experience and behavior, which might be affected if participants know they are being watched. Museums and research at the

Figure 8. Various OSN's widely available

confluence of art and technology can raise ethical problems since the difference between study participants and event attendees is not apparent.

Concerning vulnerable user demographics, such as elderly folks, people with impairments, immigrants, and socially isolated individuals as well as patients and children is another point of care for HCI research. This includes managing participants' misunderstandings about technology and correcting any unrealistic or too optimistic expectations about it, as well as addressing any potential problems that may arise when the technology does not work as anticipated (Agarwal & Whig, 2016).

New concerns have arisen as a result of recent technological advancements regarding the use of internet data in HCI research, including the use of data without participants' agreement. As a result, the question arises as to whether researchers are authorized to use publicly available data without permission. It is still unclear exactly what founds community data also what are the finest procedures obtaining well-versed agreement Anonymous participation is also a challenge because studies have shown that anonymized data can be revealed when combined with other information

1.   Social Network

Information security is a key problem in online social networks (OSNs), and it's an issue that is being discussed across all technical disciplines. A human right to privacy includes intimacy, the right not to be observed and preserved, as well as the right to govern one's personal information, including how it is distributed. A various online social network is shown in Figure 8.

Data retention difficulties, the potential of OSN workers to access private material, the sale of data, and targeted marketing are all privacy concerns with OSNs. People divulge personal information despite their privacy concerns, a phenomenon known as the "privacy paradox".

These considerations include: OSN use has become ingrained into daily life; perceived advantages exceed observable hazards. Individuals do not make information-sharing decisions as totally free agents. (Rupani et al., 2017). Using OSNs for

Figure 9. HCI In health sector

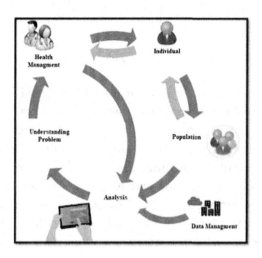

sensitive applications makes privacy in OSNs even more critical Online social networks (OSNs) are characterized by two fundamentally opposing characteristics: privacy and content sharing.

Regulation 2016/679 of the General Data Protection Regulation (GDPR) was published by the European Parliament and Council of the European Union to promote awareness and safeguard user rights.

2.   Healthcare Sector

To facilitate information exchange and to generate media material that can be shared with specialized groups, social media is widely used in the context of healthcare IT. There are ethical problems about the usage of social media by children, seniors, and for research purposes such as collecting patient-reported data or conducting online surveys and recruiting participants in this regard. (Chacko & Whig, 2016). Since after covid HCI Place a very important role in Healthcare sector and lot of development using the machine are going on a hot area of research. The flow of HCI in the Health sector is shown in Figure 9.

Another feature of all of the technologies mentioned above is the predominance of persuasive tactics for changing people's behavior. While certain health-related goals are typically beneficial and desirable, persuasive technology can be used to deceive individuals or encourage them to participate in bad behavior under the wrong conditions. Mobile goods and social media are particularly susceptible to these distortions, and as technologies advance and mature, they must be evaluated.

An in-depth examination of technology that promotes well-being, health, and human potential, including ethical considerations (Rupani et al., 2016).

3.   VR and AR

Vr is a technical realm that elicits two key social and ethical issues because of the illusion it creates: I the goals of the VR environment designer, which may be obscene VR allows the user to experience a "reality" that can be synthetic and produced digitally, or it can be a frozen moment in time that has been digitally captured.

With its marriage certificate asserting the union of a man and a virtual character, hologram company has ignited a wide-ranging debate about the inalienable freedom of the individual, how technology influences free will, and ethical dilemmas and responsibilities for those who create and desecrate technology. Over-attachment to virtual agents may be less of a concern than how VR might affect social interactions, leading to individuals opting out of social activities or permitting the possibility of digitally prolonging one's life beyond physical death, for example.

4.   Internet of Things

The Internet of Things paradigm is defined by varied skills, such as smart plans that are networked and collaborate through the Internet infrastructure, enabling a wide range of new services and making buildings, cities, and transportation smarter. New privacy and security concerns emerge in this highly linked and diverse world, where any interaction between humans, gadgets, and autonomous entities is possible.

Privacy will become increasingly additional crucial in future clever hybrid cities. People can utilize false identities and anonymization services in the virtual world. In the actual world, this will be difficult, if not impossible. Data around persons in the simulated world is now supplemented and integrated with data from the actual world, and vice versa as shown in Figure 10. People entering a business or a restaurant with known locations are photographed by public and private Closed Circuit Television (CCTV) cameras, and facial recognition is used to identify human identities. Because real items are marked, sensors in the environment will detect what individuals are wearing, carrying, using, and buying. Increased vehicle instrumentation in the context of autonomous driving has an impact on privacy. When walking with a smartphone, one's walking behavior is visible. IoT-enabled scenarios will make it increasingly difficult to evade tracking of items and people, and privacy will be a major concern in both the real and hybrid worlds.

5.   IoT along with Big Data

Figure 10. Comparison of past and future in HCI with IoT

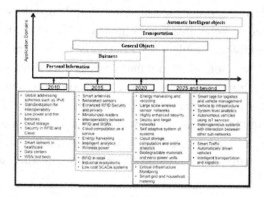

Big data and the Internet of Things are both recent technical advances that will undoubtedly form the basis of future technologically enhanced settings. Big data plans extra threats to privacy, such as automatic choice-making, which raises concerns about discrimination, self-determination, and the narrowing of choices, as a result of the reaping of big groups of individual data combined with the usage of advanced analytics. Predictive analytics, for example, may have negative consequences for those who are prone to disease, criminality, or other socially undesirable qualities or behaviors.

6.   Ambience Intelligence

All technical areas are affected by ethics, privacy, and trust. Their basic concerns are the same. Despite this, the diverse domains bring additional issues that must be addressed. However, biometrics creates an extra moral issue since biocentric data affects someone accurately to regulate the usage along with the temperament of someone.

Because intelligent settings, like other new technologies, raise concerns about how individuals see themselves and our place in the world, they pose ethical issues. Many risks are associated with intelligent systems, such as user identification based on collected data, the permanence of personal/sensitive information, profiling, implicit deduction and attribution of new properties to individuals, the use of data for monitoring, misinterpretation of data, the public disclosure of confidential information, and the use of persuasion.

The topic of accountability for AI systems and autonomous agents, as well as the moral, social, and legal consequences of their actions and decisions, is one of the most serious ethical concerns. A multidisciplinary branch of research, ethical decision-making in AI, is entrusted with finding answers to these dilemmas and safeguarding our future. Usual factors and moral standards guide human moral decision-making; holy values learned from earlier examples and cultural considerations are common.

Humans will need to know that autonomous intelligent entities' judgments are trustworthy and morally justifiable when they make more complicated and critical ethical decisions. As a result, whether it manifests as traceability, verifiability, non-deception, or intelligibility, transparency is a need so that humans can understand, predict, and correctly trust AI. Intelligent AI, in particular, will aid humans in detecting AI errors and facilitating meaningful human control. However, depending on how the explanations are utilized, a balance in the degree of detail must be established, since complete transparency may be too overpowering in some situations.

7. Cyber Skill

The concerns raised above are primarily concerned with ethics and privacy, and they highlight obstacles and potential dangers. However, privacy is linked to cybersecurity, a topic that has gained traction for two reasons. To begin with, the transformation of our society as a result of the growth of digital technology creates greater chances for cybercrime. Residential units, as well as public organizations and institutions, are now heavily computerized. Every element of human activity, including "in-person" meetings, is controlled, recorded, and tracked in the digital domain. Second, cyber-attacks are low-cost and have no geographical boundaries (Kautish et al. 2022)

As a result of the huge number of connected devices, traditional security measures are rendered useless. Because most commercial IoT devices lack appropriate security safeguards, they might be an easy target for hacking, blocking, altering communication, changing settings, or issuing fraudulent orders because they lack suitable security protections on board. Data breaches and privacy violations, as well as attacks on devices or software on both devices and servers, are the most significant security concerns (Moorthy et al. 2022).

From a technical standpoint, the conversation on cyber security in the background of IoT and smart cities is comprehensive, highlighting difficulties, offering designs, and recommending future research initiatives. Despite technological improvements that should be sought, it has been acknowledged that the human agent, whether through error or ignorance, is the major weak spot in compromised security. A human-centered approach to cyber security becomes more essential in establishing useable cyber security, in educating individuals on how to raise their awareness, and in training businesses and organizations on the human side of cyber security (Madhu et al. 2022).

CONCLUSION AND FUTURE WORKS

This chapter has explored seven major difficulties that exist in today's socio-technical world, to use the growing availability of interaction intelligence to meet pressing human and societal demands. Despite being sparked by current technology breakthroughs and intelligence, the conversation has mostly argued for a future technological fabric in which intelligence would be used to better serve and empower humanity. In this environment, the HCI community is called upon to perform a significant task: to create a future in which intelligence integration does not undermine human self-efficacy and control, but rather enhances it.

HCI will lead efforts to improve the quality of life of diverse groups, including the disabled and the elderly, in new technology-augmented environments, as it has always centered on humans. Smart cities, not only smart homes and offices, will be the technical settings of the future. Given that technology will be an integral part of every daily activity, catering to human wants, wealth, and well-being, the stakes for universal access are now much greater than they were previously. To ensure that the new technologies do not exclude or isolate someone, special attention must be made to anyone who is a danger of exclusion.

Finally, the crucial times we live in, as well as anticipated future gloomy scenarios, have already pushed research toward developing technology to help mankind cope with key social issues like resource shortages, climate change, poverty, and disasters. In this framework, civic engagement, social fairness, and democracy are goals that should be actively pursued and realized. In this regard, the dynamics of new technologies present problems as well as opportunities, particularly in terms of sustainability, public participation, and democracy. Promises will be kept or problems will turn into disasters based on current and future actions and behaviors.

REFERENCES

Agarwal, P., & Whig, P. (2016). Low Delay Based 4 Bit QSD Adder/Subtraction Number System by Reversible Logic Gate. *2016 8th International Conference on Computational Intelligence and Communication Networks (CICN)*, 580–584.

Ahmad, S. N. (2012). Pawan Whig. *Journal of Mobile and Adhoc Network*.

Ahmad, S. N., & Whig, P. (2011). *On the Performance of ISFET-based Device for Water Quality Monitoring*. Academic Press.

Ahmad, P. W., & S. N. (2019). Novel Photo Catalytic Sensor Output Calibration Technique. *SSRG International Journal of VLSI & Signal Processing, 6*(1).

Ajay Rupani, P. (2019). The development of big data science to the world. *Engineering Reports*, 2(2), 1–7.

Alkali Y. Routray I. Whig P. (2022). Study of various methods for reliable, efficient and Secured IoT using Artificial Intelligence. *Available at* SSRN 4020364. doi:10.2139/ssrn.4020364

Anand, M., Velu, A., & Whig, P. (2022). Prediction of Loan Behaviour with Machine Learning Models for Secure Banking. *Journal of Computing Science and Engineering: JCSE*, 3(1), 1–13.

Aparicio, J. H. V., de León, H. R. M. P., Arroyo, L. O., & Herrera, J. Á. O. (n.d.). *Dual Reciprocity-Boundary Element Method Applied to the Solution of the Equation of Helmholtz*. Academic Press.

Arun Velu, P. W. (2021). Impact of Covid Vaccination on the Globe using data analytics. *International Journal of Sustainable Development in Computing Science*, 3(2).

Asopa, P., Purohit, P., Nadikattu, R. R., & Whig, P. (2021). Reducing carbon footprint for sustainable development of smart cities using IoT. *2021 Third International Conference on Intelligent Communication Technologies and Virtual Mobile Networks (ICICV)*, 361–367. 10.1109/ICICV50876.2021.9388466

Bhargav, R., & Whig, P. (2021). More Insight on Data Analysis of Titanic Data Set. *International Journal of Sustainable Development in Computing Science*, 3(4), 1–10.

Bhateja, V., Tavares, J. M. R. S., Rani, B. P., Prasad, V. K., & Raju, K. S. (2018). *Proceedings of the Second International Conference on Computational Intelligence and Informatics: ICCII 2017* (Vol. 712). Springer.

Bhatia, V., & Bhatia, G. (2013). Room temperature based fan speed control system using pulse width modulation technique. *International Journal of Computers and Applications*, 81(5).

Bhatia, V., & Gupta, R. (2015). Design of a GSM based electronic voting machine with voter tracking. *BVICA M's International. Journal of Information Technology*, 7(1), 799.

Chacko, J. B., & Whig, P. (2016). Low Delay Based Full Adder/Subtractor by MIG and COG Reversible Logic Gate. *2016 8th International Conference on Computational Intelligence and Communication Networks (CICN)*, 585–589.

Chopra, G., & Whig, P. (2021). Analysis of Tomato Leaf Disease Identification Techniques. *Journal of Computing Science and Engineering: JCSE*, 2(2), 98–103.

Chopra, G., & Whig, P. (2022). Smart Agriculture System Using AI. *International Journal of Sustainable Development in Computing Science, 1*(1).

Chouhan, S. (2019). Using an Arduino and a temperature, humidity sensor, Automate the fan speed. *International Journal of Sustainable Development in Computing Science, 1*(2).

Agarwal & P. W. (2016). A Review-Quaternary Signed Digit Number System byReversible Logic Gate. *International Journal on Recent and Innovation Trends in Computing and Communication, 4*(3).

Chouhan, S., Chaudhary, S., Upadhay, T., Rupani, A., & Whig, P. (2017). Comparative Study of Various Gates Based in Different Technologies. *Int Rob Auto J, 3*(2), 00046.

George, N., Muiz, K., Whig, P., & Velu, A. (2021). Framework of Perceptive Artificial Intelligence using Natural Language Processing (PAIN). *Artificial & Computational Intelligence.*

Kautish, S., Reyana, A., & Vidyarthi, A. (2022). SDMTA: Attack Detection and Mitigation Mechanism for DDoS Vulnerabilities in Hybrid Cloud Environment. *IEEE Transactions on Industrial Informatics.*

Khera, Y., Whig, P., & Velu, A. (2021). efficient effective and secured electronic billing system using AI. *Vivekananda Journal of Research, 10*, 53–60.

Kumavat, M. K. S., Sao, A. K., Khedekar, H., Panpaliya, C., & Korde, S. (n.d.). *Social Distancing Detector using YOLO v3 Image Processing Algorithm.* Academic Press.

Madhu, G., Govardhan, A., & Ravi, V. (2022). DSCN-net: a deep Siamese capsule neural network model for automatic diagnosis of malaria parasites detection. *Multimed Tools Appl.* doi:10.1007/s11042-022-13008-6

Mamza, E. S. (2021). Use of AIOT in Health System. *International Journal of Sustainable Development in Computing Science, 3*(4), 21–30.

Mathurkar, G., Parkhi, C., Utekar, M., & Chitte, P. H. (2021). Ensuring social distancing using machine learning. *ITM Web of Conferences, 40*, 03049.

Moorthy, T. V. K., Budati, A. K., Kautish, S., Goyal, S. B., & Prasad, K. L. (2022). Reduction of satellite images size in 5G networks using Machinelearning algorithms. *IET Communications, 16*, 584–591. https://doi.org/10.1049/cmu2.12354

Nadikattu, R. R. (2014). Content analysis of American & Indian Comics on Instagram using Machine learning. *International Journal of Creative Research Thoughts*, 2320–2882.

Nadikattu, R. R. (2020a). A Comparative Study between a Simulation of Machine Learning and Extreme Learning Machine Techniques on Breast Cancer Diagnosis. *Global Journal of Computer Science and Technology*.

NadikattuR. R. (2020b). A Comparative Study between Simulation of Machine Learning and Extreme Learning Techniques on Breast Cancer Diagnosis. *Available at* SSRN 3615092. doi:10.2139/ssrn.3615092

Nadikattu, R. R., Bhandari, R., & Whig, P. (2021). Improved Pattern of Adaptive Rood-Pattern Search Algorithm for Motion Estimation in Video Compression. In *Innovations in Cyber Physical Systems* (pp. 441–448). Springer. doi:10.1007/978-981-16-4149-7_39

Nadikattu, R. R., Mohammad, S. M., & Whig, P. (2020a). *Novel economical social distancing smart device for covid-19. International Journal of Electrical Engineering and Technology*.

Nadikattu, R. R., Mohammad, S. M., & Whig, P. (2020b). Novel economical social distancing smart Device for COVID-19 (*SSRN* Scholarly Paper ID 3640230). *Social Science Research Network*. Https://Papers. Ssrn. Com/Abstract,3640230

Parihar, V., & Yadav, S. (n.d.). *Comparison estimation of effective consumer future preferences with the application of AI*. Academic Press.

Reddy, R. (2019). Purification of indoor air using a novel pseudo PMOS ultraviolet photocatalytic oxidation (PP-UVPCO) sensor. *International Journal of Sustainable Development in Computing Science*, *1*(3).

Ruchin, C. M., & Whig, P. (2015). Design and Simulation of Dynamic UART Using Scan Path Technique (USPT). *International Journal of Electrical, Electronics & Computing in Science & Engineering*.

Rupani, A., & Kumar, D. (2020). *Temperature Effect On Behaviour of Photo Catalytic Sensor (PCS)*. Used For Water Quality Monitoring.

Rupani, A., Saini, D., Sujediya, G., & Whig, P. (2016). A Review of Technology Paradigm for IOT on FPGA. *IJARCCE-International Journal of Advanced Research in Computer and Communication Engineering*, *5*(9).

Rupani, A., Whig, P., Sujediya, G., & Vyas, P. (2017). A robust technique for image processing based on interfacing of Raspberry-Pi and FPGA using IoT. *2017 International Conference on Computer, Communications and Electronics (Comptelix)*, 350–353. 10.1109/COMPTELIX.2017.8003992

Rupani, A., Whig, P., Sujediya, G., & Vyas, P. (2018). Hardware implementation of iot-based image processing filters. *Proceedings of the Second International Conference on Computational Intelligence and Informatics*, 681–691. 10.1007/978-981-10-8228-3_63

Sharma, H., Rao, N., & Sharma, M. (2016). Analysis of astrology and scientific calculation through orbital period. *2016 3rd International Conference on Computing for Sustainable Global Development (INDIACom)*, 236–239.

Shrivastav, P., Whig, P., & Gupta, K. (n.d.). *Bandwidth Enhancement by Slotted Stacked Arrangement and its Comparative Analysis with Conventional Single and Stacked Patch Antenna*. Academic Press.

Sinha, R., & Ranjan, A. (2015). Effect of Variable Damping Ratio on design of PID Controller. *2015 4th International Conference on Reliability, Infocom Technologies and Optimization (ICRITO)(Trends and Future Directions)*, 1–4.

Sowmya, K. B., Gomes, S., & Tadiparthi, V. R. (2020). Design of UART module using ASMD technique. *2020 5th International Conference on Communication and Electronics Systems (ICCES)*, 176–181.

Srivastava, J., Bhagat, R., & Kumar, P. (2020). Analog inverse filters using OTAs. *2020 6th International Conference on Control, Automation and Robotics (ICCAR)*, 627–631.

Velu, A., & Whig, P. (2021). Protect Personal Privacy And Wasting Time Using Nlp: A Comparative Approach Using Ai. *Vivekananda Journal of Research*, *10*, 42–52.

Velu, A., & Whig, P. (n.d.). *Studying the Impact of the COVID Vaccination on the World Using Data Analytics*. Academic Press.

Verma, T. (2019). A comparison of different R2R D/A converters. *International Journal of Sustainable Development in Computing Science, 1*(2).

Whig, P. (2019a). Artificial intelligence and machine learning in business. *Engineering Reports*, *2*(2), 8–13.

Whig, P. (2019b). Machine Learning Based Techniques for Communication and Signal Processing Problem. *International Journal of Machine Learning for Sustainable Development*, *1*(3), 1–10.

Whig, P. (2019c). Prediction of Smart Building Indoor Temperature Using IoT and Machine Learning. *International Journal of Machine Learning for Sustainable Development*, *1*(4), 1–10.

Whig, P. (2021). IoT Based Novel Smart Blind Guidance System. *Journal of Computing Science and Engineering: JCSE*, 2(2), 80–88.

Whig, P., & Ahmad, S. N. (2017). Fuzzy logic implementation of photo catalytic sensor. *Int. Robot. Autom. J*, 2(3), 15–19.

Whig, P., & Ahmad, S. N. (2018). Comparison analysis of various R2R D/A converter. *Int J Biosen Bioelectron*, 4(6), 275–279.

Whig, P., & Ahmad, S. N. (2019). Methodology for Calibrating Photocatalytic Sensor Output. *International Journal of Sustainable Development in Computing Science*, 1(1), 1–10.

Whig, P., Nadikattu, R. R., & Velu, A. (2022). COVID-19 pandemic analysis using application of AI. *Healthcare Monitoring and Data Analysis Using IoT: Technologies and Applications*, 1.

Whig Priyam, & Ahmad. (2018). Simulation & performance analysis of various R2R D/A converter using various topologies. *International Robotics & Automation Journal*, 4(2), 128–131.

ADDITIONAL READING

Bhatia, V., & Whig, P. (2013). A secured dual tune multi frequency based smart elevator control system. *International Journal of Research in Engineering and Advanced Technology*, 4(1), 1163–2319.

Culnan, M. J. (1987). Mapping the intellectual structure of MIS, 1980–1985: A co-citation analysis. *Management Information Systems Quarterly*, 11(3), 341–353. doi:10.2307/248680

Goodhue, D. L. (1998). Development and measurement validity of a task-technology fit instrument for user evaluations of information systems. *Decision Sciences*, 29(1), 105–137. doi:10.1111/j.1540-5915.1998.tb01346.x

Pervan, G. P. (1998). A review of research in Group Support Systems: Leaders, approaches and directions. *Decision Support Systems*, 23(2), 149–159. doi:10.1016/S0167-9236(98)00041-4

Rupani, A., Whig, P., Sujediya, G., & Vyas, P. (2017). A robust technique for image processing based on interfacing of Raspberry-Pi and FPGA using IoT. *2017 International Conference on Computer, Communications and Electronics (Comptelix)*, 350–353. 10.1109/COMPTELIX.2017.8003992

Sharma, A., Kumar, A., & Whig, P. (2015). On the performance of CDTA based novel analog inverse low pass filter using 0.35 µm CMOS parameter. International Journal of Science. *Technology & Management, 4*(1), 594–601.

Singh, A. K., Gupta, A., & Senani, R. (2018). OTRA-based multi-function inverse filter configuration. *Advances in Electrical and Electronic Engineering, 15*(5), 846–856. doi:10.15598/aeee.v15i5.2572

Venkatesh, V., & Davis, F. (2000). A theoretical extension of the technology acceptance model: Four longitudinal field studies. *Management Science, 46*(2), 186–204. doi:10.1287/mnsc.46.2.186.11926

Whig, P., & Ahmad, S. N. (2012). Performance analysis of various readout circuits for monitoring quality of water using analog integrated circuits. *International Journal of Intelligent Systems and Applications, 4*(11), 103. doi:10.5815/ijisa.2012.11.11

Whig, P., & Ahmad, S. N. (2014). Simulation of linear dynamic macro model of photo catalytic sensor in SPICE. *COMPEL: The International Journal for Computation and Mathematics in Electrical and Electronic Engineering.*

Zhang, P., & Dillon, A. (2003). HCI and MIS: Shared Concerns, Editorial Introduction. *International Journal of Human-Computer Studies, 59*(4), 397–402. doi:10.1016/S1071-5819(03)00109-5

KEY TERMS AND DEFINITIONS

AI: Artificial intelligence (AI) is the ability of a computer or a robot controlled by a computer to do tasks that are usually done by humans because they require human intelligence and discernment.

AR: AR transforms how you work, learn, play, shop and connect with the world around you.

Big Data: Big data is a combination of structured, semi structured, and unstructured data collected by organizations that can be mined for information and used in machine learning projects, predictive modeling and other advanced analytics applications.

Health Sector: The healthcare industry is an aggregation and integration of sectors within the economic system that provides goods and services to treat patients with curative, preventive, rehabilitative, and palliative care.

Human-Computer Interaction (HCI): HCI (human-computer interaction) is the study of how people interact with computers and to what extent computers are or are not developed for successful interaction with human beings.

IoT: The term IoT, or Internet of Things, refers to the collective network of connected devices and the technology that facilitates communication between devices and the cloud, as well as between the devices themselves.

Machine Learning: Machine learning is a branch of artificial intelligence (AI) and computer science which focuses on the use of data and algorithms to imitate the way that humans learn, gradually improving its accuracy.

VR: Virtual reality (VR) is a simulated experience that can be similar to or completely different from the real world.

Chapter 7

Protect Nature and Reduce the Carbon Footprint With an Application of Blockchain for IIoT

Pawan Whig
Vivekananda Institute of Professional Studies, India

Arun Velu
Equifax, USA

Ashima Bhatnagar Bhatia
Vivekananda Institute of Professional Studies, India

ABSTRACT

The cumulative amount of greenhouse gases that are shaped by our actions is a carbon footmark. In the US, the total carbon footmark of a humanoid is 16 tonnes, one of the largest amounts in the world. The average is closer to 4 tonnes worldwide. The average universal carbon footmark per year requirements is to drop below 3 tonnes by 2050 to have the utmost chance of stopping a 2°C point rise in worldwide temperature. Rahul et al. already predicted that the carbon footprint reduced by 17% with the use of IoT-enabled services. In this research study a novel approach to reduce carbon footprint using IoT with reinforcement AI learning is presented, which further reduced carbon footprint by 5% when using and nearly 7% when it is done using Q-Learning. The detailed findings are included to demonstrate the result.

DOI: 10.4018/978-1-6684-3733-9.ch007

INTRODUCTION

A carbon footmark is the quantity of greenhouse vapours emitted by a single humanoid operation into the atmosphere, mainly carbon dioxide (Whig et al., 2022). A carbon footprint may be a large measure that can be attributed to an individual's behaviour, a family, a case, an entity, or even a country as a whole (Anand et al., 2022). Tons of CO_2 corresponding gases, counting methane, nitrous oxide, and other greenhouse vapours, are typically measured as tonnes of CO_2 produced each year, an amount that can be augmented with tonnes of CO_2 corresponding vapours (Alkali et al., 2022; Chopra & WHIG, 2022).

Many variables are taken into account when assessing a carbon footprint some are shown in Figure.1. Pouring to the grocery supply, for instance, burns a sure quantity of gasoline, and the main foundations of greenhouse gases are fossil fuels (Chopra & Whig, 2022b, 2022a; Madhu & WHIG, 2022). Yet the grocery shop is operated by gas, and the workers have probably gone to work, meaning the store has a carbon footprint of its own. In addition, all the items that the store offers have been delivered there, meaning that the overall carbon emissions must also be taken into account (Bhargav & Whig, 2021; George et al., 2021; Khera et al., 2021; Mamza, 2021; Pawar, 2021; Whig & Rupani, 2020). In comparison, the berries, potatoes and essences produced by the supermarket were all cultivated or raised on plantations, a methane producing operation that has a greenhouse effect 25 times greater than CO_2 (Arun Velu, 2021; Reddy, 2019; Velu & Whig, 2021; verma, 2019; Whig, 2019b, 2019a). The carbon foot print is well defined by Figure 1.

As of Dec 2020, carbon dioxide (CO2) makes up 411 ppm of the Earth's heaven, according to NASA. The United States receives about 81 percent of its overall electricity from the combustion of fossil fuels, according to the National Academy of Sciences (chouhan, 2019; Mathurkar et al., 2021; Nadikattu et al., 2020b, 2021; Ruchin & Whig, 2015; Sharma et al., 2016; Shrivastav et al., n.d.). One of the key reasons that green energy still needs to take off in the United States, or internationally, is that it is still impossible to store renewable energy sources. IoT has the ability to transform electricity grids by smart metering and forecasts to be powered by renewable sources such as wind and solar power. By converting from fossil fuels to clean energy sources, big cities are expected to reduce their carbon dioxide emissions by more than half (Chopra & Whig, 2021; Nadikattu et al., 2020a; Velu & Whig, n.d.; Whig2*, 2020). New technologies, in Industry 4.0 like AI, IoT and ML have been seen as a boon to reducing Carbon footprint. IoT Plays an important role in reducing Carbon Footprint (S. N. Ahmad & Whig, 2011; Pawan Whig 2 Anupam Priyam3, 2018; Whig & Ahmad, 2018).

In addition to cleaner electricity sources, IoT will also allow the automation of HVAC energy in houses, which, according to the International Energy Agency, is

Figure 1. Carbon foot print

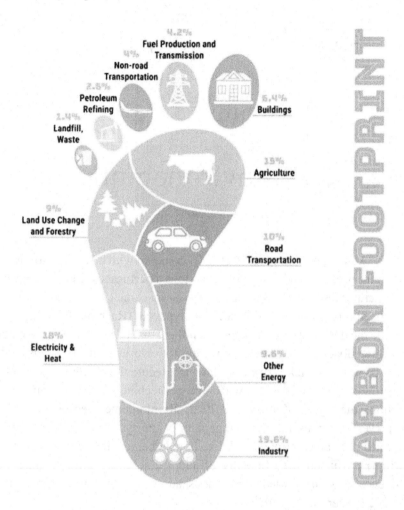

one of the main drivers of global electricity demand. In order to improve energy efficiency, smart HVAC systems can efficiently monitor the temperature in large buildings, maintaining track of occupancy and other variables (Bhatia & Whig, 2013; Chacko & Whig, 2016; Rupani et al., 2016, 2017, 2018; Whig, 2017; Whig & Ahmad, 2016).

REINFORCEMENT LEARNING

In an unpredictable, possibly complex environment, the agent learns to attain a target. Artificial intelligence faces a game-like scenario in reinforcement learning (P. W.

Figure 2. Reinforcement learning block diagram

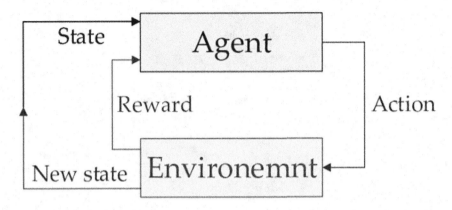

and S. N. Ahmad, n.d.; ahmad, 2016). To come up with a solution to the problem, the machine uses trial and error. For the actions it performs, the artificial intelligence receives either rewards or penalties to get the machine to do what the programmer wants. Its aim is to optimize the cumulative payout (Rashmi Sinha, 2015).

While the designer sets the incentive policy, that is, the game rules, he gives the model no feedback or suggestions about how to solve the game (Moorthy et.al, 2022).

It is up to the model to work out how to execute the challenge, beginning with entirely random trials and ending with advanced techniques and superhuman abilities, to optimize the payout (Kautish et.al,2022). Reinforcement learning is probably the most powerful way to hint at the ingenuity of the system by using the strength of search and several experiments. Unlike human beings, if a reinforcement learning algorithm is run on a sufficiently efficient computing infrastructure, artificial intelligence will gain knowledge from thousands of simultaneous gameplays (Alferaidi et.al., 2022; Sharma et.al 2022).

Blockchain

We may envisage a biosphere in which agreements are written in numerical code and stowed in clear, communal records that are endangered from removal, modification, and amendment by blockchain. In this environment, every contract would have a numerary record and autograph that could be detected. People, businesses, robots, and procedures would be free to transact and interconnect with ace extra.

Almost everybody has caught the argument that blockchain would transform commercial and reshape organisations and frugalities. Many barriers—technical, governance, organisational, and even societal—will have to collapse if there is to be a blockchain revolution, according to our experience researching technology innovation. It would be a mistake to dive headfirst into blockchain technology without first knowing how it will spread.

We believe that true blockchain-led corporate and government change is still several years away. This is due to the fact that block chain is not a "disruptive" skill that container occurrence a outdated business perfect with a low cost key and swiftly overrun existing businesses. Blockchain is a foundational technology, with the ability to build new economic and social institutions on top of it. However, though blockchain will have a huge influence, it determination income decades to pervade financial and social substructure. As waves of technical and institutional change acquire speed, adoption will be gradual and steady, rather than abrupt.

Both blockchain and the Internet of Things (IoT) are frequently touted as significant digital transformation technologies. But what if you used a mix of the two? End of 2019, Gartner identified blockchain adoption in conjunction with IoT adoption as a DX sweet spot, particularly in the United States. And nothing has changed.

Since about 2014, blockchain technology, a kind of Distributed Ledger Technology, has gotten a lot of attention in fields other than cryptocurrency.

Blockchain is intended to serve as the foundation for apps that include transactions and interactions. As a result, blockchain technology may enhance not just IoT compliance, but also IoT features and cost-efficiency.

Benefits of Blockchain and IoT

The dispersed ledger of a blockchain is interfere proof, reducing the need for the parties involved to trust one another, according to Andres Ricaurte, senior vice president and worldwide head of payments at an IT services business. As a result, no solitary entity has switch ended the vast volume of data produced by IoT strategies Because of blockchain encryption, it is nearly difficult for anybody to alter existing data records. Furthermore, storing IoT data on blockchain adds another layer of protection to prevent hostile attackers from getting access to the network.

According to Vipul Parekh, senior director at management consulting company Alvarez & Marsal, one of the most difficult challenges for IoT providers is protecting information throughout the IoT ecosystem. IoT devices' security flaws brand them an informal board for assaults, malevolent attackers, and data breaches.

According to Parekh, the combination of IoT with blockchain opens the door to new possibilities that decrease inefficiencies, improve security, and increase transparency for all involved parties while enabling safe machine-to-machine transactions. The combination of these technologies enables a physical asset to be monitored from the time raw materials are mined, for example, and along the supply chain until it reaches the end customer.

Figure 3. Benefit of blockchain with iot

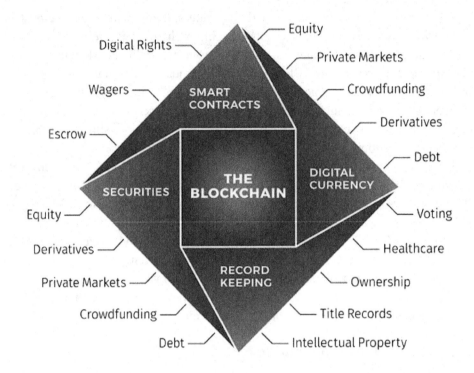

Increased security. Blockchain technology integrates security by allowing trusted parties to verify and approve transactions, as well as encryption while data is being sent and stored. Blockchain technology gives visibility into who has access, who is transacting, and a record of all interactions. Furthermore, blockchain provides a layer of security through encryption, the elimination of single points of failure, and the capacity to rapidly identify the weakest link in the whole network.

Cost savings. The entire ecosystem may be made more proactive at a lower cost by automating the transaction validation and processing processes on blockchain.

Transactional speed. This is especially true for supply chain transactions involving many suppliers, manufacturers, distributors, and customers. Because the blockchain functions as a shared ledger to some extent, untrusted parties may exchange data directly with one another, reducing manual processes and boosting transaction speed.

"While at Amazon, we handled this problem using a strategy known as 'working backwards,' in which we began with the consumer and moved backwards to the solution," Rossman explained. "Blockchain is an example of a technology that seems like a transformative technology, but substantial adoption outside of cryptocurrencies has not fulfilled the expectations. Let us begin with the consumer and move backwards to see how blockchain might help the Internet of Things."

Costs, security, privacy, and data sharing are all issues that must be addressed in IoT implementations.

According to Rossman, blockchain is encrypted and safe by design, with multiple independent nodes validating modifications to the chain prior to upgrades to avoid malicious acts. This is designed to be secure. The blockchain can be viewed and confirmed by all stakeholders, which helps to enhance data access and trust without adding cumbersome and expensive bureaucratic layers. This significantly increases accessibility, trust, and affordability.

Use Cases for Blockchain

Smart contracts/supply chain According to John Thielens, CTO of Cleo, IoT and blockchain may be integrated for quality assurance in the supply chain. Perishable commodities, such as wine or rare delicacies, are frequently exposed to changing temperatures and light exposures as they travel through transportation and warehousing networks. "By integrating IoT and blockchain, we can record the path of perishable commodities from manufacturer to retailer," Thielens explained. "At the case or pallet level, location and temperature data may be gathered and put into the blockchain, providing the ability to verify the history of the product as it goes through the supply chain and refuse accepting the goods and transferring it.

Aside from storing data, certain blockchain models enable companies to store and operate immutable algorithms in a distributed and decentralised manner, according to Carvahlo. These algorithms, often known as smart contracts, allow businesses to automatically codify business and domain rules.

IoT devices, such as temperature sensors, can continually check the temperature of shipments and communicate data to a running smart contract, which can notify stakeholders of any temperature decline in real time," Carvahlo explained. "Because the smart contract is operating on top of blockchain, the underlying temperature data are saved in an immutable data structure, which aids in data tampering prevention."

Leasing a truck According to the Gartner Inc. study "Integrating Blockchain With IoT Strengthens Trust in Multiparty Processes," IoT sensors installed in leased vehicles may record critical events on a blockchain to assist monitor fleet whereabouts and returns, as well as to enable more meaningful invoicing methods.

"With IoT sensors on board vehicles, truck leasing firms may charge renters' costs based on the torque of the loads rather than distance, as is now the practise," according to the study. "The blockchain distributed ledger technology enables people to share a single, shared version of the truth. There is no single body in charge of the data, and truckers and leasing firms can all be independent.

Figure 4. Flow chart to represent smart contract

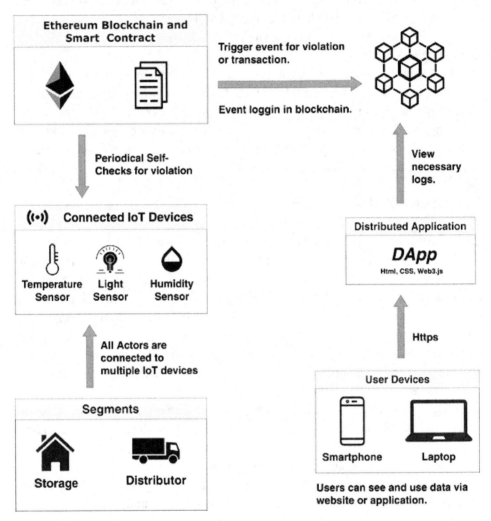

Field service and oil operations According to the Garter research, IoT sensors on oil and water wells may help oil firms control the performance of hauling businesses that pick up and distribute oil and water from wells and carry it to various destinations, including environmental waste dumping grounds.

"The IoT sensors on the wells assist oil firms in scheduling truck pickups and allowing them to monitor the amount of material picked up and delivered to avoid fraud and false representations," according to the article. "The blockchain distributed ledger technology records critical events in the logistics chain and provides a shared single version of independently verifiable truth throughout the entire logistics chain."

Figure 5. Blockchain and iot in transportation

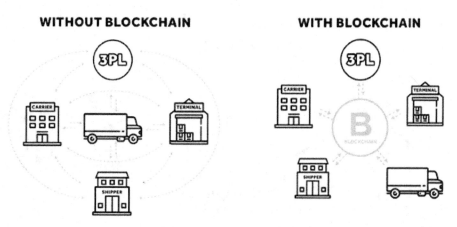

According to the Gartner study, using blockchain in this use case may help oil firms save money and run their pickup and delivery operations more effectively. Furthermore, by providing regulators with access to data such as the volume of water transported to a water dumping site vs the amount taken up from a water well, blockchain distributed ledger technology will assist the oil firm in managing its compliance reporting obligations.

The Difficulties of Integrating Blockchain Technology with IoT

One of the most difficult aspects of combining blockchain with IoT is the restrictions associated with the low battery life of some IoT devices.

"Some IoT devices are always linked to electricity and Wi-Fi, so there aren't really any significant constraints," he explained. "However, many IoT devices are not. And you can't run a compute- and bandwidth-intensive blockchain transaction system on a little device. As a result, they may need to employ some form of server-based architecture.

MATHEMATICAL MODELLING

In this research studies the initial calculation has been done on the basis of building without use of any advanced technologies i.e IoT

After calculating the result without IoT the carbon foot print is again calculated with the application of IoT enabled building for summer using IoT and reinforcement

Figure 6. Difficulties of integrating blockchain technology with IoT

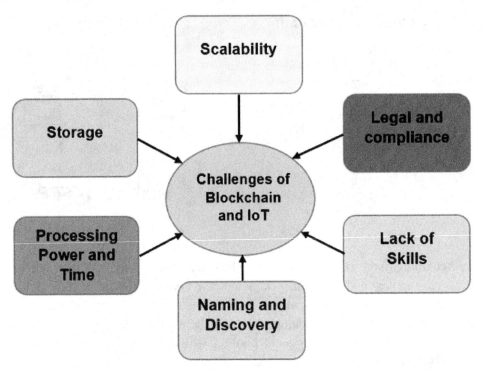

learning markov's decision process and Q learning. The mathematical calculations are sown below

(2.058 tonnes – 2940kwh of electricity at 0.708KgCO$_2$/kwh, 0.336 tonnes – 235.2liter of LPG)

The summary of above data is presented in a Table -1 below

RESULT

It is observed that with the use of IOT the Carbon Footprint of the house went down by 23% as compared to the Footprint without use of IOT, moreover when Reinforcement Learning (Markov decision process) was applied with IOT the graph went down by 28% as compared to house without IOT implementation as shown in given figure. When IOT with Reinforcement Learning (Q-Learning) was applied Carbon Footprint graph showed a fall of 30% as compared to graph of a system without IOT. It clearly shows that a house installed with IOT and Reinforcement Learning (Q-Learning) is the most efficient system to reduce the Carbon Footprint than any other.

Figure 7. FF

Carbon Footprint per year of house without IOT

- Electrical Appliances – 4194kwh
- LPG – 336 litres

Total House footprint – 4.86 tonnes of CO_2

(2.94 tonnes – 4194kwh of electricity at 0.708KgCO_2/kwh, 1.92 tonnes – 336 litres of LPG)

Carbon Footprint per year of house with IOT

- Electrical Appliances – 3234kwh
- LPG – 252 litres

Total House footprint – 2.64 tonnes of CO_2

(2.28 tonnes – 3234kwh of electricity at 0.708KgCO_2/kwh, 0.36 tonnes – 252 litres of LPG)

The above graph shown in Figure 9 represents the Carbon Footprint of a house (Monthly) in summer without IOT, with IOT, with IOT and Reinforcement Learning (Markov decision process), with IOT and Reinforcement Learning (Q-Learning).

Representation of the Carbon Footprint (Monthly) in the winter without IOT, with IOT, with IOT and Reinforcement Learning (Markov decision process) and with IOT and Reinforcement Learning (Q-Learning) is shown in Figure 10

Detailed representation of the Carbon Footprint made by a house in a year with different technologies installed to reduce the Carbon emission is shown in Figure 11. It is observed that the house installed with IOT and Reinforcement Learning (Q-Learning) is the most efficient and fruitful to reduce the Carbon Footprint by 30% as compared to any of the other technology implementation.

Representation of the increase in the Carbon Footprint per year from 1965-2019 is shown in Figure 12. It is observed that there is drastic increase in the carbon Footprint graph. There is not such a rapid change in the methane emission but the energy per capita and primary energy consumption have changed remarkably. This shows that energy consumption is increasing rapidly with increase in population resulting in increase in the Carbon Footprint.

Figure 8.

Carbon Footprint per year of house with IOT and Reinforcement Learning (Markov Decision Process)

- Electrical Appliances – 3024kwh
- LPG – 241.92 litres

Total House footprint – 2.4624 tonnes of CO_2

(2.1168 tonnes – 3024kwh of electricity at 0.708$KgCO_2$/kwh, 0.3456 tonnes – 241.92 litres of LPG)

Carbon Footprint per year of house with IOT and Reinforcement Learning (Q-Learning)

- Electrical Appliances – 2940kwh

- LPG – 235.2 litres

Total House footprint – 0.28 tonnes of CO_2

It is observed that methane emission is not well affect by the years but the energy per capita and primary energy consumption are increased drastically being a major cause in the increase in carbon level.

The graph sown in Figure 14 is the comparison between Energy per capita and Primary energy consumption and it is observed that R^2= 0.9533. It is observed

Table 1. Carbon foot print of the year

Carbon Footprint per year of a house (in tonnes)			
Technology Implemented	**Electronic Appliances**	**LPG**	**Total**
Without IOT	2.94	1.92	4.86
With IOT	2.28	0.36	2.64
With IOT and Reinforcement Learning (Markov decision process)	2.1168	0.3456	2.4624
With IOT and Reinforcement Learning (Q-Learning)	2.058	0.336	2.394

Figure 9. Summer analytics of carbon footprint

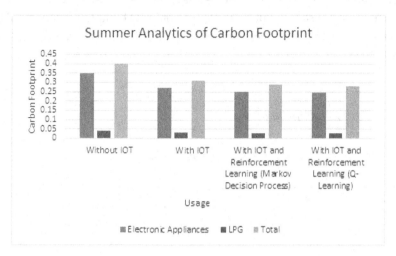

that the Energy per capita is 95% similar to Primary energy per capita and is 5% dissimilar to it.

Figure 10. Winter analytics of carbon footprint

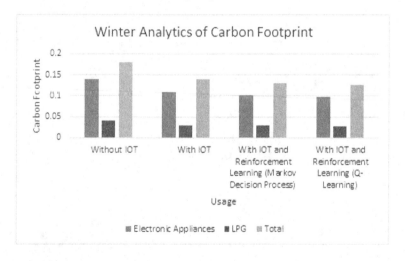

CONCLUSION

Thus, it is concluded that the use of IOT with Reinforcement Learning (Q-Learning) is the most efficient and fruitful to reduce the Carbon Footprint as compared to any other technology implementation because it reduces the Carbon emission by 30% as compared to a house without IOT whereas only IOT implementation reduces it by 23% and IOT with Reinforcement Learning (Markov decision process) reduces it by 28%.

Figure 11. Carbon foot print analysis

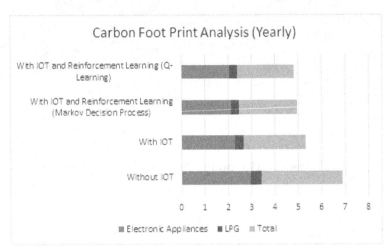

Figure 12. Carbon footprint since 1965

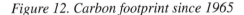
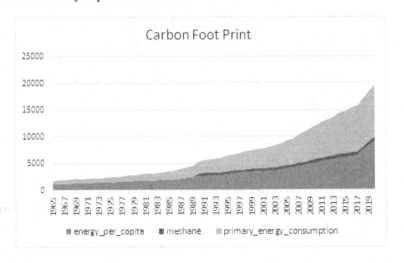

Figure 13. Comparison between the rate of increase in energy per capita, methane and primary energy consumption

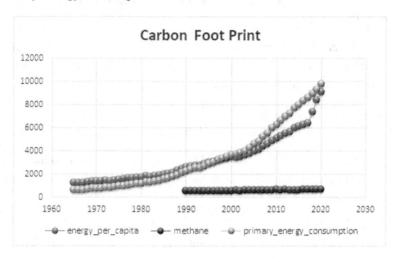

Figure 14. Primary energy consumption Vs Energy Per Capita

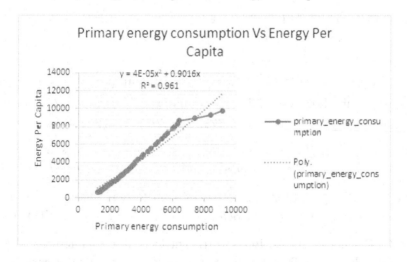

REFERENCES

Ahmad, P. W., & S. N. (2016). A Novel Pseudo NMOS Integrated CC -ISFET Device for Water Quality Monitoring. *Journal of Integrated Circuit and System, 8*(2), 1–6.

Ahmad, S. N., & Whig, P. (2011). *On the Performance of ISFET-based Device for Water Quality Monitoring*. Academic Press.

Ahmad & Naseem. (2016). Simulation and Performance Analysis of Low Power Quasi Floating Gate PCS Model. *The International Journal of Intelligent Engineering and Systems, 9*(2), 8–13.

Alferaidi, A., Yadav, K., Alharbi, Y., Viriyasitavat, W., Kautish, S., & Dhiman, G. (2022). Federated Learning Algorithms to Optimize the Client and Cost Selections. *Mathematical Problems in Engineering.*

Alkali, Y., Routray, I., & Whig, P. (2022). *Study of various methods for reliable, efficient and Secured IoT using Artificial Intelligence.* Available at SSRN 4020364.

Anand, M., Velu, A., & Whig, P. (2022). Prediction of Loan Behaviour with Machine Learning Models for Secure Banking. *Journal of Computing Science and Engineering: JCSE, 3*(1), 1–13.

Arun Velu, P. W. (2021). Impact of Covid Vaccination on the Globe using data analytics. *International Journal of Sustainable Development in Computing Science, 3*(2).

Bhargav, R., & Whig, P. (2021). More Insight on Data Analysis of Titanic Data Set. *International Journal of Sustainable Development in Computing Science, 3*(4), 1–10.

Bhatia, V., & Whig, P. (2013). A secured dual tune multi frequency based smart elevator control system. *International Journal of Research in Engineering and Advanced Technology, 4*(1), 1163–2319.

Chacko, J. B., & Whig, P. (2016). Low Delay Based Full Adder/Subtractor by MIG and COG Reversible Logic Gate. *2016 8th International Conference on Computational Intelligence and Communication Networks (CICN)*, 585–589.

Chopra, G., & Whig, P. (2022). A clustering approach based on support vectors. *International Journal of Machine Learning for Sustainable Development, 4*(1), 21–30.

Chopra, G., & Whig, P. (2021). Analysis of Tomato Leaf Disease Identification Techniques. *Journal of Computing Science and Engineering: JCSE, 2*(2), 98–103.

Chopra, G., & Whig, P. (2022a). Energy Efficient Scheduling for Internet of Vehicles. *International Journal of Sustainable Development in Computing Science, 4*(1).

Chopra, G., & Whig, P. (2022b). Smart Agriculture System Using AI. *International Journal of Sustainable Development in Computing Science, 1*(1).

Chouhan, S. (2019). Using an Arduino and a temperature, humidity sensor, Automate the fan speed. *International Journal of Sustainable Development in Computing Science, 1*(2).

George, N., Muiz, K., Whig, P., & Velu, A. (2021). Framework of Perceptive Artificial Intelligence using Natural Language Processing (PAIN). *Artificial & Computational Intelligence.*

Kautish, S., Reyana, A., & Vidyarthi, A. (2022). SDMTA: Attack Detection and Mitigation Mechanism for DDoS Vulnerabilities in Hybrid Cloud Environment. *IEEE Transactions on Industrial Informatics.*

Khera, Y., Whig, P., & Velu, A. (2021). efficient effective and secured electronic billing system using AI. *Vivekananda Journal of Research*, *10*, 53–60.

Madhu, M., & Whig, P. (2022). A survey of machine learning and its applications. *International Journal of Machine Learning for Sustainable Development*, *4*(1), 11–20.

Mamza, E. S. (2021). Use of AIOT in Health System. *International Journal of Sustainable Development in Computing Science*, *3*(4), 21–30.

Mathurkar, G., Parkhi, C., Utekar, M., & Chitte, P. H. (2021). Ensuring social distancing using machine learning. *ITM Web of Conferences, 40*, 03049.

Moorthy, T. V. K., Budati, A. K., Kautish, S., Goyal, S. B., & Prasad, K. L. (2022). Reduction of satellite images size in 5G networks using Machine learning algorithms. *IET Communications*, *16*, 584–591. https://doi.org/10.1049/cmu2.12354

Nadikattu, R. R., Bhandari, R., & Whig, P. (2021). Improved Pattern of Adaptive Rood-Pattern Search Algorithm for Motion Estimation in Video Compression. In *Innovations in Cyber Physical Systems* (pp. 441–448). Springer.

Nadikattu, R. R., Mohammad, S. M., & Whig, P. (2020a). *Novel economical social distancing smart device for covid-19. International Journal of Electrical Engineering and Technology.*

Nadikattu, R. R., Mohammad, S. M., & Whig, P. (2020b). Novel economical social distancing smart Device for COVID-19 (SSRN Scholarly Paper ID 3640230). *Social Science Research Network.* Https://Papers. Ssrn. Com/Abstract,3640230

Pawar, V. S. (2021). IoT architecture with embedded AI. *International Journal of Sustainable Development in Computing Science*, *3*(4), 11–20.

Rashmi Sinha, S. P., & P. W. (2015). Effect of Output Error on Fuzzy Interface for VDRC of Second Order Systems. *International Journal of Computers and Applications*, *125*(13), 11–16.

Reddy, R. (2019). Purification of indoor air using a novel pseudo PMOS ultraviolet photocatalytic oxidation (PP-UVPCO) sensor. *International Journal of Sustainable Development in Computing Science, 1*(3).

Ruchin, C. M., & Whig, P. (2015). Design and Simulation of Dynamic UART Using Scan Path Technique (USPT). *International Journal of Electrical, Electronics & Computing in Science & Engineering.*

Rupani, A., Saini, D., Sujediya, G., & Whig, P. (2016). A Review of Technology Paradigm for IOT on FPGA. *IJARCCE-International Journal of Advanced Research in Computer and Communication Engineering, 5*(9).

Rupani, A., Whig, P., Sujediya, G., & Vyas, P. (2017). A robust technique for image processing based on interfacing of Raspberry-Pi and FPGA using IoT. *2017 International Conference on Computer, Communications and Electronics (Comptelix)*, 350–353.

Rupani, A., Whig, P., Sujediya, G., & Vyas, P. (2018). Hardware implementation of iot-based image processing filters. *Proceedings of the Second International Conference on Computational Intelligence and Informatics*, 681–691.

Sharma, C., Sharma, S., Kautish, S., Alsallami, S. A., Khalil, E. M., & Mohamed, A. W. (2022). A new median-average round Robin scheduling algorithm: An optimal approach for reducing turnaround and waiting time. *Alexandria Engineering Journal, 61*(12), 10527–10538.

Sharma, H., Rao, N., & Sharma, M. (2016). Analysis of astrology and scientific calculation through orbital period. *2016 3rd International Conference on Computing for Sustainable Global Development (INDIACom)*, 236–239.

Shrivastav, P., Whig, P., & Gupta, K. (2012). *Bandwidth Enhancement by Slotted Stacked Arrangement and its Comparative Analysis with Conventional Single and Stacked Patch Antenna.* Academic Press.

Velu, A., & Whig, P. (2021). Protect Personal Privacy And Wasting Time Using Nlp: A Comparative Approach Using AI. *Vivekananda Journal of Research, 10*, 42–52.

Velu, A., & Whig, P. (2022). *Studying the Impact of the COVID Vaccination on the World Using Data Analytics.* Academic Press.

Verma, T. (2019). A comparison of different R2R D/A converters. *International Journal of Sustainable Development in Computing Science, 1*(2).

Whig, P. (2017). Temperature and Frequency Independent Readout Circuit for PCS System. *SF J Material Res Let, 1*(3), 8–12.

Whig, P. (2019a). A Novel Multi-Center and Threshold Ternary Pattern. *International Journal of Machine Learning for Sustainable Development*, *1*(2), 1–10.

Whig, P. (2019b). Prediction of Smart Building Indoor Temperature Using IoT and Machine Learning. *International Journal of Machine Learning for Sustainable Development*, *1*(4), 1–10.

Whig, P., & Ahmad, S. N. (2016). Modelling and simulation of economical water quality monitoring device. *Journal of Aquaculture & Marine Biology*, *4*(6), 1–6.

Whig, P., & Ahmad, S. N. (2018). Novel pseudo PMOS ultraviolet photo catalytic oxidation (PP-UVPCO) sensor for air purification. *Int Rob Auto J*, *4*(6), 393–398.

Whig, P., Nadikattu, R. R., & Velu, A. (2022). COVID-19 pandemic analysis using application of AI. *Healthcare Monitoring and Data Analysis Using IoT: Technologies and Applications*, 1.

Whig, P., & Rupani, A. (2020). Novel Economical Social Distancing Smart Device for COVID19. *International Journal of Electrical Engineering and Technology*, 2.

Whig, K. K., & P. (2020). Macroeconomic Implications of the Monetary Policy Committee Recommendations: An IS-LM Framework. *ACTA Scientific Agriculture*, *4*(2).

Whig, Priyam, & Ahmad. (2018). Simulation & performance analysis of various R2R D/A converter using various topologies. *International Robotics & Automation Journal*, *4*(2), 128–131.

ADDITIONAL READING

Bhatia, V., & Whig, P. (2013). A secured dual tune multi frequency based smart elevator control system. *International Journal of Research in Engineering and Advanced Technology*, *4*(1), 1163–2319.

Fenner, A. E., Kibert, C. J., Woo, J., Morque, S., Razkenari, M., Hakim, H., & Lu, X. (2018). The carbon footprint of buildings: A review of methodologies and applications. *Renewable & Sustainable Energy Reviews*, *94*, 1142–1152. doi:10.1016/j.rser.2018.07.012

Giaccherini, F., Munz, G., Dockhorn, T., Lubello, C., & Rosso, D. (2017). Carbon and energy footprint analysis of tannery wastewater treatment: A Global overview. *Water Resources and Industry*, *17*, 43–52. doi:10.1016/j.wri.2017.03.001

Gui, F., Ren, S., Zhao, Y., Zhou, J., Xie, Z., Xu, C., & Zhu, F. (2019). Activity-based allocation and optimization for carbon footprint and cost in product lifecycle. *Journal of Cleaner Production, 236*, 117627. doi:10.1016/j.jclepro.2019.117627

Rosati, F., & Faria, L. G. D. (2019). Addressing the SDGs in sustainability reports: The relationship with institutional factors. *Journal of Cleaner Production, 215*, 1312–1326. doi:10.1016/j.jclepro.2018.12.107

Sharma, A., Kumar, A., & Whig, P. (2015). On the performance of CDTA based novel analog inverse low pass filter using 0.35 μm CMOS parameter. International Journal of Science. *Technology & Management, 4*(1), 594–601.

Singh, A. K., Gupta, A., & Senani, R. (2018). OTRA-based multi-function inverse filter configuration. *Advances in Electrical and Electronic Engineering, 15*(5), 846–856. doi:10.15598/aeee.v15i5.2572

Whig, P., & Ahmad, S. N. (2012). Performance analysis of various readout circuits for monitoring quality of water using analog integrated circuits. *International Journal of Intelligent Systems and Applications, 4*(11), 103. doi:10.5815/ijisa.2012.11.11

KEY TERMS AND DEFINITIONS

AI: Artificial intelligence (AI) is the ability of a computer or a robot controlled by a computer to do tasks that are usually done by humans because they require human intelligence and discernment.

Carbon Footprint: A carbon footprint is the total amount of greenhouse gases (including carbon dioxide and methane) that are generated by our actions.

IIoT: The industrial internet of things (IIoT) is the use of smart sensors and actuators to enhance manufacturing and industrial processes.

IoT: The term IoT, or Internet of Things, refers to the collective network of connected devices and the technology that facilitates communication between devices and the cloud, as well as between the devices themselves.

Machine Learning: Machine learning is a branch of artificial intelligence (AI) and computer science which focuses on the use of data and algorithms to imitate the way that humans learn, gradually improving its accuracy.

Markov Decision: Markov decision process (MDP) is a discrete-time stochastic control process.

Q-Learning: Q-learning is a model-free reinforcement learning algorithm to learn the value of an action in a particular state.

Reinforcement Learning: Reinforcement learning is a machine learning training method based on rewarding desired behaviors and/or punishing undesired ones.

Chapter 8

Demystifying Federated Learning for Blockchain:
A Case Study

Pawan Whig
Vivekananda Institute of Professional Studies, India

ARUN Velu
Equifax, USA

Pavika Sharma
Bhagwan Parshuram Institute of Technology, India

ABSTRACT

Blockchain genuinely has the power to revolutionise the energy market mechanism by introducing smart PPAs (purchase power agreements), smart micro grids, and REC certificates. By converting energy resources into digital commodities that can be exchanged on a blockchain, new investment and trading possibilities that allow new players to join easily and encourage innovations will be enabled. It may also contribute to a shift driven by the organisation to address the issue of last mile connectivity. While recent grid developments have broadened the use of advanced control techniques, the next-generation grid requires technology that makes it simpler to connect distributed energy services (DERs) for users who both acquire and sell power seamlessly. This chapter will present a case study of a blockchain-based optimization paradigm and framework for crowd-sourced operations.

DOI: 10.4018/978-1-6684-3733-9.ch008

INTRODUCTION

Modern renewable energy is a prominent answer as energy and climate are constantly addressing the worldwide looming challenge (Anand et al., 2022). Because it emits less pollutants and is renewable, clean energy is referred to as green energy that may be used to counterbalance conventional energy. As a result, green energy infrastructure and platforms are being created at an increasing rate, and there is a growing demand for renewable energy growth (Alkali et al., 2022; Chopra & WHIG, 2022).

In this Chapter, we leverage the block chain to develop a novel trading mechanism for unlocking fresh energy resources that might be employed in the future. Blockchain is an open leader in which all online transactions are logged and all transactions can bind, submit, or check. Blockchain is a digitalised accounting records scheme in which all transactions are documented in full in accordance with a set of cryptographic rules to prevent unauthorised intervention (Chopra & Whig, 2022; Madhu & WHIG, 2022).

Each node in a block chain becomes a prosumer, capable of generating, selling, and buying electricity as well as exchanging it over a peer-to-peer network without the need for a central organization (WHIG, 2022).

Because smart contracts are used, trading may be done remotely and without the involvement of a third party. There are other exchange criteria that may be established, but the most basic way of trading is when the sell and purchase amounts match based on a price determined by the total energy level (George et al., 2021; Mamza, 2021). This enables us to make better use of energy by developing a non-traditional active energy trading network (Bhargav & Whig, 2021; Sinha & Ranjan, 2015; Whig & Rupani, 2020).

During this time, as the quantity of power and transaction records recorded in the blockchain network grows, we construct private networks that engage only in the permitted nodes without fear of failure or attack, in order to prevent attacking nodes purchasing and selling indiscreet resources (Velu & Whig, 2021).

BLOCKCHAIN

The blockchain is a peer-to-peer data network infrastructure. The blockchain is named as the blocks are grouped into chains. Each network user distributes and saves data from the history of transactions in block format on the blockchain. Because each node has a unique private and public key, the secret key and hash function may be used to perform a cryptographic signature on the transaction. Each node checks that the transaction has been signed by the digital signature subject using the public key (Whig, 2019). This transaction is included in a block that contains a structure of "chains" that are always linked after a particular cycle during the time flow. Because every user has a transaction history, each user may evaluate their transaction history by reading their own logs. Transactions that have not been authenticated cannot be stored in the block. As a result, blockchain has three characteristics: Confidentiality, security, and decentralisation of data (Whig & Ahmad, 2019).

Corporate material is now in use. The higher the speed and accuracy, the better. The more precisely. Blockchain is appropriate for providing information because it delivers information that can be instantaneously saved in an immutable ledger, shared, and completely open, and which can only be viewed by permitted network users. A blockchain network will keep track of orders, transactions, accounts, development, and much more. And, because all players have a single knowledge of the facts, all transaction information is end-to-end, providing you with enhanced interest and new efficiency (Arun Velu, 2021; Reddy, 2019; verma, 2019).

Main Elements of Block Chain

1. Distributed ledger

DLT is a digital asset transaction structure in which transactions and their data are logged in several locations at the same time. The transaction can only be registered via DLT. Unlike traditional databases, distributed ledgers do not have a centralised storage or administrative function (Nadikattu et al., 2021).

Each node on a distributed ledger processes and verifies each item, resulting in a record of each item and agreement on its veracity. A distributed directory can be used to store static records such as a register and dynamic transactions.

This computing architecture shows a significant change in record keeping by altering record collecting and communication (Srivastava et al., 2020).

Source of the Ledgers Books

For thousands of years, ledgers — primarily transaction records and accompanying numbers – have been kept on paper. With the introduction of computers towards the end of the twentieth century, they were digitised, and electronic books typically mirrored what used to appear on paper (Jumaa et al., 2018; Nadikattu et al., 2020). The legitimacy of transactions reported in the records, on the other hand, must be confirmed by a central authority during the period. Banks, for example, must verify money transfers.

All network members have access to the distributed directory and its unchangeable transaction log. This mutual directory only records transactions once, reducing the duplication of effort that is common in traditional business networks. Figure 1 depicts the workflow in a distributed ledger as shown inn Fig 1(Shrivastav et al., 2020.).

Figure 1. Distributed ledger technology

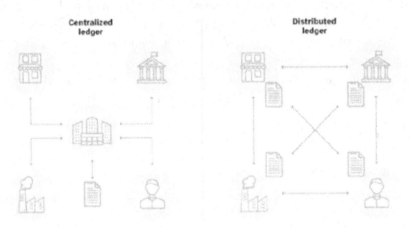

IMPORTANCE

Because distributed ledger technology eliminates the need for a central agency or middleman, transactions will be faster. Similarly, dispersed booklets will lower transaction costs.

Experts also believe that distributed ledger technical information is considerably secure when each network node has data, resulting in a method that is more difficult to attack or target successfully (Kaushik et al., 2018)

Many people consider a distributed block to be a far more open approach of keeping records since the content is transferred and so observed in a network (Mehta et al., 2014)

Early on, the use of distributed ledger technology in financial transactions was critical. This is understandable given the widespread use of blockchain bitcoin, while also demonstrating that DLT can operate. Early innovation also occurred in banks and other financial institutions in this chamber (Whig, 2021)

However, DLT supporters argue that, in addition to financial purchases, digital books may still be utilised in other domains, such as government and business.

Figure 2. Futures of DL systems

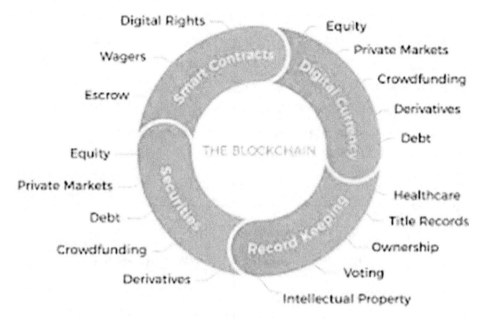

According to experts, automated leads will be utilised to collect taxes, pass land titles, administer social services, and even vote (Asopa et al., 2021).

They also claim that DLT may be utilised to process and implement legal papers and other documents of the kind (Chopra & Whig, 2021).

Some say that this technology may be used to gather, monitor, and selectively share personal data as appropriate. Medical records and commercial supply chains are two examples of use cases.

Proponents also claim that digital booklets will aid in the monitoring of intellectual property rights and possession of books, commodities, songs, movies, and other forms of intellectual property (Velu & Whig, 2022)

FUTURES OF DL SYSTEMS

The topic of whether distributed leading developments, like as blockchain, can transform the way economies, organisations, and enterprises work is still being debated (Ajay Rupani, 2019). Articles in the academic and financial press questioned whether distributed ledger systems, as they now exist, are safe enough to be extensively utilised. This current style of trading, as well as security concerns, are not governed by any government (Rupani & Kumar, 2020).

Figure 3. Representation of immutable record

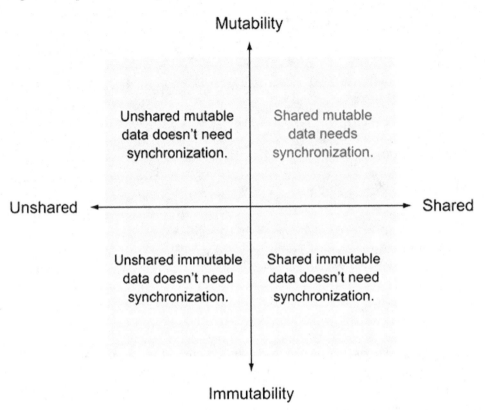

1. Immutable Records

No one can change or modify a transaction after it has been recorded in the public ledger. If a mistake occurs in a transaction log, it must be corrected by adding a new transaction, after which all transactions are available. Figure 2 depicts the representation of an immutable record (Purva Agarwall, 2016).

The word "immutable" can almost always be found across hundreds of posts and discussions surrounding Blockchain. Immutability—the ability to remain a constant, unchanging and unalterable transaction background for a blockchain leader—is a definite attribute that blockchain evangelists emphasize as an important advantage. Immutability will turn the audit process into a quick, reliable and cost-effective process to increase confidence and integrity in the use and sharing of data companies on a daily basis(Whig & Ahmad, 2018a).

Trillions of dollars would be spent on strategies for cybersecurity that can secure our confidential data out of our sight. However, we seldom fight the domestic cyber protection fight: to ensure that our data is not compromised, substituted or falsified by a corporation or its employees. In certain instances, we clearly depend on methods such as private keys and user permissions as to correct data (Whig & Ahmad, 2018b). Yet in fact, methodologically or mathematically, one cannot prove the knowledge is clearly flawless in a typical program database. The next (and costly) line of security is auditing (Whig & Ahmad, 2017b).

The introduction of Blockchain will provide a regular degree of confidence for data companies — immutability gives credibility (both in its technical and primary definition). Blockchain allows customers to show that the information we use to have is not manipulated and at the same time the audit process can be turned into an effective, sensible and economical operation (Ahmad & Whig, 2011; Pawan Whig Anupam Priyam, 2018; Whig & Ahmad, 2017a).

What is Immutability?

A brief introduction to hazardous cryptography

We need to consider crypto graphical hatching before diving into blockchain immutability. The fundamentals are here:

A hash function takes the current data and outputs a "Checksum" — a number and letter string which serves as digital signatures (an entry such as the 'Blockchain is Disruptive' in the examples below...).

The check amount is guaranteed to indicate your exact data entry — if any one byte differs from two files, the outputs are absolutely two strings after hacking. This can be associated with an avalanche effect — you can dramatically modify the performance in a limited way.

SHA 2 (and its variants: Sha-256 is the most common in blockchain world) is probably the most popular hashing algorithm. It was developed by the NSA.

Cryptography + Blockchain Hashing Process = Immutability

Of transaction validated by the Blockchain network is time-marked and inserted in a "block" of records, encrypted by a hacking mechanism that links the hash in the previous block and integrates it into the chain as a sequential update (Rupani et al., 2018)

Includes metadata from the previous block hash output will be still in the hash method for a new block (Whig & Ahmad, 2016). This connection during the hacking process renders the chain "unbreakable" – after validation, data cannot be manipulated or deleted so the subsequent blocks in the chain deny the change attempted. In other words, as data is manipulated, the blockchain breaks down and

Figure 4. Block diagram to represent smart contract

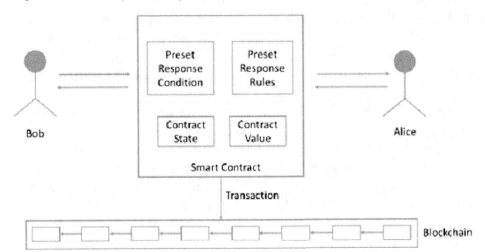

the cause can be found easily. This feature is not present in conventional databases where details can be easily changed or erased (Chacko & Whig, 2016).

At a certain time, the blockchain is simply a reference of truth. For Bitcoin, these details include Bitcoin transmission detail. The picture below illustrates how as part of the header the check-summation of the transaction data has been applied to and becomes a checksum for the whole block (Rupani et al., 2016).

2. Smart agreements

A customary of instructions, recognized as a smart agreement, is recorded happening the block chain and implemented mechanically to rapidity up and around connections. Smart agreement can stipulate the footings for communal bond transmissions, as well as the terms for portable assurance expenditures, among other things. Figure 3 is a block diagram of a smart contract (Sharma et al., n.d.).

Intelligent contracts are self-executing contracts that include the conditions of a peer-to-peer agreement. The arrangement's provisions must be included in the code. The intelligent contract operates on the Ethereum blockchain's open network. The arrangements make it simpler to exchange capital, shares, property, or other commodities. Solidity and Serpent are two programming languages that are extensively utilised in Ethereum smart contracts. Solidity is a sophisticated programming language that is used on the Ethereum blockchain platform to integrate intelligent contracts. It enables blockchain engineers to evaluate the software rather than build it at runtime (Kautish et al. 2022)

As two parties enter into a transaction, they generally employ the knowledge of a credible third party to carry out the arrangement. This is how it has been done for millennia. The deployment of intelligent contracts and their accompanying applications, on the other hand, automates a complex manual task. This Chapter discusses the technology underlying intelligent contracts as well as how they may be employed (Moorthy et al. 2022). Let us first examine some of the primary advantages of intelligent contracts over traditional contracts:

Savings

The sheer quantity of lower and middle levels causes the process to take days, if not weeks, to complete.

Because smart contracts are automated and programmable, they may be completed in minutes on a computer in predetermined contexts. There is no third-party participation.

Safety

Contacts with typical contracts have concerns regarding privacy and stability. With too many intermediate parties engaged, safety might be threatened at any time. Encryption, public key, and private key are used to maintain security while utilising smart contracts. When data is kept in a decentralised setting, it is nearly impossible to modify. Using private keys, intelligent agreements are entered upon remotely. The public key that the participants exchanged cannot be deciphered (Sharma et al. 2022; Rajawat et al. 2022)

Precision and Openness

An intelligent contract's conditions and terms are established and pre-integrated. When a condition is met, the transmission occurs and is automatically registered. If every transfer is part of a traditional contract, it is a manual operation with permission procedures. Traditionally, responsibility is dictated by the organisations involved, as well as peripheral entities and mediators. It's a fault in the gadget. Intelligent contracts, on the other hand, are completely open and accessible connected 24 hours a day, seven existences a week. Anyone determination be talented to review and verify the transactions that have been preserved. Traditional contracts are impossible to preserve since they are offline, rely on paper, and are retained (Whig & Ahmad, 2015).

Fare

Traditional contracts are more expensive than smart contracts because all middlemen must be paid for. Smart contracts have no middlemen, and only the exchange expenses are derived from the underlying smart contract network networks.

BENEFITS OF BLOCKCHAIN

What needs to be changed: Activities take time to keep duplicate records and authenticate third parties. Cyber-assault and theft can occur in record-keeping systems. Limited clarity can stymie weak data verification. And, with the introduction of IoT, transaction rates skyrocketed. All of this is slowing down industry and emptying the ultimate result, suggesting that we need a new strategy. Here are some of the advantages of Blockchain.

Trust

As part of a Network-Only, you should ensure that you get trustworthy and timely data from blockchain, and that private information may only be transferred with network users to whom you have particular access.

Security

Both network participants need a security consensus on data accuracy, and all authenticated transactions cannot be changed since they are forever registered. Nobody can uninstall a transaction, not even a system administrator.

Sustainability

The time-consuming record reconciliation is avoided with a public ledger exchanged by users of a network. And a series of laws — known as an intelligent contract — may be saved and exceeded instantly in a blockchain for pace transactions.

ESS Requirement

ESSs can help to improve the Distributed Generation (DG) operation and electricity delivery and help to eliminate system uncertainties. Conventional energy systems depended only on spinning reserves and auxiliary services rotational generators. Most DG micro-sources, especially renewable generation units, are not however able

Figure 5. Block diagram to represent ESS

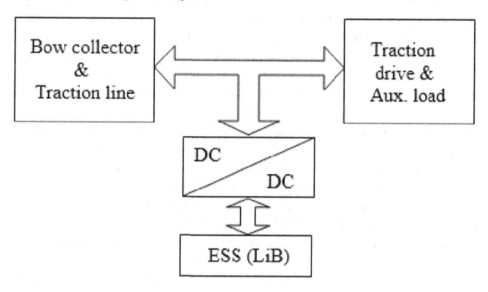

to meet these requirements, and therefore depends on outside storage. The following are some of the requirements of the ESS in DG systems. The block diagram of ESS is shown in Figure 5.

Fuel-powered plants are often maintained standing to assure the spinning reserve, although they still require a significant amount of time to reply. In the lack of a rotating standby in renewable energy systems, the ESS can help to ramp up the power supply in times of necessity. The capacity of modern smart storage systems may be increased in seconds to minutes. As a result, a well accomplished ESS can effectively substitute a considerably bigger rotating standby. They container too be used to collection liveliness during temporary authority outages. They reply slowly but may be commissioned in about an hour.

Charging and peak shaving: Typically, utilities use top capitals and producers to encounter crowning power request. It mainly uses burning locomotives and gas fired control plants, which have poorer efficiency and advanced releases. Labours are existence made to minimise the top of the request bend by enhancing end operator energy efficiency, informing about request rejoinder, and employing highest price schemes. Keeping energy in storage is an enticing strategy to regulate the demand peak curve. They have the ability to store energy at low peak times and then release it during peak times. As a result, it is a actual sensitive and adaptable peak standby. Storage is particularly vital for request reply programmes, which will allow for agreed upon and coordinated direct control over end-user needs. ESS will also result in a reduction in peak emissions.

Inclusion of DG renewable sources: When request is low, wind control is typically shaped at night. The storage and transmission of this energy during times of need thereby improves the competence of the DG scheme. When the similar storage devices are providing on the operator's adjacent, any extra wind energy (low congestion period) may be transported at night and stored close to the supply point. Congestion on T&D lines during peak hours will also be reduced, resulting in fewer breakdowns and failures. Similarly, solar energy is only accessible when the sun is shining brightly, allowing generation to be stored during peak hours and generation to occur at night.

As solar energy penetration increased, a critical scenario known as the cane curve developed. The system providers encountered significant difficulties in ramping up alternative generators to accommodate rapid demand fluctuations. In such cases, ESS can assist level the demand curve and enhance supply at peak periods. They can also assist to increase penetration by removing the unpredictability and intermittent usage of renewable sources.

Support for power quality: The integration of renewable energy faces a wide range of power quality issues, ranging from swells, swells, and slugs to variations and spikes. To maintain grid code power quality criteria, storage technologies accomplished of fast replying to system oscillations, like as flywheels and extreme condensers, container remain deployed. In addition, the ESS may be used to reduce harmonics, LVRT, and transient response. Flywheels, superconductors, and fast-response batteries are frequently used in DG to manage frequency and voltage and enhance energy quality.

Annex services: Grid operators require annex services to sustain stable and dependable grid operation. Frequency control is a critical component of auxiliary services such as load tracking and energy arbitrage. A platform for energy arbitrators will be built in preparation for future market deregulation and the implementation of time-based pricing. It comprises the fee for low storage during peak periods and the delivery at higher costs during peak times. Peak shaving and peak shaving go hand in hand, but the latter focuses on the greatest possible marketing of saved energy.

Though, this one is vital to remember that storing schemes rummage-sale for controlling then loading subsequent must be very sensitive and well-organized, or different storage up/down fatalities would outweigh the gains. Traditional generators used for auxiliary services are often run at less than their rated capacity, resulting in reduced efficiency and higher emissions. As a result, ESS container remain the less expensive release allowed choice aimed at auxiliary facilities, release producers to function at peak efficiency.

Figure 6. Global share of different installed capacity-based energy storage technologies

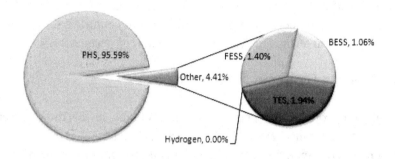

ESS Type

For many decades, humanity has been practising energy storage and conservation. The traditional electricity storage faces were hydro storage and electrochemical batteries. The various ESS can be classified as shown in Figure 2 based on the technology used. Figure 6 demonstrates the global share of different installed capacity-based energy storage technologies.

Hydro-Storage Pumped

The grid-scale storage is commercially installed and most widely operated. PHS uses two reservoirs at various highs that use off-peak cheap grid electricity, which pumps water from lower to upper reservoir. The stored water is discharged into the lower tank if necessary and electricity is generated by rotating turbines. They have long lifetime of around 50-60 years and are able to store enormous energy capacity for many months. Depending on the capacity of the plant, height difference, and type of turbine, their efficiency is between 70–80%. They require a long period of investment and planning and gestation. New features in hydropumping include speed pumping, which increases system reaction time for ramping applications even further.

Storage of Air Power Compressed

Beaten air is stowed by way of a source of possible liveliness in big subterranean caves and excavations. When necessary, combined with normal fume and overdone to create power using expansion turbines. This sort of CAES is commonly referred to as Diabatic CAES, and it has a low efficiency value of roughly 50%. An adiabetical

CAES occurs when heat is saved during compression and used to heat air during the discharge phase as some sort of thermal energy. These systems are currently being researched, but when implemented, they will have a actual in height competence of roughly 77%. It is widely rummage-sale in several countries. CAES provides significant benefits in terms of energy capacity and long-term storage.

Energy Storage Systems for Flywheel

As an accelerating rotor or spinning cylinders in a rotating device, they store energy in the form of electromechanical kinetic energy. The notion is founded on the practice of motorized apathy stored in a revolving thing. Once loading, the flywheel accelerates, and when the opposite procedure is discharged, the flywheel functions by way of a frequency. Progressive FESS has tall haste rotors composed of bright heaviness, in height resistance carbon resources that spin at 20-50,000 rpm under vacuum. It has a high power rating and a fast reaction time, making it perfect for ramping and rotating standby requests.

Additional appealing topographies of FESS are great efficiency, tall power, extended life, and little to not at all upkeep. Primary disadvantage is the excessive self release induced by braking and robust coil fatalities.

Storage of Hydrogen

The hydrogen generated is held under pressure in separate tanks, and electricity is utilised in electrolyzers to split water into hydrogen and oxygen. This hydrogen is necessary for the creation of electrons and water in a fuel cell via oxygen/air. Because the only byproducts of the entire process are water and heat, it is truly a type of highly clean energy. This is also known as a regeneration fuel cell. They're very modular, scalable, energy-efficient, and powerful. They do, however, have a 50% poor to medium efficiency and are vulnerable to self-deployment.

BESSs are the greatest frequently deployed and commercially utilised storing schemes in control scheme requests. The rudimentary concept is to transform power into some electrochemical procedure and store it by way of electrolytes within the lockup. During discharge, the electrolytes respond with the conductors of the cell, and the opposite response produces electrical power. A multitude of battery types with diverse properties have been produced throughout the years, making battery storage technology incredibly adaptable and versatile. Non-rechargeable batteries, also known as primary batteries, are primarily employed in medical and military applications. Various types of BSES are shown in Fig. 7.

In the 1890s, lead acid batteries were developed to increase battery performance and shorten servicing time, as were recent advances like as valve-regulated batteries

Figure 7. Various types of BESS

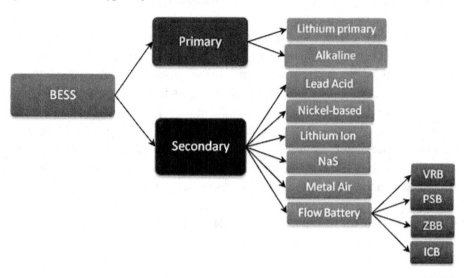

and absorbent glass mat batteries. Nickel cadmium batteries have been employed in wind stabilising applications but are prohibited by cadmium disposal owing to environmental hazards. Because of its great power density, lithium-ion batteries are commonly employed in portable electronic equipment. Recently developed lithium-polymer systems with high renewable integration properties are also being developed. Increased use of NaS batteries in high-energy, energy-efficient renewable systems. Recent research into metal–air batteries. Lithium-air batteries are the most appealing due to their high specific energies and zinc-air batteries. Metal air batteries, on the other hand, are extremely flammable due to strong metal reactivity and air. Flow batteries are renew sequences that stock fluid electrolytes outside in distinct containers. This assistances to boost the power capacity of the plugs. They may increase their power capacity by adding electrode cells, which is extremely flexible and scalable. The electrolytes in the tank may be easily changed by performing an immediate recharge. Because of the recyclable electrolytes that function over hundreds of cycles, the system is extremely efficient. Because the battery interacts with reduction-oxidation during charge-unloading, they are also known as redox batteries. Vanadium redox, bromide polysulphide, zinc bromide, and iron-chromium batteries are examples of flow batteries. A thorough examination of the properties of battery storage systems was conducted.

Magnetic Energy Store Super-Conducting

Each SMES unit is equipped with a low temperature superconducting belt, a power conditioning unit, and a refrigeration system. When supercooled metals demonstrated superconductivity, electromagnetic electricity was discovered many years ago. This property for electrical energy storage was first investigated in the late 1960s, when robust attractive turfs created by high-temperature superconducting loops such as Kelvin were investigated. Recent research has resulted in materials that can also operate at 100 degrees Celsius. The system is incredibly efficient, but it is becoming less and less powerful. Furthermore, cooling systems raise system expenses and maintenance and are still in the early phases of development.

Dual Layer Electric Condensers or Super Condensers

Electrostatic charges are used to store electricity in these devices. It is typically made of a dielectric parallel plate structure that holds the charge. Because of their huge battery-comparable energy capacity, this technology bridges the gap between ordinary electrical condensers and batteries. Because they are not converted, they are incredibly fast and can do fast load and release series. They are extremely well-organized, ecologically safe, simple to recycle, and can handle frequent applications. They have a very from head to foot personality release and are increasingly employed in electric cars and grip schemes.

Storage of Thermal Energy

Through augmented solar energy diffusion, current storing consumes acquired a ration of traction. Excess warmth energy container be saved for later use in structures stored secondary energy carriers. The ice and melted saline machineries are existence industrialized, and when operational, it is projected to share a major portion of the electricity need for heating. Thermal storage on ice, which includes latent heat storage, is said to reach exceptional efficiency when employed in solar generating.

Energy Management ESSs for DGs

The paragraph discusses the numerous issues that arise during the integration of renewable energy systems and the accompanying ESS needs. It provided an overview of the numerous applications that can benefit from ESSs. Some applications, such as power smoothing and frequency regulation, necessitate the use of short-term storage devices capable of charging and unloading large amounts of power. Arbitration and peak shaving applications need more energy capacity in order to preserve low-self-discharge energy from stored energy. Depending on the applications, the suitable storage type and size must be selected and scaled for integration. Because storage schemes are luxurious, must be efficiently achieved to safeguard length and presentation; otherwise, can create F&E issues, decreased performance, and premature failure.

Effective administration of both storage and generating devices is required to guarantee that DERs are used effectively. As a result, energy management has become a hot issue among renewable vigour researchers and producers. Fig. 8 portrays the mechanisms of an energy organization scheme.

Figure 8. Mechanisms of an energy organization scheme

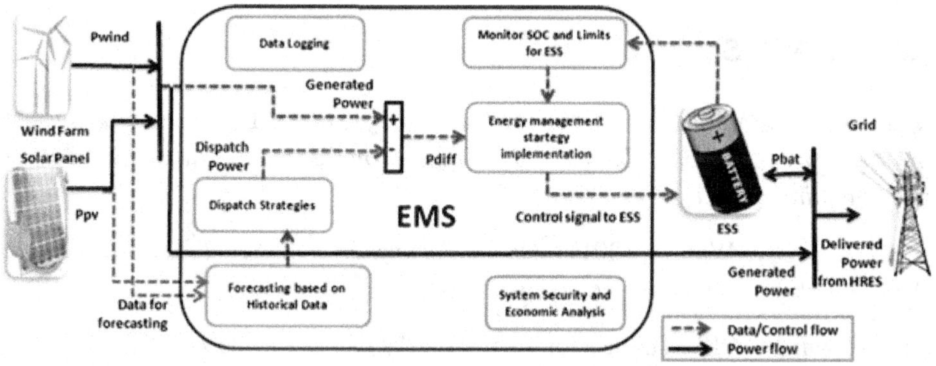

EMS are a critical component in preparation an autonomous and independent renewable energy system. A storing scheme may be run to meet numerous requests as defined in a micro grid, and a organization approach will be presented to fulfil the default goals without harming both the storage system and the system. According to Nykamp et al., from the perspective of a Distribution Scheme Operative, the utilisation of a storage system is mostly aimed to peak shaving and renewable addition requests.

A secluded liveliness seller intends to exploit the storing scheme to maximise revenues through arbitration and ancillary services. The simulation results on a sharp comparison of the various applications of the same storage in a distribution grid were reported. In order to minimise charging issues, energy management is often dependent on the state of charge (SOC) of energy storage devices. Reihani et al. developed a simulation of battery ride-scale storage for the purposes of peak load shaving, power smoothing, and distribution system voltage regulation.

CONCLUSION

The rise of large measure multi gathering Machine Leaning assignments and disseminated records for scaling consensus has resulted in binary powerful then fast-moving tendencies. Many designs is based on the intersection of these two elements. To the finest of our information, this is the first answer to enable confidentiality preservative P2P ML using a secure layer-1 distributed blockchain ledger. In contrast to previous work, this casestudy not depend on on a centralised service, trusted implementation surroundings, or specialised hardware to enable adversary protections. A novel paradigm of blockchain-based decentralised Federated Learning, in order to bridge the knowledge gap between deployment and developers.

REFERENCES

Agarwal & P. W. (2016). A Review-Quaternary Signed Digit Number System byReversible Logic Gate. *International Journal on Recent and Innovation Trends in Computing and Communication, 4*(3).

Ahmad, S. N., & Whig, P. (2011). *On the Performance of ISFET-based Device for Water Quality Monitoring*. Academic Press.

Ajay Rupani, P. (2019). The development of big data science to the world. *Engineering Reports, 2*(2), 1–7.

Alkali Y. Routray I. Whig P. (2022). Study of various methods for reliable, efficient and Secured IoT using Artificial Intelligence. *Available at* SSRN 4020364. doi:10.2139/ssrn.4020364

Anand, M., Velu, A., & Whig, P. (2022). Prediction of Loan Behaviour with Machine Learning Models for Secure Banking. *Journal of Computing Science and Engineering: JCSE, 3*(1), 1–13.

Arun Velu, P. W. (2021). Impact of Covid Vaccination on the Globe using data analytics. *International Journal of Sustainable Development in Computing Science, 3*(2).

Asopa, P., Purohit, P., Nadikattu, R. R., & Whig, P. (2021). Reducing carbon footprint for sustainable development of smart cities using IoT. *2021 Third International Conference on Intelligent Communication Technologies and Virtual Mobile Networks (ICICV)*, 361–367. 10.1109/ICICV50876.2021.9388466

Bhargav, R., & Whig, P. (2021). More Insight on Data Analysis of Titanic Data Set. *International Journal of Sustainable Development in Computing Science*, *3*(4), 1–10.

Chacko, J. B., & Whig, P. (2016). Low Delay Based Full Adder/Subtractor by MIG and COG Reversible Logic Gate. *2016 8th International Conference on Computational Intelligence and Communication Networks (CICN)*, 585–589.

Chopra, G., & Whig, P. (2022). A clustering approach based on support vectors. *International Journal of Machine Learning for Sustainable Development*, *4*(1), 21–30.

Chopra, G., & Whig, P. (2021). Analysis of Tomato Leaf Disease Identification Techniques. *Journal of Computing Science and Engineering: JCSE*, *2*(2), 98–103.

Chopra, G., & Whig, P. (2022). Smart Agriculture System Using AI. *International Journal of Sustainable Development in Computing Science*, *1*(1).

George, N., Muiz, K., Whig, P., & Velu, A. (2021). Framework of Perceptive Artificial Intelligence using Natural Language Processing (PAIN). *Artificial & Computational Intelligence*.

Jumaa, N. K., Abdulhameed, O. A., & Abbas, R. H. (2018). A Theoretical Background of IoT Platforms based on FPGAs. *Communications on Applied Electronics*, *7*(23), 6–10. doi:10.5120/cae2018652797

Kaushik, S., Chouhan, Y. S., Sharma, N., Singh, S., & Suganya, P. (2018). Automatic fan speed control using temperature and humidity sensor and Arduino. *International Journal of Advanced Research*, *4*(2), 453–467.

Madhu, M., & Whig, P. (2022). A survey of machine learning and its applications. *International Journal of Machine Learning for Sustainable Development*, *1*(1), 11–20.

Mamza, E. S. (2021). Use of AIOT in Health System. *International Journal of Sustainable Development in Computing Science*, *3*(4), 21–30.

Mehta, R., Bhattacharya, N., & Goyal, S. (2014). RFID and ASP.NET based Campus Management System. *International Journal of Computers and Applications*, *88*(4).

Nadikattu, R. R., Bhandari, R., & Whig, P. (2021). Improved Pattern of Adaptive Rood-Pattern Search Algorithm for Motion Estimation in Video Compression. In *Innovations in Cyber Physical Systems* (pp. 441–448). Springer. doi:10.1007/978-981-16-4149-7_39

Nadikattu, R. R., Mohammad, S. M., & Whig, P. (2020). Novel economical social distancing smart Device for COVID-19 (*SSRN* Scholarly Paper ID 3640230). *Social Science Research Network*. Https://Papers. Ssrn. Com/Abstract,3640230

Reddy, R. (2019). Purification of indoor air using a novel pseudo PMOS ultraviolet photocatalytic oxidation (PP-UVPCO) sensor. *International Journal of Sustainable Development in Computing Science, 1*(3).

Rupani, A., & Kumar, D. (2020). *Temperature Effect On Behaviour of Photo Catalytic Sensor (PCS)*. Used For Water Quality Monitoring.

Rupani, A., Saini, D., Sujediya, G., & Whig, P. (2016). A Review of Technology Paradigm for IOT on FPGA. *IJARCCE-International Journal of Advanced Research in Computer and Communication Engineering, 5*(9).

Rupani, A., Whig, P., Sujediya, G., & Vyas, P. (2018). Hardware implementation of iot-based image processing filters. *Proceedings of the Second International Conference on Computational Intelligence and Informatics*, 681–691. 10.1007/978-981-10-8228-3_63

Sharma, N. K., Shrivastava, S., & Whig, P. (n.d.). *Optimization of Process Parameters for Developing Stresses in Square Cup by Incremental Sheet Metal (ISM) Technique uses Finite Element Methods*. Academic Press.

Shrivastav, P., Whig, P., & Gupta, K. (n.d.). *Bandwidth Enhancement by Slotted Stacked Arrangement and its Comparative Analysis with Conventional Single and Stacked Patch Antenna*. Academic Press.

Sinha, R., & Ranjan, A. (2015). Effect of Variable Damping Ratio on design of PID Controller. *2015 4th International Conference on Reliability, Infocom Technologies and Optimization (ICRITO)(Trends and Future Directions)*, 1–4.

Srivastava, J., Bhagat, R., & Kumar, P. (2020). Analog inverse filters using OTAs. *2020 6th International Conference on Control, Automation and Robotics (ICCAR)*, 627–631.

Velu, A., & Whig, P. (2021). Protect Personal Privacy And Wasting Time Using Nlp: A Comparative Approach Using Ai. *Vivekananda Journal of Research, 10*, 42–52.

Velu, A., & Whig, P. (n.d.). *Studying the Impact of the COVID Vaccination on the World Using Data Analytics*. Academic Press.

Verma, T. (2019). A comparison of different R2R D/A converters. *International Journal of Sustainable Development in Computing Science, 1*(2).

Whig, P. (2022). More on Convolution Neural Network CNN. *International Journal of Sustainable Development in Computing Science, 1*(1).

Whig, P. (2019). A Novel Multi-Center and Threshold Ternary Pattern. *International Journal of Machine Learning for Sustainable Development*, *1*(2), 1–10.

Whig, P. (2021). IoT Based Novel Smart Blind Guidance System. *Journal of Computing Science and Engineering: JCSE*, *2*(2), 80–88.

Whig, P., & Ahmad, S. N. (2015). Novel FGMOS based PCS device for low power applications. *Photonic Sensors*, *5*(2), 123–127.

Whig, P., & Ahmad, S. N. (2016). Modelling and simulation of economical water quality monitoring device. *Journal of Aquaculture & Marine Biology*, *4*(6), 1–6.

Whig, P., & Ahmad, S. N. (2017a). Controlling the Output Error for Photo Catalytic Sensor (PCS) Using Fuzzy Logic. *Journal of Earth Science & Climatic Change*, *8*(4), 1–6.

Whig, P., & Ahmad, S. N. (2017b). Fuzzy logic implementation of photo catalytic sensor. *Int. Robot. Autom. J*, *2*(3), 15–19.

Whig, P., & Ahmad, S. N. (2018a). Comparison analysis of various R2R D/A converter. *Int J Biosen Bioelectron*, *4*(6), 275–279.

Whig, P., & Ahmad, S. N. (2018b). Novel pseudo PMOS ultraviolet photo catalytic oxidation (PP-UVPCO) sensor for air purification. *Int Rob Auto J*, *4*(6), 393–398.

Whig, P., & Ahmad, S. N. (2019). Methodology for Calibrating Photocatalytic Sensor Output. *International Journal of Sustainable Development in Computing Science*, *1*(1), 1–10.

Whig, P., & Rupani, A. (2020). Novel Economical Social Distancing Smart Device for COVID19. *International Journal of Electrical Engineering and Technology*, *2*.

Whig, Priyam, & Ahmad. (2018). Simulation & performance analysis of various R2R D/A converter using various topologies. *International Robotics & Automation Journal*, *4*(2), 128–131.

ADDITIONAL READING

Bhatia, V., & Whig, P. (2013). A secured dual tune multi frequency based smart elevator control system. *International Journal of Research in Engineering and Advanced Technology*, *4*(1), 1163–2319.

Dannen, C. (2017). *Introducing Ethereum and Solidity: Foundations of Cryptocurrency and Blockchain Programming for Beginners* (1st ed.). Apress. doi:10.1007/978-1-4842-2535-6

Rupani, A., Whig, P., Sujediya, G., & Vyas, P. (2017). A robust technique for image processing based on interfacing of Raspberry-Pi and FPGA using IoT. *2017 International Conference on Computer, Communications and Electronics (Comptelix)*, 350–353.

Sharma, A., Kumar, A., & Whig, P. (2015). On the performance of CDTA based novel analog inverse low pass filter using 0.35 μm CMOS parameter. *International Journal of Science. Technology & Management*, *4*(1), 594–601.

Singh, A. K., Gupta, A., & Senani, R. (2018). OTRA-based multi-function inverse filter configuration. *Advances in Electrical and Electronic Engineering*, *15*(5), 846–856.

Whig, P., & Ahmad, S. N. (2012). Performance analysis of various readout circuits for monitoring quality of water using analog integrated circuits. *International Journal of Intelligent Systems and Applications*, *4*(11), 103.

Whig, P., & Ahmad, S. N. (2014). Simulation of linear dynamic macro model of photo catalytic sensor in SPICE. *COMPEL: The International Journal for Computation and Mathematics in Electrical and Electronic Engineering*.

KEY TERMS AND DEFINITIONS

Bitcoin: Bitcoin (₿) is a decentralized digital currency that can be transferred on the peer-to-peer bitcoin network.

Blockchain: A blockchain platform allows users and developers to create novel uses of an existing blockchain infrastructure.

Crypto: A cryptocurrency is an encrypted data string that denotes a unit of currency.

Ethereum: Ethereum is a technology that's home to digital money, global payments, and applications.

Holochain: Holochain is an eco-aware peer-to-peer network.

IoT: The term IoT, or Internet of Things, refers to the collective network of connected devices and the technology that facilitates communication between devices and the cloud, as well as between the devices themselves.

NFT: NFT, known as non-fungible tokens (NFTs), these cryptographic assets are based on blockchain technology and have unique identification codes and metadata that set them apart from each other.

Smart Contracts: A smart contract is a computer program or a transaction protocol which is intended to automatically execute, control or document legally.

Chapter 9
Digital Twins and Federated Learning for Smart Cities and Their Applications

Surabhi Shanker

(iD) https://orcid.org/0000-0001-7160-9049

Trinity Institute of Professional Studies, Guru Gobind Singh Indraprastha University, India

ABSTRACT

This chapter is written with the intent to explore the history, architecture, applications, and challenges in the implementation of digital twin with IoT competences. Digital twins are considered to be a fundamental starting point for today's smart city construction. The chapter initiates with a brief description of the concepts of digital twins and digital twin for cities and smart homes, discusses the relationship between digital twins and smart cities, analyses the characteristics of smart cities and homes based on digital twins, and focuses on the main applications of smart cities based on digital twins. This chapter sheds light on the future development of smart cities and smart homes based on digital twins.

INTRODUCTION

The concept of "twin" was introduced by NASA's Apollo program, which designed and manufactured two real identical space vehicles. One of them was launched into the air space to perform the mission, while the other remained on Earth, agreeing engineers to mirror the conditions of the launched one (Boschert & Rosen, 2016). In the white paper written by Grieves (Glaegen & Stargel, 2012), the Digital Twins

DOI: 10.4018/978-1-6684-3733-9.ch009

Figure 1. The complete development history of DT can be divided into three stages

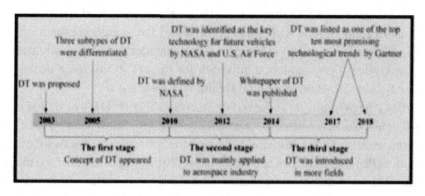

was first projected at his executive course on product lifecycle management (PLM). With technical enhancements, the DT was introduced into the aerospace industry by National Aeronautics and Space Administration (NASA) and U.S. Air Force (Tuegel et al., 2011). Consequently, the space vehicle remaining on Earth could be replaced by a digital mirror model to provide more insights through high-fidelity simulation. Nowadays, the DT has been applied to more fields and has become a most demanding technology. In the figure:1 the complete development history of DT can be divided into three stages.

In the inception stage i.e. first stage, the concept of Digital Twin was introduced by Grieves in 2003 according to the Whitepaper written by him (Glaegen & Stargel, 2012). It was explained in three dimensions, including a physical entity, a digital counterpart, and a linking that connect the two parts together (Glaegen & Stargel, 2012).

In 2005, Grieves set forth another idea and told that the Digital Twin could be classified into three subtypes, including: DT prototype, DT instance, and DT aggregate (Tac, 2012). However, due to technical and perceptive limitations, we are having very few related reports in the following 5 years. But fortunately, during this period, the New IT has arisen and developed, which established the frameworks for the future development of the Digital Twins.

In 2010, NASA established the definition and function of Digital Twins for space vehicles in detail in the Draft Modelling, Simulation, Information Technology and Processing Roadmap (Allare, 2014). In 2011, the U.S. Air Force discovered the application of DT in the mechanical health management of aircrafts (Reifinider & Majumdar, 2013). In 2012, NASA and the U.S. Air Force jointly issued a paper about the Digital Twins, which expressed that the Digital Twin was the critical innovation for future vehicles (Tuegel et al., 2011). After that, the number of research studies on the DT in aerospace has improved gradually. For example, Tuegel proposed the

Airframe Digital Twins for design and maintenance, and deliberated the challenges for its development (Swedberg, n.d.). Allaire et al. researched a dynamic data-driven application system, which was portrayed as the execution establishment of the DT for aerospace vehicles (Menard, n.d.). Reifsnider and Majumdar introduced a multidisciplinary physics-based approach for the DT in taskforce management (Science Service Dr. Hempel Digital Health Network, n.d.).

In 2014, the Whitepaper (Glaegen & Stargel, 2012) on DT was issued and the three-dimensional structure of DT was widely revealed. Subsequently, the DT was spread the word about for more fields beyond the aerospace business, for example, automotive (Panetta, 2017), oil and gas (Panetta, 2017), and healthcare and medicine (Murray, 2018). In recent years, many recognized organizations have introduced great importance to the DT. Both in 2017 and 2018, Gartner stared the DT as one of the top 10 most auspicious technological trends in the next decade [13,14]. In 2017, Lockheed Martin Space Systems Company listed the DT as the top of six protruding technologies for future defence and aerospace (Tao, 2017). Smart Manufacturing Association of China Association for Science and Technology indicated that the DT was one of the best 10 logical and innovative advances for smart manufacturing in the world (Tao, 2017b). Based on the current inclination, it can be expected that the DT will experience a rapid development in the next few years.

DIGITAL TWIN- CONCEPT AND ARCHITECTURE

The growth of progressive technologies is concrete way for the smart cities, where all the physical objects will have embedded computing and communication capabilities so that they can sense the atmosphere and connect with each other to provide the services. These intelligent interconnections and interoperability are also termed as IoT or machine-to-machine (M2M) communications (Tao, 2017a). Some of the important areas of a smart city are the smart energy, smart home, smart transport system. and smart manufacturing. Because of the affordability and availability of the sensors and actuators, data acquisition has become relatively easier. Monitoring and diagnosing the manufacturing machines through the Internet is a challenging task. The convergence of the physical and virtual worlds of manufacturing is still one of the major challenges in the field of Cyber-Physical Systems (CPS), which needs more research. To confront these challenges, Industry 4.0 was conceptualized (Tao, 2017), which revealed that if the production systems are made intelligent and smart, they can function more competently (Tao et al., 2018; Tao, 2017b). There have been many developments to enable this, one of which is digital twin (Machine-to-Machine Communications, 2015).

Figure 2. The different stages in the architecture of digital twin service

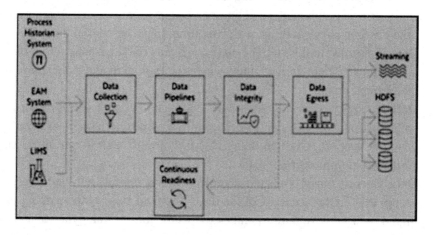

"Digital twin" is an idea that makes a model of an actual model of a physical asset for predictive maintenance. This model will continually adapt to changes in the environment or operation using real-time sensory data and can forecast the future of the corresponding physical assets (Schuh et al., 2017). It can monitor and recognize expected issues with its physical twin. In addition, it allows the prediction of the remaining useful life (RUL) of the physical twin by leveraging a combination of physics-based models and data-driven analytics. It consists of three main parts: (i) physical products in real space (ii) virtual products in virtual space, and (iii) the connections of data and information that will tie the virtual and real products together. Therefore, collecting and analysing a large volume of manufacturing data to find the information and connections has become the key to smart manufacturing.

The concept of digital twin presented by Grieves at one of his presentations in 2003 on Product Lifecycle Management (PLM) at University of Michigan (Ribeiro & Björkman, 2017). GE has started its digital transformation journey cantered on Digital Twin, by building critical jet engine components that predict the business outcomes associated with the remaining life of those components (Qin et al., 2016).

The work done in (Uhlemann et al., 2017) was the first initiative to come up with a dynamic Bayesian network approach for digital twin, where they utilized the concept of digital twin for tracking the evolution of time-dependent variables to monitor aircraft structure.

The different stages in the architecture of digital twin service involve:

- **Data collection**: The first stage is the Data collection. The industrial digital transformation begins with building operational digital twins. These are comprised of two types of data: Model data and Time series data. Model data is used to construct the digital representation of real world's things by constricting a graph model and time series data represents observations of the state of some physical thing at a given time. It can be continuing or discrete.

- **Data Pipelines**: In this step the dissimilar array of data sources from the data collection phase are merged into a single intelligible model and exported into the element graph.

- **Data Integrity**: It also looks at the actual data stream to detect issues with collaboration, connectivity, or even physical issues with the instrumentation which collect the physical data. This is a set of analysis on either single variant or multiple variant data.

- **Data Egress**: Once collected organized into a digital twin and analyze to ensure trust in the accuracy of the data. The final stage is the making use of digital twin we have built to unlock the whole range of analytic value.

UNDERLYING TECHNOLOGIES ENABLING DIGITAL TWINS

There are five underlying technology trends which are used to develop in a complimentary way to enable digital twins. These are:

- **Internet of things**: High precision sensors enable continuous collection of machine data, state and condition from the physical asset to the digital twin to the real life via wireless network.

- **Cloud computing**: It allows storage and processing of large volumes of machine data from its asset and its digital twin in the real time.

- **API and open standards**: It provide the necessary tool to extract, share and harmonize data from multiple systems that contribute to a single digital twin.

- **Artificial Intelligence**: It leverages historical and real time data paired with the Machine learning frameworks to make predictions about future scenarios or events that will occur within the context of the asset.

- **Augmented, Mixed and Virtual reality**: They render the special model and visualization of the digital twin providing the medium for collaboration and interaction with it.

DIGITAL TWINS AND ITS IMPORTANCE FOR SMART CITY

It is known that the Digital Twin is a replication process that makes full use of physical models, sensors, past data of operation, etc. to assimilate information of multi-discipline, scale and probability. It assists as a replication process for physical products in virtual space. There are presently many diverse understandings of the concept of digital twins, and a consensus definition has not yet been defined. Though, it is common thought that physical entities, virtual models, data, connections and services are the fundamental elements of digital twins (Tao et al., 2019). The core of digital twins is a bi-directional mapping relationship that occurs between physical space and virtual space. This bi-directional mapping is different to the unidirectional mapping. The uni-directional mapping maps data in one direction i.e. from physical entities to digital objects. It is also known as digital shadow (Kritzinger, 2018) In this case "a change in state of the physical object leads to a change in the digital object, but not vice versa." (Kritzinger, 2018) Though, digital twins empower virtual objects to control physical entities without human intervention (Enders & Hoßbach, 2019), which is a characteristic that digital shadows do not have.

As a key way to understand the bidirectional mapping, dynamic interaction, and realtime linking between the virtual and the real, the digital twin can plot the physical entities and attributes, structure, state, performance, function and behaviour of systems to the virtual world (Tao et al., 2019) creating a high-fidelity dynamic multidimensional, multi-scale, multi-physical quantity model, which will offer an actual way for observing, recognizing, understanding, controlling and converting the physical world (Tao et al., 2019).

Digital twins first showed up and played a role in industries of product and manufacturing design, and later arose in different industries such as aerospace, automation, shipbuilding, medical and energy. In recent years, with the quick advancement of technologies and industries such as the Internet of Things(IoT), big data (Tao et al., 2019), cloud computing and artificial intelligence(AI), the construction basis of smart city has progressively advanced from the original static 3D modelling level towards the digital twin level that combines dynamic digital technology and static 3D model,, which frames another idea that digital twin city assists smart city construction.

Noticeably, the digital twin city is a wide application of the digital twin concept at the city level. It targets at constructing a complex giant system between the physical world and the virtual space that can plan each other and incorporate with each other in both directions. It can match the physical city to the paralleled "twin city", creating a pattern of coexistence of both and incorporation of physical cities in the physical dimension and digital cities in the information dimension. The building of a digital twin city requires a data foundation and a technical foundation. The data foundation refers to the huge urban big data that is uninterruptedly generated every day from various sensors and cameras everywhere in the city, as well as the digital subsystems consecutively built by the municipal management departments.

Technical groundwork refers to relevant technologies such as the IoT, cloud computing, big data, and AI, including 5G. In a digital twin city, the data of functioning status of infrastructure, the placement of municipal resources, and the flow of people, logistics and vehicles will be composed through sensors, cameras, and various digital subsystems. With technologies including 5G transporting them to the cloud and the city government, the city will be well-organized. The building of digital twin cities will trigger great innovations in urban intelligent planning, management and services, and converted a "new starting point" for the construction of smart cities. This will help accomplish the goal of imagining of all-element information of the city and the intelligent city planning, management and services. The digital twin city is not only the goal of a digital city, but also a key component of a smart city. It is a significant facility and basic ability that enable the city to realize smartness. It is also a landmark in the transformation of urban informatization from qualitative variation to quantitative variation determined by technology, which provides the creation of smart cities more room for innovation.

As the Internet of Things (IoT) began to upsurge, it saw the implementation and popularity of digital twins in other industries, due to its cost-effectiveness and ease of use. The idea of the smart city through digital twins is apparent. From urban planning to land-use optimization, digital twin provides the power to govern the city in an effective manner. Digital twins permit the simulation of strategies before implementing them, exposing problems before they become a reality.

Although Singapore is amongst the most tech-savvy countries in the world, Thomas Pramotedham, CEO of Esri Singapore has faith in that creating a digital twin is paramount for any city embarking on the journey of the digital conversion. According to Pramotedham, "Just with a digital twin set up, can government agencies effectively analyse what can be done with the data and advance citizen living, create economic opportunity and revive a closer community." The concept is still new for many countries, but it is foreseen to become main stream within the next five to ten years.

THE BENEFITS OF DEVELOPING DIGITAL TWIN POWERED CITIES

More competent traffic systems and housing structures will be the main benefits of developing smart cities.

There is no distrust that the cities proficient to leverage this technology and harness the benefits will be the ones that grow. Apart from technological accomplishment, they will become more environmentally, economically and socially bearable. However, a few analysts have raised up questions about how this innovation would conquest traditional approaches. Digital twin experts have replied that while Computer Aided Design currently designs and provide visions regarding the design process – the digital twin would offer the same thing but also a physical corresponding item with which they can interact. Having a corresponding part would enable the designers to predict any potential problem. Relating virtual technology with smart maps driven by geospatial analytics is alternative prime example of how this innovation betters' current practices. The purpose of these maps is to lodge users in visualizing, processing, and analysing multiple, large and complex geo referenced data. Again, the digital twin proposes the same service, but it also represents an in-service physical object, which forcefully changes in neighbouring real-time as the state of the physical object changes.

ADVANCED DIGITAL TWIN APPLICATIONS IN SMART CITIES

The objective of Digital twin technology is to improve the productivity and sustainability of energy consumption, security, traffic control, public epidemic services, urban planning and flood monitoring.

Smart Grid Digital Twin Services

The Smart Grid Digital Twin is a replication with numerous physical quantities, numerous temporal and spatial scales and numerous probabilities, which makes full use of the physical model, online measurement data and historical operation data of the power system, and assimilates multi-disciplinary knowledge such as electricity, computers, communications, climate, and economics. It reproduces the entire life cycle process of the smart grid by plotting it in the virtual space. Due to the growing demand for electricity by humans, the scale of power grid transmission lines is increasing year by year (Figure 3), attached with the frequent occurrence of natural disasters and the weakening of the equipment operating environment, resulting in increased pressure on power grid line check-ups. Current line inspections mainly depend on manual ways. However, this method is not only incompetent, but also has review blind spots, which gradually cannot completely meet the needs of power grid inspections (Figure 4). Modern power grids rapidly need to establish a safe, effective and intelligent inspection mode.

Grounded on the digital twin smart grid technology, we can develop a technique of on-line, real-time recognition of insulator damage and AI on-line design of tree barrier safety distance. This method can realize real-time inspection, fault interpretation, and report the output, thereby significantly minimizing labour power. In addition, depending on this technique, a software and hardware integrated system based on power corridor multi-element specific placing, identification and modelling, and 3D spatial association calculation model can also be designed, which can be used to solve the problems of power corridor security risk placing and its early warning. At present, the technique has touched 15 provinces, cities and regions in China, with a scrutiny line of about 20,000 km and an inspection mileage of more than 50,000 km, bringing economic profits of more than 200 million yuan.

Figure 3. Growth of various voltage classes in China from 2012 to 2014

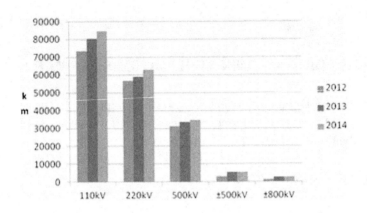

Figure 4. Staffing situation of State Grid Branch in 100 km

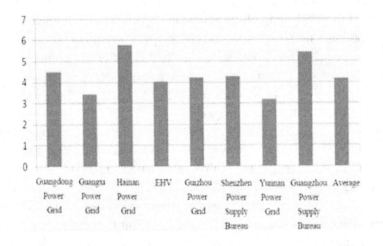

Smart City Operation Brain Management

On the basis of the digital twin city, a Smart City Operation Brain (SCOB) can be established, and the city administrators will take the lead to establish a Smart City Operation Centre (SCOC) and engage a Chief Operating Officer (COO) to take the responsibility. The SCOC is under the authority of the COO, and between them the Chief Information Officer (CIO) Joint Conference Committee is responsible for management and supervision. SCOC manages four main sectors for the urban information, including Urban IT Operation and Maintenance Centre, Big Data Centre, Urban Operation Monitoring and Command Centre, and Smart Service Centre. The main functions of SCOB include

1. Contributing in and revising the top-level plan of the city;
2. Planning and revising the overall goals, frameworks, tasks, operation and administrations of the information development of various industries;
3. Articulating relevant policies, regulations and standards;
4. Accountable for the incorporation and sharing of urban information resources;
5. Monitoring city action, multi-departmental management and facility;
6. Promoting the formation of the system of social-oriented big data open applications, services and transactions.

The Public Information Cloud Service Platform is the structure part of the SCOB (Figure 5). Once the Public Information Cloud Service Platform is established then the office of SCOB start to activate, and the officials can just use the "applications" of the platform to take the responsibility of management of the smart city.

The platform is made-up of infrastructure layer, software development and operation platform layer, and application layer. The platform uses structure such as servers, networks, and sensor equipment to acquire data, and uses cloud infrastructure, data, platforms and software as service area, and finally accomplishes the applications of cloud service platforms in various arenas such as smart urban management, smart public security, and smart tourism and many more. The platform can produce an environmental chain of data collecting, processing, storing, cleaning, mining, applying, and feedback. The smart city operation centre based on the digital twin city is the core of the smart city. It is the resource centre of urban big data and the hub of the urban IoT. It direct and monitors the operation of the city, and widely obtain the city's operation data, so as to realize the well-organized management and emergency response capabilities of cross-departmental and cross-regional systems.

Figure 6 is a graphical diagram of the structure of a smart city operation brain grounded on a digital twin city. Built on the smart city operation brain, a multi-portal unified city command and emergency centre can be built with the integration of the

Figure 5. The construction of the public information cloud service platform

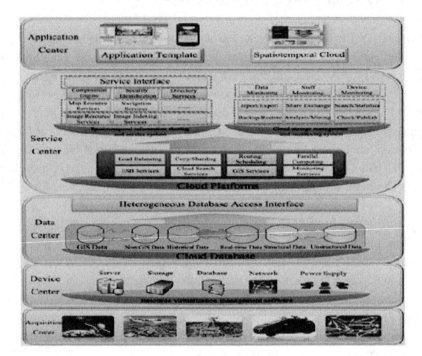

data from the cloud data centre and the digital subsystems of various departments. The centre also uses basic data analysis components such as multi-dimensional analysis and data mining, and analysis applications such as IoT perception and real-time operation monitoring.

This centre can reduce the cost of urban informatization projects and its maintenance, minimize the cost of government affairs, and upgrade urban efficiency.

Smart City Traffic Brain

The Smart City Traffic Brain is one more application of smart city created on digital twin. Hundreds of millions of big data on travel line are generated in cities every day from mobile phones, surveillance camera videos, taxies, indoor positioning systems, buses and subways, and also mobile apps. Trusting on technologies such as holographic perception, time-space analysis, and data mining, the Wuhan Road Traffic Smart Emergency System (Figure 7) is established, which is a significant part of Wuhan Smart City Traffic Brain. The system is intended to deeply assimilate multi-network resources and real-time dynamic traffic information, while linking various emergency platform resources such as city alarm system, the police, road

Figure 6. Schematic diagram of the smart city operation brain based on digital twins. (UUM: Unified Users Management)

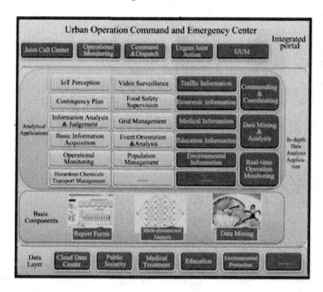

condition system, accident emergency system and traffic video system, and presenting them on the same interface. The Wuhan Road Traffic Smart Emergency System comprehends traffic big data management based on real-time traffic data flow. It developed a congestion index estimation algorithm which combines historical congestion data, traffic data, vehicle speed data and other information to realize functions such as

1. Accurate evaluation of road congestion levels;
2. Real-time ranking of road congestion;
3. Relative analysis between past congestion and real-time congestion.

The system also offers functions such as video verification, major event security, real-time scheduling and navigation, and congestion event replay. All these functions provide a decision-making mechanism to help traffic departments to discharge and clear traffic congestion with the benefit of smart traffic cloud and GIS computation.

Smart City Public Epidemic Services

A Smart City Public Epidemic Service System can be made based on mechanisms of the data cloud platform, analysis system, response system and user terminals (Li et al. 2020) (Figure 8). The patient spatiotemporal data is formed by blend of the

Figure 7. Schematic diagram of the structure and function of the smart city traffic brain based on digital twins

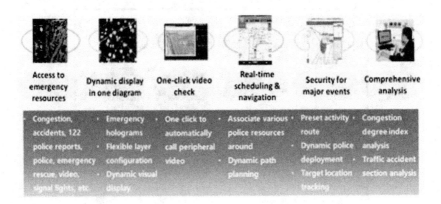

patient information provided by the hospital information system of major hospitals and the patient's spatiotemporal route data provided by the communication operator, which is kept in the patient spatiotemporal database. This database can be associated to the spatiotemporal data cloud platform and linked to the epidemic big data analysis system. The analysis system uses spatiotemporal contiguity analysis, AI analysis and other technologies to regulate the occurrence of the epidemic and determine the people in close contact, and **the** results will be transmitted to the response system. The response system connects with government departments, employers and individual users, provides the government with a reference for epidemic avoidance and control, the employers with a reference for employees' health condition testimonies, and individuals with information services for self-isolation and protection.

Smart Healthcare

The inconsistency between the limited resources and the ever-growing demand brings into view the need for effective, intelligent, and sustainable healthcare. Blockchain technology is the best solution. IoT sensors accumulate and monitor the patient's health data, such as pulse rate, blood sugar level, heart rate, respiratory rate, blood pressure, and body temperature. After that the administrators monitor the composed data and generate the patient's report. The received report is analysed by the doctors who then endorse the required treatment. Doctors may share the treatment reports using a distributed database for further analysis. The authorized report is shared in an encrypted format. The patient claims the "cloud service provider (CSP)" for retrieve to their treatment record.

Figure 8. Schematic diagram of the structure of the national public epidemic prevention and control system

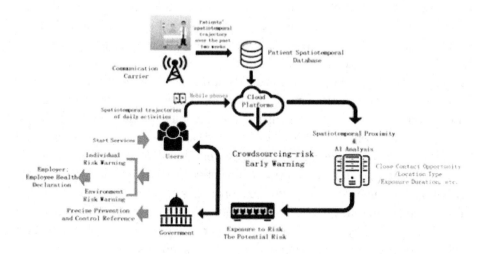

After successful authentication, the encrypted file of the treatment record is received by the patient. Patients decrypt the received encrypted file with their own private key to acquire their original treatment record.

Smart Transportation

By implementing the Blockchain technology concept we can effectively handle security and privacy matters related to the intelligent transportation system. In vehicle networks, vehicles can communicate with the roadside unit or with each other without the participation of any central authority. However, in such an independent environment, challengers might inject ambiguous or false information to exploit personal benefits. Therefore, vehicle authentication is required to guarantee secure data exchange between these vehicles. In order to do this, IoT sensors gather and monitor the information of vehicles, such as model size, speed, driving direction, and load. Then the distributed network nodes monitor the composed data and produce a real-time package for communicating. The received package will be used to calculate the behaviours of vehicles. The process of sharing will be recorded on a "CSP." Vehicles request the "CSP" for retrieve the information associated with them.

After successful authentication, vehicles will run the algorithm to determine their behaviours. Successful results will be recorded to improve the algorithm.

Smart Supply Chain

Globally, complex supply chains have empowered the manufacture and sale of several products, but the entities (e.g., retailers, distributors, transporters, and suppliers) in these supply chains have very limited knowledge about the product lifecycle. However, such product information is necessary as the customers require the information to develop their trust, and entities require the information to make business decisions or foresee market trends. Blockchain technology in digital twin cities can be a solution. Blockchains track the complete product information, avert the entry of bogus products into the market, and share information amongst various entities to optimize the decision-making process. In the process of doing this, IoT sensors gather and monitor the information of entities, such as logistics, specifications, affiliation, and value. The distributed network nodes monitor the composed data and produce a real-time package for communicating. The received package will be used to analyse the behaviours of vehicles. The process of sharing will be recorded on a "CSP." Retailers, distributors, transporters, and suppliers can retrieve the "CSP" for access to the information associated with them. After successful authentication, entities will get the information they need.

FLOOD MONITORING AND FLOOD SITUATION SERVICES FOR SMART CITIES

In the complete life cycle of flood disaster's stabilized monitoring and forecasting before disasters, dynamic monitoring and analysis during disasters, and assessment and reconstruction after disasters, an application state for real-time urban flood replication and think tank research and judgment facilities can be recognized using digital twin technology, which in that way adding service roles to the construction of smart cities (Figure 9). The smart city flood monitoring and service system based on the digital twin mostly caters three areas, namely, the regulated and dynamic big data monitoring of flood, the flood knowledge map and the flood service application. Flood big data monitoring mentions to the monitoring method of real-time assortment of flood disasters and flood big data from the urban and watershed scales in the milieu of the IoT, joint with the real-time monitoring technology of the incorporation of space, air and earth. The core point is to collect water conditions in rivers and lakes, rain conditions in urban atmospheric stations and dynamic trajectories of people and vehicles from monitoring and collection equipment such as ground sensors. This can be comprehended grounded on satellite remote sensing technology in large-scale air and sky states to monitor cloud and rain water volume,

Figure 9. Smart city flood monitoring and flood service platform

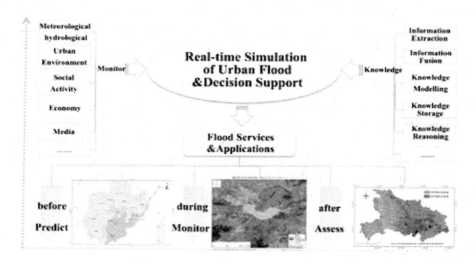

lake water volume and water level distinctions of rivers and reservoirs in the upper and lower basins.

The structure of a flood knowledge map is to launch a flood big data knowledge map through big data analysis and AI technology, which will help accomplish knowledge and discover knowledge acquired by dynamic monitoring of flood disasters and flood big data. Based on normalized and dynamic flood monitoring and flood knowledge map, a smart city flood service application can be provided, which comprises real-time replication of flood monitoring big data in urban scenes. After combining flood knowledge analysis, knowledge mining, modelling, and flood adversity prediction technologies, flood-related knowledge of the complete life cycle of urban flood disasters, it will be helpful to deliver services for urban flood control management.

CONCLUSION

As a new model for building smart cities, the digital twin will reform the city governance structures and rules and shoot up a continuous momentum for the growth and transformation of cities. Many of the developed cities around the world are planning to build and launch digital twin cities. The speedy development of digital twin technologies is one of the reasons to construct digital twin cities. The development of digital twin will create a new management design that can trace past events and explore frontier guidelines, which will be a trend for future research on Digital Twin

Cities. The digital twin city is certainly a new beginning point for the construction of modern smart cities. Smart cities built on digital twins have extensive prospects for economic transformation, urban smart management and public smart services, so that man and nature can grow more co-ordinately. The comprehension of smart cities needs the creation of more complete altitudinal information organization to ensure that various smart city applications can be used well and affordable. The big data problem of smart cities carries new opportunities and challenges. It is necessary to do a good job in technological revolution and research in order to promote the development of the digital service industry, and develop the digital economy. The building of smart city is a leading project. It is essential to do a top-level design and overall planning according to the characteristics of each city, and begin a smart city operation centre and operation brain to make the city smart.

REFERENCES

Allare, D. (2014). Multifidelity DDDAS methods with application to a self-aware aerospace vehicle. *Procedia Computer Science, 29*, 1182–1192.

Boschert & Rosen. (2016). Digital Twin-The Simulation Aspect. In Mechatronic Futures. Springer. https://doi.org/.171 doi:10.1007/978-3-319-32156-1_5

Enders & Hoßbach. (2019). Dimensions of Digital Twin Applications - A Literature Review. Conference: AMCIS.

Glaegen, E. H., & Stargel, D. S. (2012). The Digital Twin paradigm for future NASA and US Air Force vehicles. 53rd Structures, *Structural Dynamics, and Materials Conference: Special Session on the Digital Twin*, 1-14.

Kritzinger. (2018). *Digital Twin in manufacturing: A categorical literature review and classification*. 10.1016/j.ifacol.2018.08.474

Machine-to-Machine Communications. (2015). *Impact of smart city activity on IoT evitonment*. ETSI.

Menard. (n.d.). *3 ways digital twins are going to help improve oil and gas maintenance hard, and operations*. Available from: https://www.linkedin.com/pulse/3-ways-digitaltwins-going-help-improve-od-gas-sophie-menard

Murray. (2018). *Lockheed Martin forecasts tech trends for defense in 2018*. Available https://dallasinnovates.com/lockheed-martin-forecasts-tech-trends-for defense-in-2018/

Panetta. (2017). *Top 10 strategic technology trends for 2017, digital twins.* Available from: https://www.gartner.com/smarterwithgartner/gartner-top-10-strategic-technology-trends-2017/

Panetta. (2018). *Top 10 strategic technology trends for 2018: Digital twins.* Available from: https://www.gartner.com/smarterwithgartner/gartner-top-10-strategic-technology-trends-for-2018/

Qin, J., Liu, Y., & Grosvenor, R. A. (2016). categorical framework of manufacturing for industry 4.0 and beyond. *Procedia Cirp, 52,* 173-178.

Reifinider & Majumdar. (2013). Multiphysics stimulated simulation digital twin methods for fleet management. *54th AIAA/ASME/ASCE/AHS/ASC Structures, Structural Dynamics, and Materials Conference,* 1578.

Ribeiro, L., & Björkman, M. (2017). Transitioning From Standard Automation Solutions to CyberPhysical Production Systems: An Assessment of Critical Conceptual and Technical Challenges. *IEEE Systems Journal,* 1-13. https://doi.org/10.1109/JSYST.2017.2771139

Schuh, G., Anderl, R., Gausemeier, J., Hompel, M.T., & Wahlster, W. (2017). *Industrie 4.0 maturity index. Managing the digital transformation of companies.* Munich: Herbert Utz.

Science Service Dr. Hempel Digital Health Network. (n.d.). *Healthcare solution testing for future Digital Twins in healthcare.* Available from: https://www.dr-hempel-network.com/digital-health-technolgy/digital-twins-in-healthcare

Smart Manufacturing Association of China Association for Science and Technology. (n.d.). *Smart Manufacturing Association of China Association for Science and Technology releases the top ten scientific and technological advances for smart manufacturing in the world and the top ten scientific and technological advances for smart manufacturing in China.* Available from: http://www.cast.org.cn/n200705/n202961/n202993/c57776269/content.html

Swedberg. (n.d.). *Digital twins bring value to big RFID and IoT data.* Available from: http://www.rfidjournal.com/articles/vies717421

Tac, E.J. (2012). The airframe digital twin: some challenges to realization. *53rd AIAA/ASME/ASCE/AHS/ASC Structures, Structural Dynamics and Materials Conference 20th AIAA/ASME/AHS Adaptive Structures Conference 14th AIAA.*

Tao, F., Liu, W., & Liu, H. (2018). Digital twin and its potential application exploration. *Computer Integrated Manufacturing Systems, 24*(1), 1–18.

Tao, F., Qi, Q., Wang, L., & Nee, A. Y. C. (2019). Digital Twins and Cyber–Physical Systems toward Smart Manufacturing and Industry 4.0: Correlation and Comparison. *Engineering, 5*(4), 653-661. https://doi.org/10.1016/j.eng.2019.01.014

Tao, M. (2017a). Digital twin workshop: A new paradigm for future workshop. *Jisuanji Jicheng Zhizao Xitong, 23*(1), 1–9.

Tao, M. (2017b). Digital twin shop-floor a new shop-floor paradigm towards smart manufacturing. *IEEE Access: Practical Innovations, Open Solutions, 5*, 20418–20427.

Tao, Y. (2017). Theory and technologies for cyber- physical fusion in digital twin shop-floor. *Jisuanji Jicheng Zhizao Xitong, 23*(8), 1603–1611.

Tuegel, J., Ingraffea, A. R., Eason, T. G., & Spottswood, S. M. (2011). Reengineering aircraft structural life prediction using a digital twin. *Int. J. Aerosp. Eng.* https://doi.org/10.1155/2011/154798

Uhlemann, T. H. J., Lehmann, C., & Steinhilper, R. (2017). The digital twin realizing the cyber physical production system for industry 4.0. *Procedia CIRP, 61*, 335–340.

ADDITIONAL READING

Grieves, M. (2014). *Digital twin: manufacturing excellence through virtual factory replication.* White Pap.

Qi, Q., To, F., Zao, Y., & Zhao, D. (2018). Digital twin service towards smart manufacturing. *Procedia CIRP, 72*(1), 237–242. doi:10.1016/j.procir.2018.03.103

KEY TERMS AND DEFINITIONS

Artificial Intelligence: Artificial intelligence (AI) is spreading like a fire in our world. With intelligent machines enabling high level cognitive processes like thinking, perceiving, learning, problem solving and decision making, with the facility of high-level data collection and aggregation, analytics and computer processing power, Artificial Intelligence is empowering and increment human intelligence and enrich the way people be in this world and work.

Digital Twins: Digital twin is the concept of virtual replica of physical object. Digital twins duplicate the physical model for remote monitoring, viewing, and controlling based on the digital format. It is actually the alive model of the physical systems which uninterruptedly adapts to operational changes based on the real-time data from various IoT sensors and devices and predicts the future of the matching physical counterparts with the help of machine learning/artificial intelligence.

DT Prototype: Digital Twin Prototype offers the user with the panorama to modify parameters and operating conditions of different components and allows observing the response of the entire system in real time. Digital twin prototype is a great way to ease communication between product developers and end users from planning and design phase to authorizing and forms the backbone and platform for the digital twin coupled to the physical entity through IoT and live sensor data.

Federated Learning: Federated learning is a machine learning technique that allows machine learning models to obtain experience from different data sets placed in different sites (e.g., local data centers, a central server) deprived of sharing training data. This allows personal data to remain in local sites, reducing possibility of personal data breaches. Federated learning is used to train other machine learning algorithms by using multiple local datasets without exchanging data. This allows companies to create a shared global model without putting training data in a central location.

Smart City Operation Brain (SCOB): The SCOC is under the authority of the COO, and between them the Chief Information Officer (CIO) Joint Conference Committee is responsible for management and supervision. SCOC manages four main sectors for the urban information, including Urban IT Operation and Maintenance Centre, Big Data Centre, Urban Operation Monitoring and Command Centre, and Smart Service Centre.

Smart City Traffic Brain: The Smart City Traffic Brain is one more application of smart city created on digital twin. Trusting on technologies such as holographic perception, time-space analysis, and data mining, the Wuhan Road Traffic Smart Emergency System is established, which is a significant part of Wuhan Smart City Traffic Brain. The system is intended to deeply assimilate multi-network resources and real-time dynamic traffic information, while linking various emergency platform resources such as city alarm system, the police, road condition system, accident emergency system and traffic video system, and presenting them on the same interface.

Smart Supply Chain: Blockchains track the complete product information, avert the entry of bogus products into the market, and share information amongst various entities to optimize the decision-making process. In the process of doing this, IoT sensors gather and monitor the information of entities, such as logistics, specifications, affiliation, and value. The distributed network nodes monitor the composed data and produce a real-time package for communicating. The received package will be used to analyse the behaviours of vehicles. The process of sharing will be recorded on a "CSP." Retailers, distributors, transporters, and suppliers can retrieve the "CSP" for access to the information associated with them. After successful authentication, entities will get the information they need.

Chapter 10

Multi–Criteria Decision Making in Healthcare:
A Bibliometric Review

Beena John Jiby
SBES, International Institute of Management and Human Resource Development, India

Sachin Sakhare
iD https://orcid.org/0000-0003-1974-5929
Vishwakarma Institute of Information Technology, India

Mandeep Kaur
Savitribai Phule Pune University, India

Gaurav Dhiman
Graphic Era University (Deemed), India

ABSTRACT

The wellbeing of a country depends mainly on its healthcare and is also one of the most impacted frameworks from the viewpoint of decision-making with multi-objectives and inclined more to mistakes in the various activities, and multi-decision criteria analysis (MDCA) helps a lot as a tool for this interaction of various independent actions. Therefore, the present study helps to break down and incorporate articles found in the literature involving MCDA along with assessing their general issues and various strategic angles and organizing them. Investigation in the bibliographic data sets of PubMed showed 85 journal articles regarding the subject of multi-decision criteria analysis, and after a cautious verification, 85 journal articles examinations were chosen to be studied in detail.

DOI: 10.4018/978-1-6684-3733-9.ch010

INTRODUCTION

Healthcare decision making differ from others because of the allotment of limited resources as wellbeing is indispensable and irreplaceable (Postmus D et al; 2013; Drake JI et al;2017) This exception makes it hard for health services providers to settle on the best decisions as their choices have enormous impact (Blythe R et al; 2019) on patients' personal satisfaction with societal advantage. Healthcare decision makers when confronted with these complex choices may not often utilize a calculated method to arrive at decisions (Baltussen R et al; 2019; Drake JI et.al; 2017) which may or may not be for the benefit of society and patient. This sort of dynamic interaction has raised worries about its completeness as it may neglect patient inclinations, neglected requirements, and social and moral ideals. In this intricate activity choice Specifically, multi- criteria decision analysis (MCDA), has become areas of examination in numerous studies as it is a supportive decision- making tool that evaluates various unrelated conflicting information and is considered as a valuable healthcare decision making decision support tool (Barkhuizen H et al; 2015). MCDA is progressively used to help to make choices in Health care by various uncertain criteria. In spite of the fact that uncertainty is normally tended to in financial assessments, regardless of the various sources of uncertainty which are managed well with MCDA is less studied.

The issue of numerous objectives is consistently present in the issues inside the intricacy of increasing uncertain choices as decisions are not only made by a single person. In the healthcare these techniques are even more complex, since they also include financial constraints, with human variable, causing clashes of interest and upsetting final conclusion (Blythe, R et al; 2019)); Marsh, K et al (2016). In this situation, it is important to find strategies that remember the higher number of rules that aide and impact choices, to lessen mistakes. However in the vast majority of the time this technique is difficult to perform, since the decision making criteria are clashing and increases the number of uncertain last response (Guindo, L.A et al; 2012). To expand the validity and reliability of the selected choice MCDA is used widely. These techniques help in the decision process and limit the obligation of the final decision-maker, to ensure a right solution as per the criteria (Dolan, J.G. (2010).

Many studies utilizing MCDA, are done from the point of enhancing general healthcare wellbeing. A few examinations have been regarding investigating a particular application area, like the assessment in healthcare innovation some Others have studied from an empathetic view, assessing toward patient inclination and there are many studies which who go further, to know and dissect the MCDA in different manner in healthcare. In all its application, MCDA includes many strategies by utilizing different decision criteria choice in its framework, which is included in rows and columns. The rows signify alternatives to be classified, while columns signify criteria or attributes, which are the results used to assess choices being thought about and these techniques can be broadly classified into three categories: goal programming and reference point models; value measurement models and outranking models the distinction between MCDA methods lies in how the information is drawn from the matrix.

As there are an incredible number of studies including MCDA in the healthcare, this review expects to examine and integrate the data found in the literature, by assessing general and strategic perspectives and organizing it.

Till date methods to select the most appropriate MCDA techniques to be applied in healthcare services doesn't exist and the dissemination of MCDA in health care is less reported. Hence, this paper tries to understand MCDA in health care and identify publication trends in the implementation of MCDA in this area, as well as understand areas where effectively implemented by the applications of MCDA in healthcare.

For this, the model is partitioned into two phases of assessment. First the examination of the overall inquiries of the article, meaning to know and assess the situation of the MCDA concentrates in the medical services. The subsequent stage will be the primary investigation is the exploration.

OBJECTIVES OF THE STUDY

The procedure for examining the bibliometrics from the vast Bibtext set of databases is by citation analysis and the various links displayed by authors, countries, titles, etc. The citation and network analysis helps to portray how explicit disciplines, or exploration fields are structured and how they develop through time. This study used Bibliometrix, Biblioshiny, from the R package, to examine the citation information identified in this topic for data visualization purposes and identified the results. The citation and network analysis include the investigation with a view to understand the accompanying areas.

BACKGROUND

The Literature in this review depends on bibliographic data base as it is easy to examine how and for what reason the specialists and experts use MCDA to help healthcare decision making. The database searched for keywords in title, abstract and full text.

Figure 1. Sequential steps

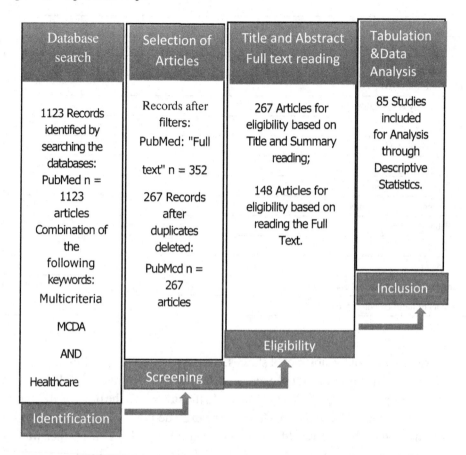

The Literature review was done in four phases, complying with some consideration and rejection measures, The examination was performed in an unbiased normalized way by two analysts and arguments were settled by consensus.

A data base Literature search in the PubMed was performed for the period in the range of 2008 and 2021 utilizing the accompanying keyword search in title, abstract and full paper and studies were downloaded which are freely accessible, and other versions in a few studies. The stages and their respective criteria are described below in

The data collected was exported to a software in R-package called bibliometrix, Biblioshiny

(I)Identification: the studies identified after the execution of each step of the techniques shown in Excel table. Study have examined 85 documents which are shown in Table

Table 1. Main information about data

Description	Results
Sources (Journals, Books, etc)	44
Documents	85
Keywords Plus (ID)	253
Author's Keywords (DE)	253
Period	2008:2021
Single-authored documents	4
Documents per Author	0.206
Authors per Document	4.86
Co-Authors per Documents	6.24
Collaboration Index	5.91
Authors	413
Author Appearances	530
Authors of single-authored documents	4
Authors of multi-authored documents	409

(II) Screening For the abstract of studies, were applied and duplicates eliminated.

(III) Eligibility After the initial articles, search by title, abstract and full text were perused. This phase comprised of two stages. In the first stage, the titles furthermore, abstracts were perused, for article which can be excluded. Assuming they addressed the essential, the full text would be downloaded. For the later stage, that was by reading, selecting and downloading the articles for inclusion. At this stage, articles that did not discuss the original research objectives were deleted.

(IV) Inclusion: Information separate from articles were incorporated in an Excel page and later research planning and the procedure was used to clarify information and the results examined in detail.

The analysis presented is carried out in the following stages:

Stage 1: Study design;
Stage 2: Data collection;
Stage 3: Initial data analysis;
Stage 4: Descriptive bibliometric analysis;
Stage 5: Network analysis;
Stage 6: Conclusions and directions for future research.

Figure 2. Word cloud of the articles

MAIN FOCUS OF THE CHAPTER

The paper addresses these research questions:

1. What is the present status of investigation on MCDA?
2. Which are the most productive nations in this area?
3. How has the studies in this area advance?
4. What are the examination gap and areas for future investigation?

RESULTS

A 'word cloud' from Figure 2 is a visual portrayal of word recurrence and shows the text examined and are being utilized as a tool to recognize the focal point of analysis. A word cloud examination was utilizing. Firstly, it very well be seen that the two most noticeable words featured are humans and decision making. This finding adjusts to the point of the study in the research articles and are more significant terms.

Figure 3. Annual scientific production

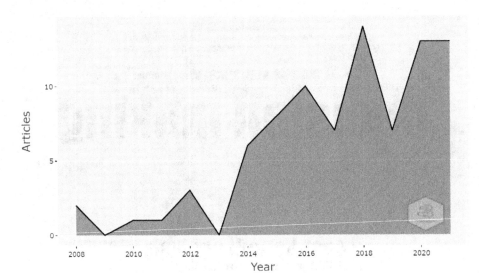

The word cloud investigation also has shown that need is given to explore areas of direct importance to patient consideration and the examination has mirrored the exceptionally different areas of decision making in healthcare with MCDA use.

The bibliometric information identified in this area was distributed mostly from year of 2008 to 2021 and less before 2008 and was extracted from PubMed by utilizing the keywords which recovered information from 85 journal articles to help in analysis. It can be observed from the Figure 3 that the yearly growth shows an exponential growth in the period from 2013. Again the distribution development has increased in 2018 than a fall in the pattern in 2019 and again its increasing.

The Figure 4 shows the thematic evolution from 2008-21 and the understanding of the various topics studied. The examination helps to recognize research interests and how they advanced across time and gives us information into future exploration direction and to foster a way to deal with the change and development in this field and recognize the many significant changes in the entire time frame.

The analysis of journal publishing most articles in multi criteria decision in healthcare. From the figure 5 it can be seen the most published journal in the subject. the various leading journal publishers in the area and had more than one article in the related area,

As indicated by Figure.6, brings the most distributed journal source on the subject of MCDA in the healthcare area. nine papers stick out in pharma economics. Considering the articles published by others are also increasing from 2016 onwards in the area of healthcare.

Figure 4. Thematic evolution

Scientific production by country is shown in Figure.7. The data was generated by "Biblioshiny", application that provides a web interface for Bibliometrix R software. The analysis uncovered the most researched authors nations in MCDA and healthcare. The outcomes show that Canada, USA and is noticeable followed

Figure 5. Published journal analysis

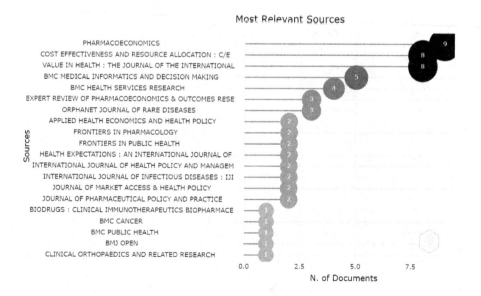

by Netherlands, USA and Germany. Fig. shows the pictorial representation of the corresponding authors.

Figure 6. Corresponding journal analysis

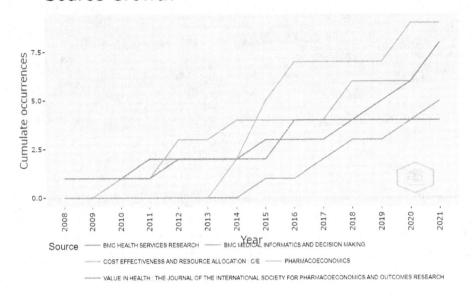

Figure 7. Country scientific production in healthcare

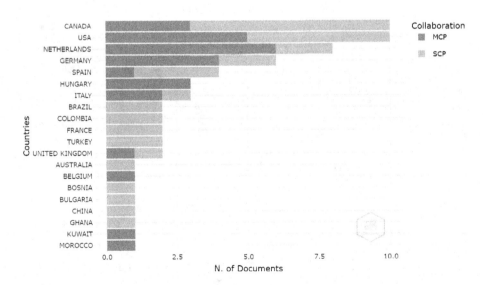

Table 2. Production and countries collaborations

Country	Articles	SCP	MCP	MCP_Ratio
Canada	10	7	3	0.3
USA	10	5	5	0.5
Netherlands	8	2	6	0.75
Germany	6	2	4	0.667
Spain	4	3	1	0.25
Hungary	3	0	3	1
Italy	3	1	2	0.667
Brazil	2	2	0	0
Colombia	2	2	0	0
France	2	2	0	0
Turkey	2	2	0	0
United Kingdom	2	1	1	0.5
Australia	1	1	0	0
Belgium	1	0	1	1
Bosnia	1	1	0	0
Bulgaria	1	1	0	0
China	1	1	0	0
Ghana	1	1	0	0
Kuwait	1	0	1	1
Morocco	1	0	1	1

Legends: Country = country of the corresponding author's affiliation.
Articles = number of articles per country of corresponding author
SCP = single country publication.
MCP = multi country publication

The article production and countries collaborations is featured in Table 2 and examination, shows the coordinated efforts who work together, however many for just a single time.

Author's production over time has been performed to comprehend the top authors in the field of multi-criteria decision making in healthcare. The outcome in Fig.8 uncovered that Wagner M has more Research Collaboration and Networking studies in multi-criteria decision making in healthcare.

A Parameter broadly utilized in the bibliographic analysis to distinguish what's the main works and the number of times it is cited. In Table 3 are the ten most cited papers out of 85 chose ones, the no of citation from the data set, in November 2021.

Figure 8. Top authors production over time

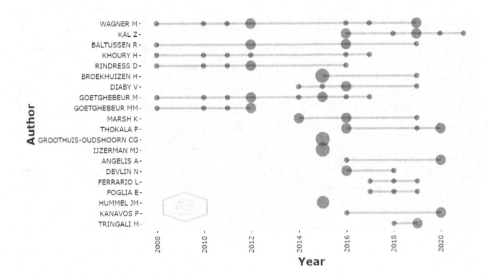

The Figure 9 Analysis of Co-Author Networks utilizing Bibliometrix Package, the examination showed other authors in this field and their collaborations. This collaborative analysis helps to highlight the most significant network between the authors widely used in various fields of this healthcare research,

The relations between the main items of three fields (e.g. authors, countries and keywords, and how they are related is shown in figure 10, Sankey diagram. In this, the applicable components are addressed in the chart by rectangles with different shading. The tallness of the shapes relies upon the significance of the relations arising between the component that the square shape addresses in the chart. The more relations the component had, the higher was the square shape addressing it. The investigation exhibited which authors were distributed most often and in which research subjects they had investigated.

Co-occurrence network examination figure 11 of author keywords (min recurrence) = 3; in the Literature helps as a guide of the primary topics in this field of healthcare with MDCA. To keep away from deviations, the dataset was separated and exposed to examination. The Co-occurrence network map created, plotted the keywords as indicated by their centrality and importance along. The round width estimates the degree of importance and is considered as a proportion of the significance of a topic. The valuable aspects of this co-reference networks are: (I) centrality of nodes, (ii) their vicinity and spread (iii) strong connections, (iv) groups (v) various connections.

Table 3. Authors citations

Sr. No	Name	Year	cite
1	Marsh K, IJzerman M, Thokala P, Baltussen R, Boysen M, Kaló Z, Lönngren T,Mussen F, Peacock S, Watkins J, Devlin N;	2016	337
2	Marsh K, Lanitis T, Neasham D, Orfanos P, Caro J.	2014	241
3	Guindo LA, Wagner M, Baltussen R, Rindress D, van Til J, Kind P, Goetghebeur MM.	2012	229
4	Goetghebeur MM, Wagner M, Khoury H, Levitt RJ, Erickson LJ, Rindress D.	2008	212
5	Dolan JG.	2010	189
6	Adunlin G, Diaby V, Xiao H.	2015	142
7	Tony M, Wagner M, Khoury H, Rindress D, Papastavros T, Oh P, Goetghebeur MM.	2011	132
8	Goetghebeur MM, Wagner M, Khoury H, Rindress D, Grégoire JP, Deal C.	2010	125
9	Broekhuizen H, Groothuis-Oudshoorn CG, van Til JA, Hummel JM, IJzerman MJ.	2015	109
10	Jehu-Appiah C, Baltussen R, Acquah C, Aikins M, d'Almeida SA, Bosu WK, Koolman X, Lauer J, Osei D, Adjei S.	2008	107

DISCUSSION AND IMPLICATION

The information collected for the investigation gives an upright outline of the latest developments and their exploration in the area of MCDA use in healthcare and its effect on the various areas across the globe. As research collaborations save time, cost, and efforts, joint research to promote at the international level by choosing cutting-edge themes in this area.

Limitations

The current study distinguished numerous applications, and the enormous work on MCDA in diverse health care decision areas. Moreover, studies that is not included in title or abstract might have been missed. Though these are possible impediments, the sample of studies gives adequate data to invigorate a discussion about the utilization of MCDA approaches in healthcare.

Figure 9. Co-authorship network analysis

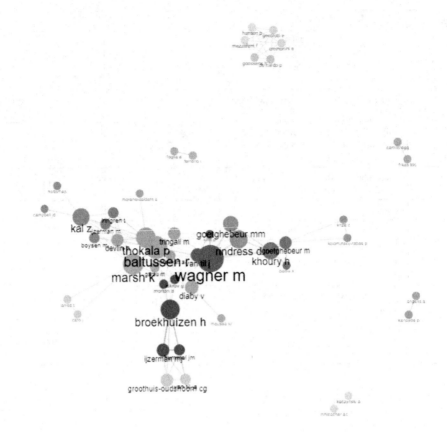

The viewpoints on which we looked at the MCDA approaches depend on previous studies, yet it is significant to recognize that for genuine independent direction different perspectives, on the particular choice and choice maker, might be pertinent. Further research is expected to more readily evaluate the handiness and explicit prerequisites of the methodologies for true direction-finding.

One clarification for this is that MCDA as of now works with an informed conversations and that this underlying vulnerability and further work is suggested to recognize ways to deal with uncertainty and ways of creating MCDA models to be incorporated in the various methodologies

Figure 10. Three fields analysis (e.g. authors, countries and keywords)

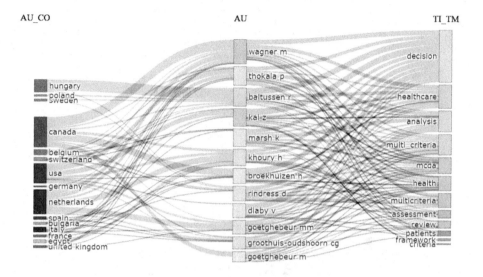

FUTURE RESEARCH DIRECTIONS

This analysis had a few limitations mainly with relation to the articles utilized and the and selected as by the representation of the articles, since articles explored were only open access. Through the analysis and information obtained in this study were of MCDA in healthcare alone and future studies can direct more new applications and methods involving MCDA in other areas of healthcare. For future work, It can include investigations where actual strategies are utilized and focusing on the systemic application of MCDA in healthcare.

CONCLUSION

The use of the MCDA procedure has been scattered what's more it is applied all over the globe and is progressively being utilized healthcare. The examinations of studies in this analysis displays the current situation, and uncovers the significance of the MCDA, application. With respect to the analysis a pattern was seen in the increasing use of these techniques, and their yearly distribution has increase and a few nations articles are more compared to others. We were unable to find the studies from developing countries. This shows that the greater part of the studies happens in the developed nations and the bibliographic analysis upheld this view. It is feasible to notice, through the information of this survey, that more multicriteria choice

Figure 11. Co-occurrence network author title words

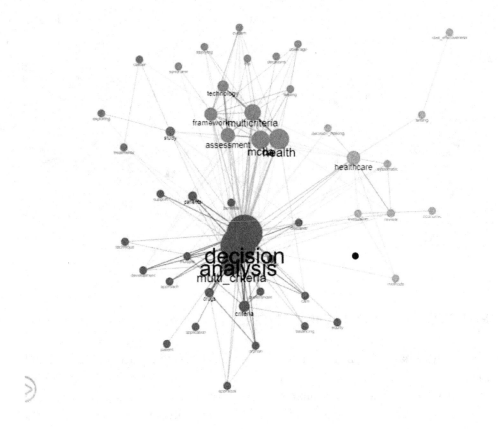

analysis model has been from the wellbeing countries and the review can direct new applications and procedures in utilizing MCDA in health care for underdeveloped and developing countries. For future work, this examination can be done, where numerical strategies are not utilized mainly focusing on the systemic application of the MCDA.

Figure 12. Authors and their used words in title in the space of healthcare MCDA use

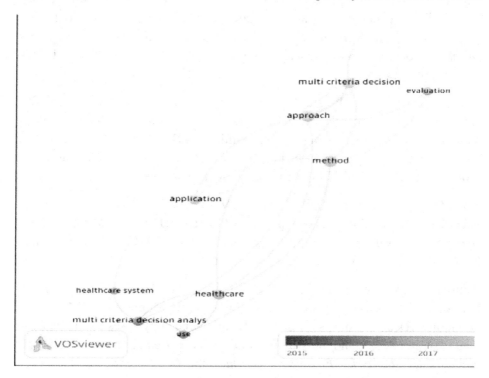

REFERENCES

Abdullah, A. H., Holtorf, A. P., Al-Hussaini, M., Lemay, J., Alowayesh, M., & Kaló, Z. (2019). Stakeholder driven development of a multi-criteria decision analysis tool for purchasing off-patent pharmaceuticals in Kuwait. *Journal of Pharmaceutical Policy and Practice*, *12*(1), 1–7. doi:10.118640545-019-0171-4 PMID:31011430

Adunlin, G., Diaby, V., & Xiao, H. (2015). Application of multicriteria decision analysis in health care: A systematic review and bibliometric analysis. *Health Expectations*, *18*(6), 1894–1905. doi:10.1111/hex.12287 PMID:25327341

Angelis, A., & Kanavos, P. (2016). Value-Based Assessment of New Medical Technologies: Towards a Robust Methodological Framework for the Application of Multiple Criteria Decision Analysis in the Context of Health Technology Assessment. *PharmacoEconomics*, *34*(5), 435–446. doi:10.100740273-015-0370-z PMID:26739955

Angelis, A., Kanavos, P., & Phillips, L.D. (2020). ICER Value Framework 2020 Update: Recommendations on the Aggregation of Benefits and Contextual Considerations. *Value in Health: The Journal of the International Society for Pharmacoeconomics and Outcomes Research, 23*(8), 1040-1048. . doi:10.1016/j. jval.2020.04.1828

Angelis, A., Thursz, M., Ratziu, V., O'brien, A., Serfaty, L., Canbay, A., Schiefke, I., Costa, J. B. E., Lecomte, P., & Kanavos, P. (2020). Early Health Technology Assessment during Nonalcoholic Steatohepatitis Drug Development: A Two-Round, Cross-Country, Multicriteria Decision Analysis. *Medical Decision Making, 40*(6), 830–845. doi:10.1177/0272989X20940672 PMID:32845234

Avila, M. L., Brandão, L. R., Williams, S., Montoya, M. I., Stinson, J., Kiss, A., & Feldman, B. M. (2016). Development of CAPTSureTM - a new index for the assessment of pediatric postthrombotic syndrome. *Journal of Thrombosis and Hemostasis, 14*(12), 2376–2385. doi:10.1111/jth.13530 PMID:27709837

Baltussen, R., Marsh, K., Thokala, P., Diaby, V., Castro, H., Cleemput, I., Garau, M., Iskrov, G., Olyaeemanesh, A., Mirelman, A., & Mobinizadeh, M. (2019). Multicriteria Decision Analysis to Support Health Technology Assessment Agencies: Benefits, Limitations, and the Way Forward. *Value in Health: The Journal of the International Society for Pharmacoeconomics and Outcomes Research, 22*(11), 1283-1288. doi:10.1016/j.jval.2019.06.014

Blythe, R., Naidoo, S., Abbott, C., Bryant, G., Dines, A., & Graves, N. (2019). Development and pilot of a multicriteria decision analysis (MCDA) tool for health services administrators. *BMJ Open, 9*(4), e025752. doi:10.1136/ bmjopen-2018-025752 PMID:31023757

Bogavac-Stanojevic, N., & Jelic-Ivanovic, Z. (2017). The Cost-effective Laboratory: Implementation of Economic Evaluation of Laboratory Testing. *Journal of Medical Biochemistry, 36*(3), 238–242. doi:10.1515/jomb-2017-0036 PMID:30568540

Bowers, J., Cheyne, H., Mould, G., Miller, M., Page, M., Harris, F., & Bick, D. (2018). A multicriteria resource allocation model for the redesign of services following birth. *BMC Health Services Research, 18*(1), 656. doi:10.118612913- 018-3430-1 PMID:30134882

Bretoni, A., Ferrario, L., & Foglia, E. (2019). HTA and innovative treatments evaluation: The case of metastatic castration-resistant prostate cancer. *ClinicoEconomics and Outcomes Research, 11*, 283–300. doi:10.2147/CEOR. S189436 PMID:31114269

Broekhuizen, H., Groothuis-Oudshoorn, C. G., Hauber, A. B., Jansen, J. P., & IJzerman, M. J. (2015). Estimating the value of medical treatments to patients using probabilistic multi criteria decision analysis. *BMC Medical Informatics and Decision Making*, *15*(1), 102. doi:10.118612911-015-0225-8 PMID:26626279

Broekhuizen, H., Groothuis-Oudshoorn, C. G., van Til, J. A., Hummel, J. M., & IJzerman, M. J. (2015). A review and classification of approaches for dealing with uncertainty in multi-criteria decision analysis for healthcare decisions. *PharmacoEconomics*, *33*(5), 445–455. doi:10.100740273-014-0251-x PMID:25630758

Camilo, D. G. G., de Souza, R. P., Frazão, T. D. C., & da Costa, J. F. Jr. (2020). Multi-criteria analysis in the health area: Selection of the most appropriate triage system for the emergency care units in natal. *BMC Medical Informatics and Decision Making*, *20*(1), 1–16. doi:10.118612911-020-1054-y PMID:32085757

Campolina, A. G. (2018). Value-based medicine in oncology: The importance of perspective in the emerging value frameworks. *Clinics (Sao Paulo, Brazil)*, *73*(suppl 1), e470s. doi:10.6061/clinics/2018/e470s PMID:30540119

Castro, H.E., Moreno-Mattar, O., & Rivillas, J.C. (2018). HTA and MCDA solely or combined? The case of priority-setting in Colombia. *Cost Effectiveness and Resource Allocation*, *16*(1), 1-7. doi:10.1186/s12962-018-0127-6

Cleemput, I., Devriese, S., Kohn, L., & Westhovens, R. (2018). A multi-criteria decision approach for ranking unmet needs in healthcare. *Health Policy*, *122*(8), 878-884. doi:10.1016/j.healthpol.2018.06.010

Clemente-Suárez, V. J., Navarro-Jiménez, E., Ruisoto, P., Dalamitros, A. A., Beltran-Velasco, A. I., Hormeño-Holgado, A., Laborde-Cárdenas, C. C., & Tornero-Aguilera, J. F. (2021). Performance of Fuzzy Multi-Criteria Decision Analysis of Emergency System in COVID-19 Pandemic. An Extensive Narrative Review. *International Journal of Environmental Research and Public Health*, *18*(10), 5208. doi:10.3390/ijerph18105208 PMID:34068866

De Nardo, P., Gentilotti, E., Mazzaferri, F., Cremonini, E., Hansen, P., Goossens, H., Tacconelli, E., Mangoni, E.D., Florio, L.L., Zampino, R., & Mele, F. (2020). Multi-Criteria Decision Analysis to prioritize hospital admission of patients affected by COVID-19 in low-resource settings with hospital-bed shortage. *International Journal of Infectious Diseases*, *98*, 494-500. . doi:10.1016/j.ijid.2020.06.082

Diaby, V., & Goeree, R. (2014). How to use multi-criteria decision analysis methods for reimbursement decision-making in healthcare: A step-by-step guide. *Expert Review of Pharmacoeconomics & Outcomes Research*, *14*(1), 81–99. doi:10.1586 /14737167.2014.859525 PMID:24328890

Diaby, V., Sanogo, V., & Moussa, K. R. (2016). ELICIT: An alternative imprecise weight elicitation technique for use in multi-criteria decision analysis for healthcare. *Expert Review of Pharmacoeconomics & Outcomes Research*, *16*(1), 141–147. doi :10.1586/14737167.2015.1083863 PMID:26361235

Diaz-Ledezma, C., Lichstein, P. M., Dolan, J. G., & Parvizi, J. (2014). Diagnosis of periprosthetic joint infection in Medicare patients: Multicriteria decision analysis. *Clinical Orthopaedics and Related Research*, *472*(11), 3275–3284. doi:10.100711999-014-3492-2 PMID:24522385

Dolan, J. G. (2010). Multi-criteria clinical decision support: A primer on the use of multiple criteria decision-making methods to promote evidence-based, patient-centered healthcare. *Patient*, *3*(4), 229–248. doi:10.2165/11539470-000000000-00000 PMID:21394218

Dowie, J., & Kaltoft, M. K. (2018). From Rapid Recommendation to Online Preference-Sensitive Decision Support: The Case of Severe Aortic Stenosis. *Medical sciences (Basel, Switzerland)*, *6*(4), E109. doi:10.3390/medsci6040109 PMID:30501062

Drake, J. I., de Hart, J. C. T., Monleón, C., Toro, W., & Valentim, J. (2017). Utilization of multiple-criteria decision analysis (MCDA) to support healthcare decision-making FIFARMA, 2016. *Journal of Market Access & Health Policy*, *5*(1), 1360545. doi: 10.1080/20016689.2017.1360545 PMID:29081919

Dubromel, A., Duvinage-Vonesch, M. A., Geffroy, L., & Dussart, C. (2020). Organizational aspect in healthcare decision-making: A literature review. *Journal of Market Access & Health Policy*, *8*(1), 1810905. doi:10.1080/20016689.2020.18 10905 PMID:32944200

Dukhanin, V., Searle, A., Zwerling, A., Dowdy, D.W., Taylor, H.A., & Merritt, M.W. (2018). Integrating social justice concerns into economic evaluation for healthcare and public health: A systematic review. *Social Science & Medicine*, *198*, 27-35. doi:10.1016/j.socscimed.2017.12.012

Fasseeh, A., Karam, R., Jameleddine, M., George, M., Kristensen, F. B., Al-Rabayah, A. A., Alsaggabi, A. H., El Rabbat, M., Alowayesh, M. S., Chamova, J., Ismail, A., Abaza, S., & Kaló, Z. (2020). Implementation of Health Technology Assessment in the Middle East and North Africa: Comparison Between the Current and Preferred Status. *Frontiers in Pharmacology*, *11*, 15. doi:10.3389/fphar.2020.00015 PMID:32153393

Frazão, T. D. C., Camilo, D. G. G., Cabral, E. L. S., & Souza, R. P. (2018). Multicriteria decision analysis (MCDA) in health care: A systematic review of the main characteristics and methodological steps. *BMC Medical Informatics and Decision Making*, *18*(1), 90. doi:10.118612911-018-0663-1 PMID:30382826

Garau, M., Hampson, G., Devlin, N., Mazzanti, N. A., & Profico, A. (2018). Applying a Multicriteria Decision Analysis (MCDA) Approach to Elicit Stakeholders' Preferences in Italy: The Case of Obinutuzumab for Rituximab-Refractory Indolent Non-Hodgkin Lymphoma (iNHL). *PharmacoEconomics Open*, *2*(2), 153–163. doi:10.100741669-017-0048-x PMID:29623625

Goetghebeur, M. M., Wagner, M., Khoury, H., Levitt, R. J., Erickson, L. J., & Rindress, D. (2008). Evidence and Value: Impact on Decision Making—the EVIDEM framework and potential applications. *BMC Health Services Research*, *8*(1), 270. doi:10.1186/1472-6963-8-270 PMID:19102752

Goetghebeur, M.M., Wagner, M., Khoury, H., Rindress, D., Grégoire, J.P., & Deal, C. (2010). Combining multicriteria decision analysis, ethics and health technology assessment: applying the EVIDEM decision-making framework to growth hormone for Turner syndrome patients. *Cost Effectiveness and Resource Allocation, 8*, 4. doi:10.1186/1478-7547-8-4

Guarga, L., Badia, X., Obach, M., Fontanet, M., Prat, A., Vallano, A., Torrent, J., & Pontes, C. (2019). Implementing reflective multicriteria decision analysis (MCDA) to assess orphan drugs value in the Catalan Health Service (CatSalut). *Orphanet Journal of Rare Diseases*, *14*(1), 1–9. doi:10.118613023-019-1121-6 PMID:31248421

Guindo, L.A., Wagner, M., Baltussen, R., Rindress, D., van Til, J., Kind, P., & Goetghebeur, M.M. (2012). From efficacy to equity: Literature review of decision criteria for resource allocation and healthcare decision making. *Cost Effectiveness and Resource Allocation*, *10*(1), 9. . doi:10.1186/1478-7547-10-9

Hall, W. (2017). Don't Discount Societal Value in Cost-Effectiveness Comment on Priority Setting for Universal Health Coverage: We Need Evidence-Informed Deliberative Processes, Not Just More Evidence on Cost-Effectiveness. *International Journal of Health Policy and Management, 6*(9), 543–545. doi:10.15171/ijhpm.2017.03 PMID:28949468

Holtorf, A. P., Kristin, E., Assamawakin, A., Upakdee, N., Indrianti, R., & Apinchonbancha, N. (2021). Case studies for implementing MCDA for tender and purchasing decisions in hospitals in Indonesia and Thailand. *Journal of Pharmaceutical Policy and Practice, 14*(1), 52. doi:10.118640545-021-00333-8 PMID:34127071

Iskrov, G., Miteva-Katrandzhieva, T., & Stefanov, R. (2016). Multi-Criteria Decision Analysis for Assessment and Appraisal of Orphan Drugs. *Frontiers in Public Health, 4*, 214. doi:10.3389/fpubh.2016.00214 PMID:27747207

Jakab, I., Whittington, M. D., Franklin, E., Raiola, S., Campbell, J. D., Kaló, Z., & McQueen, R. B. (2021). Patient and Payer Preferences for Additional Value Criteria. *Frontiers in Pharmacology, 12*, 690021. doi:10.3389/fphar.2021.690021 PMID:34248638

Janssen, I. M., Gerhardus, A., Schröer-Günther, M. A., & Scheibler, F. (2015). A descriptive review on methods to prioritize outcomes in a health care context. *Health Expectations, 18*(6), 1873–1893. doi:10.1111/hex.12256 PMID:25156207

Jehu-Appiah, C., Baltussen, R., Acquah, C., Aikins, M., d'Almeida, S.A., Bosu, W.K., Koolman, X., Lauer, J., Osei, D. & Adjei, S., (2008). Balancing equity and efficiency in health priorities in Ghana: the use of multicriteria decision analysis. *Value in Health: The Journal of the International Society for Pharmacoeconomics and Outcomes Research, 11*(7), 1081-1087. doi:10.1111/j.1524-4733.2008.00392

Karimi, M., van der Zwaan, L., Islam, K., van Genabeek, J., & Mölken, M.R. (2021). Evaluating Complex Health and Social Care Program Using Multi-Criteria Decision Analysis: A Case Study of Better Together in Amsterdam North. *Value in Health: The Journal of the International Society for Pharmacoeconomics and Outcomes Research, 24*(7), 966-75. . doi:10.1016/j.jval.2021.02.007

Karimi, M., van der Zwaan, L., Islam, K., van Genabeek, J., & Rutten-van Mölken, M. (2021). Evaluating complex health and social care program using multi-criteria decision analysis: A case study of Better Together in Amsterdam North. *Value in Health, 24*(7), 966–975. doi:10.1016/j.jval.2021.02.007 PMID:34243840

Karrer, L., Zhang, S., Kühlein, T., & Kolominsky-Rabas, P.L. (2021). Exploring physicians and patients' perspectives for current interventions on thyroid nodules using a MCDA method. *Cost Effectiveness and Resource Allocation, 19*(1), 26. doi:10.1186/s12962-021-00279-3

Klamer, S., Van Goethem, N., Thomas, D., Duysburgh, E., Braeye, T., Quoilin, S., & Geebelen, L. (2021). Prioritisation for future surveillance, prevention and control of 98 communicable diseases in Belgium: A 2018 multi-criteria decision analysis study. *BMC Public Health, 21*(1), 192. doi:10.118612889-020-09566-9 PMID:33482767

Kolasa, K., Zwolinski, K.M., Zah, V., Kaló, Z., & Lewandowski, T. (2018). Revealed preferences towards the appraisal of orphan drugs in Poland - multi criteria decision analysis. *Orphaned Journal of Rare Diseases, 13*(1), 67. . doi:10.1186/s13023-018-0803-9

Kremer, I. E. H., Jongen, P. J., Evers, S. M. A. A., Hoogervorst, E. L. J., Verhagen, W. I. M., & Hiligsmann, M. (2021). Patient decision aid based on multi-criteria decision analysis for disease-modifying drugs for multiple sclerosis: Prototype development. *BMC Medical Informatics and Decision Making, 21*(1), 123. doi:10.118612911-021-01479-w PMID:33836742

Lvovschi, V. E., Maignan, M., Tazarourte, K., Diallo, M. L., Hadjadj-Baillot, C., Pons-Kerjean, N., Lapostolle, F., & Dussart, C. (2020). Multiple criteria decision analysis approach to consider therapeutic innovations in the emergency department: The methoxyflurane organizational impact in acute trauma pain. *PLoS One, 15*(4), e0231571. doi:10.1371/journal.pone.0231571 PMID:32294125

Marsh, K., IJzerman, M., Thokala, P., Baltussen, R., Boysen, M., Kaló, Z., Lönngren, T., Mussen, F., Peacock, S., Watkins, J. & Devlin, N (2016). Multiple Criteria Decision Analysis for Health Care Decision Making--Emerging Good Practices: Report 2 of the ISPOR MCDA Emerging Good Practices Task Force. *Value in Health: The Journal of the International Society for Pharmacoeconomics and Outcomes Research, 19*(2), 125-37. doi:10.1016/j.jval.2015.12.016

Marsh, K., Lanitis, T., Neasham, D., Orfanos, P., & Caro, J. (2014). Assessing the value of healthcare interventions using multi-criteria decision analysis: A review of the literature. *PharmacoEconomics, 32*(4), 345–365. doi:10.100740273-014-0135-0 PMID:24504851

Milsom, I., Wagg, A., Oelke, M., & Chapple, C. (2021). Which drugs are best for overactive bladder? From patients' expectations to physicians' decisions. *International Journal of Clinical Practice, 75*(4), e13870. doi:10.1111/ijcp.13870 PMID:33251651

Miot, J., Wagner, M., Khoury, H., Rindress, D., & Goetghebeur, M.M. (2012). Field testing of a multicriteria decision analysis (MCDA) framework for coverage of a screening test for cervical cancer in South Africa. *Cost Effectiveness and Resource Allocation, 10*(1), 2. doi:10.1186/1478-7547-10-2

Mirelman, A., Mentzakis, E., Kinter, E., Paolucci, F., Fordham, R., Ozawa, S., Ferraz, M., Baltussen, R. & Niessen, L.W. (2012). Decision-making criteria among national policymakers in five countries: a discrete choice experiment eliciting relative preferences for equity and efficiency. *Value in Health: The Journal of the International Society for Pharmacoeconomics and Outcomes Research, 15*(3), 534-539. . doi:10.1016/j.jval.2012.04.001

Mokrini, A. E., & Aouam, T. (2020). A fuzzy multi-criteria decision analysis approach for risk evaluation in healthcare logistics outsourcing: Case of Morocco. *Health Services Management Research, 33*(3), 143–155. doi:10.1177/0951484820901668 PMID:31994906

Moreno-Calderón, A., Tong, T. S., & Thokala, P. (2020). Multi-criteria Decision Analysis Software in Healthcare Priority Setting: A Systematic Review. *PharmacoEconomics, 38*(3), 269–283. doi:10.100740273-019-00863-9 PMID:31820294

Morton, A. (2014). Aversion to health inequalities in healthcare prioritisation: A multicriteria optimisation perspective. *Journal of Health Economics, 36*, 164–173. doi:10.1016/j.jhealeco.2014.04.005 PMID:24831800

Mühlbacher, A. C., & Kaczynski, A. (2016). Making Good Decisions in Healthcare with Multi-Criteria Decision Analysis: The Use, Current Research and Future Development of MCDA. *Applied Health Economics and Health Policy, 14*(1), 29–40. doi:10.100740258-015-0203-4 PMID:26519081

Németh, B., Molnár, A., Bozóki, S., Wijaya, K., Inotai, A., Campbell, J. D., & Kaló, Z. (2019). Comparison of weighting methods used in multicriteria decision analysis frameworks in healthcare with focus on low- and middle-income countries. *Journal of Comparative Effectiveness Research, 8*(4), 195–204. doi:10.2217/cer-2018-0102 PMID:30767661

Nicholas, L., Fischbein, R., Falletta, L., & Baughman, K. (2018). Twin-Twin Transfusion Syndrome and Maternal Symptomatology-An Exploratory Analysis of Patient Experiences When Reporting Complaints. *Journal of Patient Experience, 5*(2), 134–139. doi:10.1177/2374373517736760 PMID:29978030

Oliveira, M. D., Mataloto, I., & Kanavos, P. (2019). Multi-criteria decision analysis for health technology assessment: Addressing methodological challenges to improve the state of the art. *The European Journal of Health Economics*, *20*(6), 891–918. doi:10.100710198-019-01052-3 PMID:31006056

Ottardi, C., Damonti, A., Porazzi, E., Foglia, E., Ferrario, L., Villa, T., Aimar, E., Brayda-Bruno, M., & Galbusera, F. (2017). A comparative analysis of a disposable and a reusable pedicle screw instrument kit for lumbar arthrodesis: Integrating HTA and MCDA. *Health Economics Review*, *7*(1), 1–10. doi:10.118613561-017-0153-7 PMID:28470542

Öztürk, N., Tozan, H., & Vayvay, Ö. (2020). A New Decision Model Approach for Health Technology Assessment and A Case Study for Dialysis Alternatives in Turkey. *International Journal of Environmental Research and Public Health*, *17*(10), E3608. doi:10.3390/ijerph17103608 PMID:32455609

Piaggio, D., Castaldo, R., Cinelli, M., Cinelli, S., Maccaro, A., & Pecchia, L. (2021). A framework for designing medical devices resilient to low-resource settings. *Globalization and Health*, *17*(1), 64. doi:10.118612992-021-00718-z PMID:34158072

Pinazo, M. J., Cidoncha, A., Gopal, G., Moriana, S., Saravia, R., Torrico, F., & Gascon, J. (2021). Multi-criteria decision analysis approach for strategy scale-up with application to Chagas disease management in Bolivia. *PLoS Neglected Tropical Diseases*, *15*(3), e0009249. doi:10.1371/journal.pntd.0009249 PMID:33770076

Postmus, D., Richard, S., Bere, N., van Valkenhoef, G., Galinsky, J., Low, E., Moulon, I., Mavris, M., Salmonsson, T., Flores, B., Hillege, H., & Pignatti, F. (2018). Individual Trade-Offs Between Possible Benefits and Risks of Cancer Treatments: Results from a Stated Preference Study with Patients with Multiple Myeloma. *The Oncologist*, *23*(1), 44–51. doi:10.1634/theoncologist.2017-0257 PMID:29079638

Postmus, D., Tervonen, T., van Valkenhoef, G., Hillege, H. L., & Buskens, E. (2014). A multi-criteria decision analysis perspective on the health economic evaluation of medical interventions. *The European journal of health economics. HEPAC Health Economics in Prevention and Care*, *15*(7), 709–716. doi:10.100710198-013-0517-9 PMID:23843123

Puška, A., Stević, Ž., & Pamučar, D. (2021). Evaluation and selection of healthcare waste incinerators using extended sustainability criteria and multi-criteria analysis methods. *Environment, Development and Sustainability*, 1–31. doi:10.100710668-021-01902-2 PMID:34720689

Ruggeri, M., Cadeddu, C., Roazzi, P., Mandolini, D., Grigioni, M., & Marchetti, M. (2020). Multi-Criteria-Decision-Analysis (MCDA) for the Horizon Scanning of Health Innovations an Application to COVID 19 Emergency. *International Journal of Environmental Research and Public Health, 17*(21), E7823. doi:10.3390/ijerph17217823 PMID:33114587

Sarwar, A., & Imran, M. (2021). Prioritizing Infection Prevention and Control Activities for SARS-CoV-2 (COVID-19): A Multi-Criteria Decision-Analysis Method. *Journal of Healthcare Leadership, 13*, 77–84. doi:10.2147/JHL.S292606 PMID:33664608

Schey, C., Krabbe, P. F., Postma, M. J., & Connolly, M. P. (2017). Multi-criteria decision analysis (MCDA): Testing a proposed MCDA framework for orphan drugs. *Orphanet Journal of Rare Diseases, 12*(1), 10. doi:10.118613023-016-0555-3 PMID:28095876

Suner, A., Oruc, O. E., Buke, C., Ozkaya, H. D., & Kitapcioglu, G. (2017). Evaluation of infectious diseases and clinical microbiology specialists' preferences for hand hygiene: Analysis using the multi-attribute utility theory and the analytic hierarchy process methods. *BMC Medical Informatics and Decision Making, 17*(1), 129. doi:10.118612911-017-0528-z PMID:28859640

Tony, M., Wagner, M., Khoury, H., Rindress, D., Papastavros, T., Oh, P., & Goetghebeur, M. M. (2011). Bridging health technology assessment (HTA) with multicriteria decision analyses (MCDA): Field testing of the EVIDEM framework for coverage decisions by a public payer in Canada. *BMC Health Services Research, 11*(1), 329. doi:10.1186/1472-6963-11-329 PMID:22129247

van den Bogaart, E.H.A., Kroese, M.E.A.L., Spreeuwenberg, M.D., Ruwaard, D., & Tsiachristas, A. (2021). Economic Evaluation of New Models of Care: Does the Decision Change Between Cost-Utility Analysis and Multi-Criteria Decision Analysis. *Value in Health: The Journal of the International Society for Pharmacoeconomics and Outcomes Research, 24*(6), 795-803. . doi:10.1016/j.jval.2021.01.014

van Til, J., Groothuis-Oudshoorn, C., Lieferink, M., Dolan, J., & Goetghebeur, M. (2014). Does technique matter; a pilot study exploring weighting techniques for a multi-criteria decision support framework. *Cost Effectiveness and Resource Allocation, 12*, 22. . doi:10.1186/1478-7547-12-22

Vettoretto, N., Foglia, E., Ferrario, L., Arezzo, A., Cirocchi, R., Cocorullo, G., Currò, G., Marchi, D., Portale, G., Gerardi, C., Nocco, U., Tringali, M., Anania, G., Piccoli, M., Silecchia, G., Morino, M., Valeri, A., & Lettieri, E. (2018). Why laparoscopists may opt for three-dimensional view: A summary of the full HTA report on 3D versus 2D laparoscopy by S.I.C.E. (Società Italiana di Chirurgia Endoscopica e Nuove Tecnologie). *Surgical Endoscopy, 32*(6), 2986–2993. doi:10.100700464-017-6006-y PMID:29368286

Villanueva, V., Carreño, M., Gil-Nagel, A., Serrano-Castro, P.J., Serratosa, J.M., Toledo, M., Álvarez-Barón, E., Gil, A. & Subías-Labazuy, S. (2021). Identifying key unmet needs and value drivers in the treatment of focal-onset seizures (FOS) in patients with drug-resistant epilepsy (DRE) in Spain through Multi-Criteria Decision Analysis (MCDA). *Epilepsy & Behavior, 122*, 108222. doi:10.1016/j.yebeh.2021.108222

Wagner, M., Khoury, H., Bennetts, L., Berto, P., Ehreth, J., Badia, X., & Goetghebeur, M. (2017). Appraising the holistic value of Lenvatinib for radio-iodine refractory differentiated thyroid cancer: A multi-country study applying pragmatic MCDA. *BMC Cancer, 17*(1), 272. doi:10.118612885-017-3258-9 PMID:28412971

Wagner, M., Khoury, H., Willet, J., Rindress, D., & Goetghebeur, M. (2016). Can the EVIDEM Framework Tackle Issues Raised by Evaluating Treatments for Rare Diseases: Analysis of Issues and Policies, and Context-Specific Adaptation. *PharmacoEconomics, 34*(3), 285–301. doi:10.100740273-015-0340-5 PMID:26547306

Wagner, M., Samaha, D., Casciano, R., Brougham, M., Abrishami, P., Petrie, C., Avouac, B., Mantovani, L., Sarría-Santamera, A., Kind, P., Schlander, M., & Tringali, M. (2019). Moving Towards Accountability for Reasonableness - A Systematic Exploration of the Features of Legitimate Healthcare Coverage Decision-Making Processes Using Rare Diseases and Regenerative Therapies as a Case Study. *International Journal of Health Policy and Management, 8*(7), 424–443. doi:10.15171/ijhpm.2019.24 PMID:31441279

Wahlster, P., Goetghebeur, M., Kriza, C., Niederländer, C., & Kolominsky-Rabas, P. (2015). Balancing costs and benefits at different stages of medical innovation: A systematic review of multi-criteria decision analysis (MCDA). *BMC Health Services Research, 15*(1), 262. doi:10.118612913-015-0930-0 PMID:26152122

Wahlster, P., Goetghebeur, M., Schaller, S., Kriza, C., & Kolominsky-Rabas, P. (2015). Exploring the perspectives and preferences for HTA across German healthcare stakeholders using a multi-criteria assessment of a pulmonary heart sensor as a case study. *Health Research Policy and Systems, 13*(1), 24. doi:10.118612961-015-0011-1 PMID:25928535

Wang, J., Chen, H., Lin, X., Ji, C., & Chen, B. (2020). Multiple cross displacement amplification-a more applicable technique in detecting Pseudomonas aeruginosa of ventilator-associated pneumonia (VAP). *Critical Care (London, England), 24*(1), 306. doi:10.118613054-020-03003-4 PMID:32513206

Watson, M. (2018). Panel discussion on the application of MCDA tools. *Cost Effectiveness and Resource Allocation, 16*(Suppl 1), 40. . doi:10.1186/s12962-018-0130-y

Yang, C., Wang, Y., Hu, X., Chen, Y., Qian, L., Li, F., ... Chai, X. (2021). Improving Hospital Based Medical Procurement Decisions with Health Technology Assessment and Multi-Criteria Decision Analysis. *Inquiry, 58*. . doi:10.1177/00469580211022911

Zamora, B., Garrison, L.P., Unuigbe, A., & Towse, A. (2021). Reconciling ACEA and MCDA: is there a way forward for measuring cost-effectiveness in the U.S. healthcare setting. *Cost Effectiveness and Resource Allocation, 19*(1), 13. . doi:10.1186/s12962-021-00266-8

Zozaya, N., Martínez-Galdeano, L., Alcalá, B., Armario-Hita, J.C., Carmona, C., Carrascosa, J.M., Herranz, P., Lamas, M.J., Trapero-Bertran, M., & Hidalgo-Vega, Á. (2018). Determining the Value of Two Biologic Drugs for Chronic Inflammatory Skin Diseases: Results of a Multi-Criteria Decision Analysis. *BioDrugs, 32*(3), 281-91. doi:10.1007/s40259-018-0284-3

ADDITIONAL READING

Carnero, M. C., & Gómez, A. (2016). A multicriteria decision making approach applied to improving maintenance policies in healthcare organizations. *BMC Medical Informatics and Decision Making, 16*(1), 1–22. doi:10.118612911-016-0282-7 PMID:27108234

Diaby, V., Campbell, K., & Goeree, R. (2013). Multi-criteria decision analysis (MCDA) in health care: A bibliometric analysis. *Operations Research for Health Care, 2*(1-2), 20–24. doi:10.1016/j.orhc.2013.03.001

Marsh, K., Caro, J. J., Hamed, A., & Zaiser, E. (2017). Amplifying each patient's voice: A systematic review of multi-criteria decision analyses involving patients. *Applied Health Economics and Health Policy*, *15*(2), 155–162. doi:10.100740258-016-0299-1 PMID:27928659

Tanios, N., Wagner, M., Tony, M., Baltussen, R., van Til, J., Rindress, D., Kind, P., & Goetghebeur, M. M. (2013, October). Which Criteria Are Considered in HealthcareDecisions? Insights From an International Survey of Policy and Clinical Decision *Makers*. *International Journal of Technology Assessment in Health Care*, *29*(4), 456–465. doi:10.1017/S0266462313000573 PMID:24290340

KEY TERMS AND DEFINITIONS

Criteria: Criteria are specific and measurable outcomes. A standard by and large demonstrates the heading in which to improve.

Elements of MCDA Problem: Decision maker(s), alternatives, and criteria.

Goal: Goal connect with expected performance outcomes later on.

MCDA: Multiple-criteria decision analysis is a dynamic examination that assesses numerous (conflicting) criteria in the decision process.

MCDA Procedures: Value scaling (or standardization), criterion weighting, and combination (decision) rule.

Objective: Objective is something to be pursued to its fullest level or it might demonstrate the direction of wanted change.

Compilation of References

Panetta. (2017). *Top 10 strategic technology trends for 2017, digital twins.* Available from: https://www.gartner.com/smarterwithgartner/gartner-top-10-strategic-technology-trends-2017/

Panetta. (2018). *Top 10 strategic technology trends for 2018: Digital twins.* Available from: https://www.gartner.com/smarterwithgartner/gartner-top-10-strategic-technology-trends-for-2018/

Murray. (2018). *Lockheed Martin forecasts tech trends for defense in 2018.* Available https://dallasinnovates.com/lockheed-martin-forecasts-tech-trends-for defense-in-2018/

Smart Manufacturing Association of China Association for Science and Technology. (n.d.). *Smart Manufacturing Association of China Association for Science and Technology releases the top ten scientific and technological advances for smart manufacturing in the world and the top ten scientific and technological advances for smart manufacturing in China.* Available from: http://www.cast.org.cn/n200705/n202961/n202993/c57776269/content.html

Tao, M. (2017a). Digital twin workshop: A new paradigm for future workshop. *Jisuanji Jicheng Zhizao Xitong, 23*(1), 1–9.

Tao, Y. (2017). Theory and technologies for cyber- physical fusion in digital twin shop-floor. *Jisuanji Jicheng Zhizao Xitong, 23*(8), 1603–1611.

Tao, M. (2017b). Digital twin shop-floor a new shop-floor paradigm towards smart manufacturing. *IEEE Access : Practical Innovations, Open Solutions, 5,* 20418–20427.

Tao, F., Liu, W., & Liu, H. (2018). Digital twin and its potential application exploration. *Computer Integrated Manufacturing Systems, 24*(1), 1–18.

Machine-to-Machine Communications. (2015). *Impact of smart city activity on IoT evitonment.* ETSI.

Schuh, G., Anderl, R., Gausemeier, J., Hompel, M.T., & Wahlster, W. (2017). *Industrie 4.0 maturity index. Managing the digital transformation of companies.* Munich: Herbert Utz.

Boschert & Rosen. (2016). Digital Twin-The Simulation Aspect. In Mechatronic Futures. Springer. https://doi.org/.171 doi:10.1007/978-3-319-32156-1_5

Ribeiro, L., & Björkman, M. (2017). Transitioning From Standard Automation Solutions to CyberPhysical Production Systems: An Assessment of Critical Conceptual and Technical Challenges. *IEEE Systems Journal*, 1-13. https://doi.org/10.1109/JSYST.2017.2771139

Qin, J., Liu, Y., & Grosvenor, R. A. (2016). categorical framework of manufacturing for industry 4.0 and beyond. *Procedia Cirp, 52*, 173-178.

Uhlemann, T. H. J., Lehmann, C., & Steinhilper, R. (2017). The digital twin realizing the cyber physical production system for industry 4.0. *Procedia CIRP, 61*, 335–340.

Kritzinger. (2018). *Digital Twin in manufacturing: A categorical literature review and classification*. 10.1016/j.ifacol.2018.08.474

Tao, F., Qi, Q., Wang, L., & Nee, A. Y. C. (2019). Digital Twins and Cyber–Physical Systems toward Smart Manufacturing and Industry 4.0: Correlation and Comparison. *Engineering, 5*(4), 653-661. https://doi.org/10.1016/j.eng.2019.01.014

Enders & Hoßbach. (2019). Dimensions of Digital Twin Applications - A Literature Review. Conference: AMCIS.

Glaegen, E. H., & Stargel, D. S. (2012). The Digital Twin paradigm for future NASA and US Air Force vehicles. 53rd Structures, *Structural Dynamics, and Materials Conference: Special Session on the Digital Twin*, 1-14.

Tuegel, J., Ingraffea, A. R., Eason, T. G., & Spottswood, S. M. (2011). Reengineering aircraft structural life prediction using a digital twin. *Int. J. Aerosp. Eng*. https://doi.org/10.1155/2011/154798

Tac, E. J. (2012). The airframe digital twin: some challenges to realization. *53rd AIAA/ASME/ASCE/AHS/ASC Structures, Structural Dynamics and Materials Conference 20th AIAA/ASME/AHS Adaptive Structures Conference 14th AIAA*.

Allare, D. (2014). Multifidelity DDDAS methods with application to a self-aware aerospace vehicle. *Procedia Computer Science, 29*, 1182–1192.

Reifinider & Majumdar. (2013). Multiphysics stimulated simulation digital twin methods for fleet management. *54th AIAA/ASME/ASCE/AHS/ASC Structures, Structural Dynamics, and Materials Conference*, 1578.

Swedberg. (n.d.). *Digital twins bring value to big RFID and loT data*. Available from: http://www.rfidjournal.com/articles/vies717421

Menard. (n.d.). *3 ways digital twins are going to help improve oil and gas maintenance hard, and operations*. Available from: https://www.linkedin.com/pulse/3-ways-digitaltwins-going-help-improve-od-gas-sophie-menard

Science Service Dr. Hempel Digital Health Network. (n.d.). *Healthcare solution testing for future Digital Twins in healthcare*. Available from: https://www.dr-hempel-network.com/digital-health-technolgy/digital-twins-in-healthcare

Abdullah, A. H., Holtorf, A. P., Al-Hussaini, M., Lemay, J., Alowayesh, M., & Kaló, Z. (2019). Stakeholder driven development of a multi-criteria decision analysis tool for purchasing off-patent pharmaceuticals in Kuwait. *Journal of Pharmaceutical Policy and Practice*, *12*(1), 1–7. doi:10.118640545-019-0171-4 PMID:31011430

Adunlin, G., Diaby, V., & Xiao, H. (2015). Application of multicriteria decision analysis in health care: A systematic review and bibliometric analysis. *Health Expectations*, *18*(6), 1894–1905. doi:10.1111/hex.12287 PMID:25327341

Agarwal & P. W. (2016). A Review-Quaternary Signed Digit Number System byReversible Logic Gate. *International Journal on Recent and Innovation Trends in Computing and Communication*, *4*(3).

Aggarwal, S., & Kumar, N. (2020). Blockchain components. In *The Blockchain Technology for Secure and Smart Applications across Industry Verticals* (1st ed.). Elsevier Inc. doi:10.1016/bs.adcom.2020.08.019

Aggarwal, V. K., Sharma, N., Kaushik, I., & Bhushan, B. (2021). *Integration of Blockchain and IoT (B-IoT): Architecture, Solutions, & Future Research Direction Integration of Blockchain and IoT (B-IoT)*. Architecture, Solutions, & Future Research Direction. doi:10.1088/1757-899X/1022/1/012103

Ahmad & Naseem. (2016). Simulation and Performance Analysis of Low Power Quasi Floating Gate PCS Model. *The International Journal of Intelligent Engineering and Systems, 9*(2), 8–13.

Ahmad, S. N., & Whig, P. (2011). *On the Performance of ISFET-based Device for Water Quality Monitoring*. Academic Press.

Ahmad, P. W., & S. N. (2016). A Novel Pseudo NMOS Integrated CC -ISFET Device for Water Quality Monitoring. *Journal of Integrated Circuit and System*, *8*(2), 1–6.

Ahmed, S. V., & Chaudhari, A. L. (n.d.). *Development of Microcontroller Based Tool for Effective Learning of Concepts in Control System*. Academic Press.

Ajay Rupani, P. (2019). The development of big data science to the world. *Engineering Reports*, *2*(2), 1–7.

Aldowah, H., Ul Rehman, S., & Umar, I. (2019). Security in internet of things: Issues, challenges and solutions. In Advances in Intelligent Systems and Computing (Vol. 843). Springer International Publishing. doi:10.1007/978-3-319-99007-1_38

Alferaidi, A., Yadav, K., Alharbi, Y., Viriyasitavat, W., Kautish, S., & Dhiman, G. (2022). Federated Learning Algorithms to Optimize the Client and Cost Selections. *Mathematical Problems in Engineering*.

Alkali, Y., Routray, I., & Whig, P. (2022). *Study of various methods for reliable, efficient and Secured IoT using Artificial Intelligence*. Available at SSRN 4020364.

AlkaliY.RoutrayI.WhigP. (2022). Study of various methods for reliable, efficient and Secured IoT using Artificial Intelligence. *Available at* SSRN 4020364. doi:10.2139/ssrn.4020364

Alphonse, A. S., & Starvin, M. S. (2020). Blockchain and Internet of Things: An Overview. In Handbook of Research on Blockchain Technology. Inc. doi:10.1016/B978-0-12-819816-2.00012-5

Al-saqqa, S., & Almajali, S. (2020). *Blockchain Technology Consensus Algorithms and Applications: A Survey Types of Blockchain.* Academic Press.

Anand, M., Velu, A., & Whig, P. (2022). Prediction of Loan Behaviour with Machine Learning Models for Secure Banking. *Journal of Computing Science and Engineering: JCSE, 3*(1), 1–13.

Angelis, A., Kanavos, P., & Phillips, L.D. (2020). ICER Value Framework 2020 Update: Recommendations on the Aggregation of Benefits and Contextual Considerations. *Value in Health: The Journal of the International Society for Pharmacoeconomics and Outcomes Research, 23*(8), 1040-1048. . doi:10.1016/j.jval.2020.04.1828

Angelis, A., & Kanavos, P. (2016). Value-Based Assessment of New Medical Technologies: Towards a Robust Methodological Framework for the Application of Multiple Criteria Decision Analysis in the Context of Health Technology Assessment. *PharmacoEconomics, 34*(5), 435–446. doi:10.100740273-015-0370-z PMID:26739955

Angelis, A., Thursz, M., Ratziu, V., O'brien, A., Serfaty, L., Canbay, A., Schiefke, I., Costa, J. B. E., Lecomte, P., & Kanavos, P. (2020). Early Health Technology Assessment during Nonalcoholic Steatohepatitis Drug Development: A Two-Round, Cross-Country, Multicriteria Decision Analysis. *Medical Decision Making, 40*(6), 830–845. doi:10.1177/0272989X20940672 PMID:32845234

Arun Velu, P. W. (2021). Impact of Covid Vaccination on the Globe using data analytics. *International Journal of Sustainable Development in Computing Science, 3*(2).

Asopa, P., Purohit, P., Nadikattu, R. R., & Whig, P. (2021). Reducing carbon footprint for sustainable development of smart cities using IoT. *2021 Third International Conference on Intelligent Communication Technologies and Virtual Mobile Networks (ICICV),* 361–367. 10.1109/ICICV50876.2021.9388466

Atlam, H. F., & Wills, G. B. (2018). Technical aspects of blockchain and IoT. In *Role of Blockchain Technology in IoT Applications* (1st ed.). Elsevier Inc., doi:10.1016/bs.adcom.2018.10.006

Avila, M. L., Brandão, L. R., Williams, S., Montoya, M. I., Stinson, J., Kiss, A., & Feldman, B. M. (2016). Development of CAPTSureTM - a new index for the assessment of pediatric postthrombotic syndrome. *Journal of Thrombosis and Hemostasis, 14*(12), 2376–2385. doi:10.1111/jth.13530 PMID:27709837

Bach, L., Mihaljevic, B., & Zagar, M. (2018). Comparitive Analysis of Blockchain Consensus Algorithms. *MIPRO,* 1545–1550.

Baltussen, R., Marsh, K., Thokala, P., Diaby, V., Castro, H., Cleemput, I., Garau, M., Iskrov, G., Olyaeemanesh, A., Mirelman, A., & Mobinizadeh, M. (2019). Multicriteria Decision Analysis to Support Health Technology Assessment Agencies: Benefits, Limitations, and the Way Forward. *Value in Health: The Journal of the International Society for Pharmacoeconomics and Outcomes Research, 22*(11), 1283-1288. doi:10.1016/j.jval.2019.06.014

Banerjee, A. (2019). Blockchain with IOT: Applications and use cases for a new paradigm of supply chain driving efficiency and cost. In Role of Blockchain Technology in IoT Applications (1st ed., Vol. 115). Elsevier Inc. doi:10.1016/bs.adcom.2019.07.007

Bayani, M., Leiton, K., Loaiza, M., & Automation, I. L. (2018). *Internet of things (IoT) advantages on e-learning in the smart original research.* Academic Press.

Bhargav, R., & Whig, P. (2021). More Insight on Data Analysis of Titanic Data Set. *International Journal of Sustainable Development in Computing Science, 3*(4), 1–10.

Bhatia, V., & Whig, P. (2013). A secured dual tune multi frequency based smart elevator control system. *International Journal of Research in Engineering and Advanced Technology, 4*(1), 1163–2319.

Bhatia, V., & Whig, P. (2013). Secure d Dual Tone Mul Mu l ti Frequency based Smart Elevator. *Control Systems (Tonbridge), 1*(4), 1–5.

Bhatia, V., Whig, P., & Ahmad, S. N. (2015). Smart PCS Based System for Oxygen Content Measurement. *International Journal of Information Technology and Computer Science, 7*(6), 45–51. doi:10.5815/ijitcs.2015.06.06

Blythe, R., Naidoo, S., Abbott, C., Bryant, G., Dines, A., & Graves, N. (2019). Development and pilot of a multicriteria decision analysis (MCDA) tool for health services administrators. *BMJ Open, 9*(4), e025752. doi:10.1136/bmjopen-2018-025752 PMID:31023757

Bogavac-Stanojevic, N., & Jelic-Ivanovic, Z. (2017). The Cost-effective Laboratory: Implementation of Economic Evaluation of Laboratory Testing. *Journal of Medical Biochemistry, 36*(3), 238–242. doi:10.1515/jomb-2017-0036 PMID:30568540

Bowers, J., Cheyne, H., Mould, G., Miller, M., Page, M., Harris, F., & Bick, D. (2018). A multicriteria resource allocation model for the redesign of services following birth. *BMC Health Services Research, 18*(1), 656. doi:10.118612913-018-3430-1 PMID:30134882

Bretoni, A., Ferrario, L., & Foglia, E. (2019). HTA and innovative treatments evaluation: The case of metastatic castration-resistant prostate cancer. *ClinicoEconomics and Outcomes Research, 11*, 283–300. doi:10.2147/CEOR.S189436 PMID:31114269

Broekhuizen, H., Groothuis-Oudshoorn, C. G., Hauber, A. B., Jansen, J. P., & IJzerman, M. J. (2015). Estimating the value of medical treatments to patients using probabilistic multi criteria decision analysis. *BMC Medical Informatics and Decision Making, 15*(1), 102. doi:10.118612911-015-0225-8 PMID:26626279

Broekhuizen, H., Groothuis-Oudshoorn, C. G., van Til, J. A., Hummel, J. M., & IJzerman, M. J. (2015). A review and classification of approaches for dealing with uncertainty in multi-criteria decision analysis for healthcare decisions. *PharmacoEconomics*, *33*(5), 445–455. doi:10.100740273-014-0251-x PMID:25630758

Camilo, D. G. G., de Souza, R. P., Frazão, T. D. C., & da Costa, J. F. Jr. (2020). Multi-criteria analysis in the health area: Selection of the most appropriate triage system for the emergency care units in natal. *BMC Medical Informatics and Decision Making*, *20*(1), 1–16. doi:10.118612911-020-1054-y PMID:32085757

Campolina, A. G. (2018). Value-based medicine in oncology: The importance of perspective in the emerging value frameworks. *Clinics (Sao Paulo, Brazil)*, *73*(suppl 1), e470s. doi:10.6061/clinics/2018/e470s PMID:30540119

Castro, H.E., Moreno-Mattar, O., & Rivillas, J.C. (2018). HTA and MCDA solely or combined? The case of priority-setting in Colombia. *Cost Effectiveness and Resource Allocation*, *16*(1), 1-7. doi:10.1186/s12962-018-0127-6

Chacko, J. B., & Whig, P. (2016). Low Delay Based Full Adder/Subtractor by MIG and COG Reversible Logic Gate. *2016 8th International Conference on Computational Intelligence and Communication Networks (CICN)*, 585–589.

Chen, X. (2018). *Blockchain challenges and opportunities : A survey Zibin Zheng and Shaoan Xie Hong-Ning Dai Huaimin Wang*. Academic Press.

Chopra, G., & Whig, P. (2022). A clustering approach based on support vectors. *International Journal of Machine Learning for Sustainable Development*, *4*(1), 21–30.

Chopra, G., & Whig, P. (2021). Analysis of Tomato Leaf Disease Identification Techniques. *Journal of Computing Science and Engineering: JCSE*, *2*(2), 98–103.

Chopra, G., & Whig, P. (2022a). Energy Efficient Scheduling for Internet of Vehicles. *International Journal of Sustainable Development in Computing Science*, *4*(1).

Chopra, G., & Whig, P. (2022b). Smart Agriculture System Using AI. *International Journal of Sustainable Development in Computing Science*, *1*(1).

Chouhan, S. (2019). Using an Arduino and a temperature, humidity sensor, Automate the fan speed. *International Journal of Sustainable Development in Computing Science, 1*(2).

Chouhan, S. (2019). Using an Arduino and a temperature, humidity sensor, Automate the fan speed. *International Journal of Sustainable Development in Computing Science, 1*(2).

Cleemput, I., Devriese, S., Kohn, L., & Westhovens, R. (2018). A multi-criteria decision approach for ranking unmet needs in healthcare. *Health Policy*, *122*(8), 878-884. doi:10.1016/j.healthpol.2018.06.010

Clemente-Suárez, V. J., Navarro-Jiménez, E., Ruisoto, P., Dalamitros, A. A., Beltran-Velasco, A. I., Hormeño-Holgado, A., Laborde-Cárdenas, C. C., & Tornero-Aguilera, J. F. (2021). Performance of Fuzzy Multi-Criteria Decision Analysis of Emergency System in COVID-19 Pandemic. An Extensive Narrative Review. *International Journal of Environmental Research and Public Health*, *18*(10), 5208. doi:10.3390/ijerph18105208 PMID:34068866

Collings, N., & Shen, Y. (2014). Development of low power Dynamic threshold PCS System. *Journal of Electrical & Electronic Systems*, *03*(03). Advance online publication. doi:10.4172/2332-0796.1000131

De Nardo, P., Gentilotti, E., Mazzaferri, F., Cremonini, E., Hansen, P., Goossens, H., Tacconelli, E., Mangoni, E.D., Florio, L.L., Zampino, R., & Mele, F. (2020). Multi-Criteria Decision Analysis to prioritize hospital admission of patients affected by COVID-19 in low-resource settings with hospital-bed shortage. *International Journal of Infectious Diseases*, *98*, 494-500. . doi:10.1016/j.ijid.2020.06.082

Diaby, V., & Goeree, R. (2014). How to use multi-criteria decision analysis methods for reimbursement decision-making in healthcare: A step-by-step guide. *Expert Review of Pharmacoeconomics & Outcomes Research*, *14*(1), 81–99. doi:10.1586/14737167.2014.8595 25 PMID:24328890

Diaby, V., Sanogo, V., & Moussa, K. R. (2016). ELICIT: An alternative imprecise weight elicitation technique for use in multi-criteria decision analysis for healthcare. *Expert Review of Pharmacoeconomics & Outcomes Research*, *16*(1), 141–147. doi:10.1586/14737167.2015.108 3863 PMID:26361235

Diaz-Ledezma, C., Lichstein, P. M., Dolan, J. G., & Parvizi, J. (2014). Diagnosis of periprosthetic joint infection in Medicare patients: Multicriteria decision analysis. *Clinical Orthopaedics and Related Research*, *472*(11), 3275–3284. doi:10.100711999-014-3492-2 PMID:24522385

Dolan, J. G. (2010). Multi-criteria clinical decision support: A primer on the use of multiple criteria decision-making methods to promote evidence-based, patient-centered healthcare. *Patient*, *3*(4), 229–248. doi:10.2165/11539470-000000000-00000 PMID:21394218

Dowie, J., & Kaltoft, M. K. (2018). From Rapid Recommendation to Online Preference-Sensitive Decision Support: The Case of Severe Aortic Stenosis. *Medical sciences (Basel, Switzerland)*, *6*(4), E109. doi:10.3390/medsci6040109 PMID:30501062

Drake, J. I., de Hart, J. C. T., Monleón, C., Toro, W., & Valentim, J. (2017). Utilization of multiple-criteria decision analysis (MCDA) to support healthcare decision-making FIFARMA, 2016. *Journal of Market Access & Health Policy*, *5*(1), 1360545. doi:10.1080/20016689.2017.1360545 PMID:29081919

Dubromel, A., Duvinage-Vonesch, M. A., Geffroy, L., & Dussart, C. (2020). Organizational aspect in healthcare decision-making: A literature review. *Journal of Market Access & Health Policy*, *8*(1), 1810905. doi:10.1080/20016689.2020.1810905 PMID:32944200

Dukhanin, V., Searle, A., Zwerling, A., Dowdy, D.W., Taylor, H.A., & Merritt, M.W. (2018). Integrating social justice concerns into economic evaluation for healthcare and public health: A systematic review. *Social Science & Medicine, 198,* 27-35. doi:10.1016/j.socscimed.2017.12.012

Fasseeh, A., Karam, R., Jameleddine, M., George, M., Kristensen, F. B., Al-Rabayah, A. A., Alsaggabi, A. H., El Rabbat, M., Alowayesh, M. S., Chamova, J., Ismail, A., Abaza, S., & Kaló, Z. (2020). Implementation of Health Technology Assessment in the Middle East and North Africa: Comparison Between the Current and Preferred Status. *Frontiers in Pharmacology, 11,* 15. doi:10.3389/fphar.2020.00015 PMID:32153393

Ferdous, S., Jabed, M., Chowdhury, M., Hoque, M. A., & Colman, A. (2020). Blockchain Consensus Algorithms. *Survey (London, England),* 1–39.

Frazão, T. D. C., Camilo, D. G. G., Cabral, E. L. S., & Souza, R. P. (2018). Multicriteria decision analysis (MCDA) in health care: A systematic review of the main characteristics and methodological steps. *BMC Medical Informatics and Decision Making, 18*(1), 90. doi:10.118612911-018-0663-1 PMID:30382826

Garau, M., Hampson, G., Devlin, N., Mazzanti, N. A., & Profico, A. (2018). Applying a Multicriteria Decision Analysis (MCDA) Approach to Elicit Stakeholders' Preferences in Italy: The Case of Obinutuzumab for Rituximab-Refractory Indolent Non-Hodgkin Lymphoma (iNHL). *PharmacoEconomics Open, 2*(2), 153–163. doi:10.100741669-017-0048-x PMID:29623625

George, N., Muiz, K., Whig, P., & Velu, A. (2021). Framework of Perceptive Artificial Intelligence using Natural Language Processing (PAIN). *Artificial & Computational Intelligence.*

Goetghebeur, M.M., Wagner, M., Khoury, H., Rindress, D., Grégoire, J.P., & Deal, C. (2010). Combining multicriteria decision analysis, ethics and health technology assessment: applying the EVIDEM decision-making framework to growth hormone for Turner syndrome patients. *Cost Effectiveness and Resource Allocation, 8,* 4. doi:10.1186/1478-7547-8-4

Goetghebeur, M. M., Wagner, M., Khoury, H., Levitt, R. J., Erickson, L. J., & Rindress, D. (2008). Evidence and Value: Impact on Decision Making—the EVIDEM framework and potential applications. *BMC Health Services Research, 8*(1), 270. doi:10.1186/1472-6963-8-270 PMID:19102752

Guarga, L., Badia, X., Obach, M., Fontanet, M., Prat, A., Vallano, A., Torrent, J., & Pontes, C. (2019). Implementing reflective multicriteria decision analysis (MCDA) to assess orphan drugs value in the Catalan Health Service (CatSalut). *Orphanet Journal of Rare Diseases, 14*(1), 1–9. doi:10.118613023-019-1121-6 PMID:31248421

Guindo, L.A., Wagner, M., Baltussen, R., Rindress, D., van Til, J., Kind, P., & Goetghebeur, M.M. (2012). From efficacy to equity: Literature review of decision criteria for resource allocation and healthcare decision making. *Cost Effectiveness and Resource Allocation, 10*(1), 9. . doi:10.1186/1478-7547-10-9

Hall, W. (2017). Don't Discount Societal Value in Cost-Effectiveness Comment on Priority Setting for Universal Health Coverage: We Need Evidence-Informed Deliberative Processes, Not Just More Evidence on Cost-Effectiveness. *International Journal of Health Policy and Management*, *6*(9), 543–545. doi:10.15171/ijhpm.2017.03 PMID:28949468

Hassan, M. U., Rehmani, M. H., & Chen, J. (2019). Privacy preservation in blockchain based IoT systems: Integration issues, prospects, challenges, and future research directions. *Future Generation Computer Systems*, *97*, 512–529. doi:10.1016/j.future.2019.02.060

Holtorf, A. P., Kristin, E., Assamawakin, A., Upakdee, N., Indrianti, R., & Apinchonbancha, N. (2021). Case studies for implementing MCDA for tender and purchasing decisions in hospitals in Indonesia and Thailand. *Journal of Pharmaceutical Policy and Practice*, *14*(1), 52. doi:10.118640545-021-00333-8 PMID:34127071

Iskrov, G., Miteva-Katrandzhieva, T., & Stefanov, R. (2016). Multi-Criteria Decision Analysis for Assessment and Appraisal of Orphan Drugs. *Frontiers in Public Health*, *4*, 214. doi:10.3389/fpubh.2016.00214 PMID:27747207

Jakab, I., Whittington, M. D., Franklin, E., Raiola, S., Campbell, J. D., Kaló, Z., & McQueen, R. B. (2021). Patient and Payer Preferences for Additional Value Criteria. *Frontiers in Pharmacology*, *12*, 690021. doi:10.3389/fphar.2021.690021 PMID:34248638

Jalali, M. S., Kaiser, J. P., Siegel, M., & Madnick, S. (2019). The Internet of Things Promises New Benefits and Risks A Systematic Analysis of Adoption Dynamics of IoT Products. *IEEE Security and Privacy*, *17*(April), 39–48. doi:10.1109/MSEC.2018.2888780

Janssen, I. M., Gerhardus, A., Schröer-Günther, M. A., & Scheibler, F. (2015). A descriptive review on methods to prioritize outcomes in a health care context. *Health Expectations*, *18*(6), 1873–1893. doi:10.1111/hex.12256 PMID:25156207

Jehu-Appiah, C., Baltussen, R., Acquah, C., Aikins, M., d'Almeida, S.A., Bosu, W.K., Koolman, X., Lauer, J., Osei, D. & Adjei, S., (2008). Balancing equity and efficiency in health priorities in Ghana: the use of multicriteria decision analysis. *Value in Health: The Journal of the International Society for Pharmacoeconomics and Outcomes Research, 11*(7), 1081-1087. doi: 10.1111/j.1524-4733.2008.00392

Jumaa, N. K., Abdulhameed, O. A., & Abbas, R. H. (2018). A Theoretical Background of IoT Platforms based on FPGAs. *Communications on Applied Electronics*, *7*(23), 6–10. doi:10.5120/cae2018652797

Karimi, M., van der Zwaan, L., Islam, K., van Genabeek, J., & Mölken, M.R. (2021). Evaluating Complex Health and Social Care Program Using Multi-Criteria Decision Analysis: A Case Study of Better Together in Amsterdam North. *Value in Health: The Journal of the International Society for Pharmacoeconomics and Outcomes Research, 24*(7), 966-75. . doi:10.1016/j.jval.2021.02.007

Karrer, L., Zhang, S., Kühlein, T., & Kolominsky-Rabas, P.L. (2021). Exploring physicians and patients' perspectives for current interventions on thyroid nodules using a MCDA method. *Cost Effectiveness and Resource Allocation, 19*(1), 26. doi:10.1186/s12962-021-00279-3

Kaushik, S., Chouhan, Y. S., Sharma, N., Singh, S., & Suganya, P. (2018). Automatic fan speed control using temperature and humidity sensor and Arduino. *International Journal of Advanced Research, 4*(2), 453–467.

Kautish, S., Reyana, A., & Vidyarthi, A. (2022). SDMTA: Attack Detection and Mitigation Mechanism for DDoS Vulnerabilities in Hybrid Cloud Environment. *IEEE Transactions on Industrial Informatics.*

Khera, Y., Whig, P., & Velu, A. (2021). efficient effective and secured electronic billing system using AI. *Vivekananda Journal of Research, 10,* 53–60.

Klamer, S., Van Goethem, N., Thomas, D., Duysburgh, E., Braeye, T., Quoilin, S., & Geebelen, L. (2021). Prioritisation for future surveillance, prevention and control of 98 communicable diseases in Belgium: A 2018 multi-criteria decision analysis study. *BMC Public Health, 21*(1), 192. doi:10.118612889-020-09566-9 PMID:33482767

Kolasa, K., Zwolinski, K.M., Zah, V., Kaló, Z., & Lewandowski, T. (2018). Revealed preferences towards the appraisal of orphan drugs in Poland - multi criteria decision analysis. *Orphaned Journal of Rare Diseases, 13*(1), 67. . doi:10.1186/s13023-018-0803-9

Kremer, I. E. H., Jongen, P. J., Evers, S. M. A. A., Hoogervorst, E. L. J., Verhagen, W. I. M., & Hiligsmann, M. (2021). Patient decision aid based on multi-criteria decision analysis for disease-modifying drugs for multiple sclerosis: Prototype development. *BMC Medical Informatics and Decision Making, 21*(1), 123. doi:10.118612911-021-01479-w PMID:33836742

Kumar, N., & Aggarwal, S. (2020). Architecture of blockchain. In *The Blockchain Technology for Secure and Smart Applications across Industry Verticals* (1st ed.). Elsevier Inc., doi:10.1016/bs.adcom.2020.08.009

Kumar, S., Tiwari, P., & Zymbler, M. (2019). Internet of Things is a revolutionary approach for future technology enhancement : A review. *Journal of Big Data, 6*(1), 111. Advance online publication. doi:10.118640537-019-0268-2

Lahade, S. V., & Hirekhan, S. R. (2015). Intelligent and adaptive traffic light controller (IA-TLC) using FPGA. *2015 International Conference on Industrial Instrumentation and Control (ICIC),* 618–623. 10.1109/IIC.2015.7150816

Lastovetska, A. (2021, August 25). *Blockchain Architecture Explained: How It Works & How to Build.* https://mlsdev.com/blog/156-how-to-build-your-own-blockchain-architecture

Latif, S., Idrees, Z., Ahmad, J., Zheng, L., & Zou, Z. (2021). Journal of Industrial Information Integration A blockchain-based architecture for secure and trustworthy operations in the industrial Internet of Things. *Journal of Industrial Information Integration, 21*(December), 100190. doi:10.1016/j.jii.2020.100190

Lvovschi, V. E., Maignan, M., Tazarourte, K., Diallo, M. L., Hadjadj-Baillot, C., Pons-Kerjean, N., Lapostolle, F., & Dussart, C. (2020). Multiple criteria decision analysis approach to consider therapeutic innovations in the emergency department: The methoxyflurane organizational impact in acute trauma pain. *PLoS One, 15*(4), e0231571. doi:10.1371/journal.pone.0231571 PMID:32294125

Madhu, M., & Whig, P. (2022). A survey of machine learning and its applications. *International Journal of Machine Learning for Sustainable Development, 4*(1), 11–20.

Mamza, E. S. (2021). Use of AIOT in Health System. *International Journal of Sustainable Development in Computing Science, 3*(4), 21–30.

Marsh, K., IJzerman, M., Thokala, P., Baltussen, R., Boysen, M., Kaló, Z., Lönngren, T., Mussen, F., Peacock, S., Watkins, J. & Devlin, N (2016). Multiple Criteria Decision Analysis for Health Care Decision Making--Emerging Good Practices: Report 2 of the ISPOR MCDA Emerging Good Practices Task Force. *Value in Health: The Journal of the International Society for Pharmacoeconomics and Outcomes Research, 19*(2), 125-37. doi:10.1016/j.jval.2015.12.016

Marsh, K., Lanitis, T., Neasham, D., Orfanos, P., & Caro, J. (2014). Assessing the value of healthcare interventions using multi-criteria decision analysis: A review of the literature. *PharmacoEconomics, 32*(4), 345–365. doi:10.100740273-014-0135-0 PMID:24504851

Mathurkar, G., Parkhi, C., Utekar, M., & Chitte, P. H. (2021). Ensuring social distancing using machine learning. *ITM Web of Conferences, 40*, 03049.

Mehta, R., Bhattacharya, N., & Goyal, S. (2014). RFID and ASP. NET based Campus Management System. *International Journal of Computers and Applications, 88*(4).

Milsom, I., Wagg, A., Oelke, M., & Chapple, C. (2021). Which drugs are best for overactive bladder? From patients' expectations to physicians' decisions. *International Journal of Clinical Practice, 75*(4), e13870. doi:10.1111/ijcp.13870 PMID:33251651

Miot, J., Wagner, M., Khoury, H., Rindress, D., & Goetghebeur, M.M. (2012). Field testing of a multicriteria decision analysis (MCDA) framework for coverage of a screening test for cervical cancer in South Africa. *Cost Effectiveness and Resource Allocation, 10*(1), 2. doi:10.1186/1478-7547-10-2

Mirelman, A., Mentzakis, E., Kinter, E., Paolucci, F., Fordham, R., Ozawa, S., Ferraz, M., Baltussen, R. & Niessen, L.W. (2012). Decision-making criteria among national policymakers in five countries: a discrete choice experiment eliciting relative preferences for equity and efficiency. *Value in Health: The Journal of the International Society for Pharmacoeconomics and Outcomes Research, 15*(3), 534-539. . doi:10.1016/j.jval.2012.04.001

Mokrini, A. E., & Aouam, T. (2020). A fuzzy multi-criteria decision analysis approach for risk evaluation in healthcare logistics outsourcing: Case of Morocco. *Health Services Management Research, 33*(3), 143–155. doi:10.1177/0951484820901668 PMID:31994906

Moorthy, T. V. K., Budati, A. K., Kautish, S., Goyal, S. B., & Prasad, K. L. (2022). Reductionof satellite images size in 5G networks using Machine learning algorithms. *IET Communications*, *16*, 584–591. https://doi.org/10.1049/cmu2.12354

Moreno-Calderón, A., Tong, T. S., & Thokala, P. (2020). Multi-criteria Decision Analysis Software in Healthcare Priority Setting: A Systematic Review. *PharmacoEconomics*, *38*(3), 269–283. doi:10.100740273-019-00863-9 PMID:31820294

Morton, A. (2014). Aversion to health inequalities in healthcare prioritisation: A multicriteria optimisation perspective. *Journal of Health Economics*, *36*, 164–173. doi:10.1016/j.jhealeco.2014.04.005 PMID:24831800

Mühlbacher, A. C., & Kaczynski, A. (2016). Making Good Decisions in Healthcare with Multi-Criteria Decision Analysis: The Use, Current Research and Future Development of MCDA. *Applied Health Economics and Health Policy*, *14*(1), 29–40. doi:10.100740258-015-0203-4 PMID:26519081

Nadikattu, R. R., Mohammad, S. M., & Whig, P. (2020). Novel economical social distancing smart Device for COVID-19 (*SSRN* Scholarly Paper ID 3640230). *Social Science Research Network*. Https://Papers. Ssrn. Com/Abstract,3640230

Nadikattu, R. R., Mohammad, S. M., & Whig, P. (2020b). Novel economical social distancing smart Device for COVID-19 (SSRN Scholarly Paper ID 3640230). *Social Science Research Network*. Https://Papers. Ssrn. Com/Abstract,3640230

Nadikattu, R. R., Bhandari, R., & Whig, P. (2021). Improved Pattern of Adaptive Rood-Pattern Search Algorithm for Motion Estimation in Video Compression. In *Innovations in Cyber Physical Systems* (pp. 441–448). Springer.

Nadikattu, R. R., Mohammad, S. M., & Whig, P. (2020). *Novel economical social distancing smart device for covid 19. International Journal of Electrical Engineering and Technology.*

Nehra, V., Sharma, A. K., & Tripathi, R. K. (2020). Blockchain Implementation for Internet of Things Applications. In *Handbook of Research on Blockchain Technology*. INC. doi:10.1016/B978-0-12-819816-2.00005-8

Németh, B., Molnár, A., Bozóki, S., Wijaya, K., Inotai, A., Campbell, J. D., & Kaló, Z. (2019). Comparison of weighting methods used in multicriteria decision analysis frameworks in healthcare with focus on low- and middle-income countries. *Journal of Comparative Effectiveness Research*, *8*(4), 195–204. doi:10.2217/cer-2018-0102 PMID:30767661

Nicholas, L., Fischbein, R., Falletta, L., & Baughman, K. (2018). Twin-Twin Transfusion Syndrome and Maternal Symptomatology-An Exploratory Analysis of Patient Experiences When Reporting Complaints. *Journal of Patient Experience*, *5*(2), 134–139. doi:10.1177/2374373517736760 PMID:29978030

Oliveira, M. D., Mataloto, I., & Kanavos, P. (2019). Multi-criteria decision analysis for health technology assessment: Addressing methodological challenges to improve the state of the art. *The European Journal of Health Economics*, *20*(6), 891–918. doi:10.100710198-019-01052-3 PMID:31006056

Ottardi, C., Damonti, A., Porazzi, E., Foglia, E., Ferrario, L., Villa, T., Aimar, E., Brayda-Bruno, M., & Galbusera, F. (2017). A comparative analysis of a disposable and a reusable pedicle screw instrument kit for lumbar arthrodesis: Integrating HTA and MCDA. *Health Economics Review*, *7*(1), 1–10. doi:10.118613561-017-0153-7 PMID:28470542

Öztürk, N., Tozan, H., & Vayvay, Ö. (2020). A New Decision Model Approach for Health Technology Assessment and A Case Study for Dialysis Alternatives in Turkey. *International Journal of Environmental Research and Public Health*, *17*(10), E3608. doi:10.3390/ijerph17103608 PMID:32455609

Panarello, A., Tapas, N., Merlino, G., Longo, F., & Puliafito, A. (2018). Blockchain and iot integration: A systematic survey. In Sensors (Switzerland) (Vol. 18, Issue 8). MDPI AG. doi:10.339018082575

Pawar, V. S. (2021). IoT architecture with embedded AI. *International Journal of Sustainable Development in Computing Science*, *3*(4), 11–20.

Piaggio, D., Castaldo, R., Cinelli, M., Cinelli, S., Maccaro, A., & Pecchia, L. (2021). A framework for designing medical devices resilient to low-resource settings. *Globalization and Health*, *17*(1), 64. doi:10.118612992-021-00718-z PMID:34158072

Pinazo, M. J., Cidoncha, A., Gopal, G., Moriana, S., Saravia, R., Torrico, F., & Gascon, J. (2021). Multi-criteria decision analysis approach for strategy scale-up with application to Chagas disease management in Bolivia. *PLoS Neglected Tropical Diseases*, *15*(3), e0009249. doi:10.1371/journal.pntd.0009249 PMID:33770076

Porkodi, S., & Kesavaraja, D. (2020). Integration of Blockchain and Internet of Things. In *Handbook of Research on Blockchain Technology*. INC. doi:10.1016/B978-0-12-819816-2.00003-4

Postmus, D., Richard, S., Bere, N., van Valkenhoef, G., Galinsky, J., Low, E., Moulon, I., Mavris, M., Salmonsson, T., Flores, B., Hillege, H., & Pignatti, F. (2018). Individual Trade-Offs Between Possible Benefits and Risks of Cancer Treatments: Results from a Stated Preference Study with Patients with Multiple Myeloma. *The Oncologist*, *23*(1), 44–51. doi:10.1634/theoncologist.2017-0257 PMID:29079638

Postmus, D., Tervonen, T., van Valkenhoef, G., Hillege, H. L., & Buskens, E. (2014). A multi-criteria decision analysis perspective on the health economic evaluation of medical interventions. *The European journal of health economics. HEPAC Health Economics in Prevention and Care*, *15*(7), 709–716. doi:10.100710198-013-0517-9 PMID:23843123

Puri, V., Kumar, R., Van Le, C., Sharma, R., & Priyadarshini, I. (2020). A Vital Role of Blockchain Technology Toward Internet of Vehicles. In *Handbook of Research on Blockchain Technology*. INC. doi:10.1016/B978-0-12-819816-2.00016-2

Puška, A., Stević, Ž., & Pamučar, D. (2021). Evaluation and selection of healthcare waste incinerators using extended sustainability criteria and multi-criteria analysis methods. *Environment, Development and Sustainability*, 1–31. doi:10.100710668-021-01902-2 PMID:34720689

Rajawat, A. S., Bedi, P., Goyal, S. B., Kautish, S., Xihua, Z., Aljuaid, H., & Mohamed, A. W. (2022). Dark Web Data Classification Using Neural Network. *Computational Intelligence and Neuroscience*.

Rashmi Sinha, S. P., & P. W. (2015). Effect of Output Error on Fuzzy Interface for VDRC of Second Order Systems. *International Journal of Computers and Applications*, *125*(13), 11–16.

Reddy, R. (2019). Purification of indoor air using a novel pseudo PMOS ultraviolet photocatalytic oxidation (PP-UVPCO) sensor. *International Journal of Sustainable Development in Computing Science*, *1*(3).

Reyna, A., Martín, C., Chen, J., Soler, E., & Díaz, M. (2018). On blockchain and its integration with IoT. Challenges and opportunities. *Future Generation Computer Systems*, *88*, 173–190. doi:10.1016/j.future.2018.05.046

Ruchin, C. M., & Whig, P. (2015). Design and Simulation of Dynamic UART Using Scan Path Technique (USPT). *International Journal of Electrical, Electronics & Computing in Science & Engineering*.

Ruggeri, M., Cadeddu, C., Roazzi, P., Mandolini, D., Grigioni, M., & Marchetti, M. (2020). Multi-Criteria-Decision-Analysis (MCDA) for the Horizon Scanning of Health Innovations an Application to COVID 19 Emergency. *International Journal of Environmental Research and Public Health*, *17*(21), E7823. doi:10.3390/ijerph17217823 PMID:33114587

Rupani, A., Saini, D., Sujediya, G., & Whig, P. (2016). A Review of Technology Paradigm for IOT on FPGA. *IJARCCE-International Journal of Advanced Research in Computer and Communication Engineering*, *5*(9)

Rupani, A., & Kumar, D. (2020). *Temperature Effect On Behaviour of Photo Catalytic Sensor (PCS)*. Used For Water Quality Monitoring.

Rupani, A., Whig, P., Sujediya, G., & Vyas, P. (2017). A robust technique for image processing based on interfacing of Raspberry-Pi and FPGA using IoT. *2017 International Conference on Computer, Communications and Electronics (Comptelix)*, 350–353. 10.1109/COMPTELIX.2017.8003992

Rupani, A., Whig, P., Sujediya, G., & Vyas, P. (2018). Hardware implementation of iot-based image processing filters. *Proceedings of the Second International Conference on Computational Intelligence and Informatics*, 681–691.

Sarmah, A., Baruah, K. K., & Baruah, A. J. (2017). *A Brief Review on Internet of Things*. Academic Press.

Sarwar, A., & Imran, M. (2021). Prioritizing Infection Prevention and Control Activities for SARS-CoV-2 (COVID-19): A Multi-Criteria Decision-Analysis Method. *Journal of Healthcare Leadership*, *13*, 77–84. doi:10.2147/JHL.S292606 PMID:33664608

Schey, C., Krabbe, P. F., Postma, M. J., & Connolly, M. P. (2017). Multi-criteria decision analysis (MCDA): Testing a proposed MCDA framework for orphan drugs. *Orphanet Journal of Rare Diseases, 12*(1), 10. doi:10.118613023-016-0555-3 PMID:28095876

Sharma, H., Rao, N., & Sharma, M. (2016). Analysis of astrology and scientific calculation through orbital period. *2016 3rd International Conference on Computing for Sustainable Global Development (INDIACom)*, 236–239.

Sharma, N. K., Shrivastava, S., & Whig, P. (n.d.). *Optimization of Process Parameters for Developing Stresses in Square Cup by Incremental Sheet Metal (ISM) Technique uses Finite Element Methods*. Academic Press.

Sharma, A., Kumar, A., & Whig, P. (2015). On the performance of CDTA based novel analog inverse low pass filter using 0.35 μm CMOS parameter. *International Journal of Science, Technology & Management, 4*(1), 594–601.

Sharma, C., Sharma, S., Kautish, S., Alsallami, S. A., Khalil, E. M., & Mohamed, A. W. (2022). A new median-average round Robin scheduling algorithm: An optimal approach for reducing turnaround and waiting time. *Alexandria Engineering Journal, 61*(12), 10527–10538.

Sharma, D. K., Kaushik, A. K., Goel, A., & Bhargava, S. (2020). Internet of Things and Blockchain: Integration, Need, Challenges, Applications, and Future Scope. In *Handbook of Research on Blockchain Technology*. INC. doi:10.1016/B978-0-12-819816-2.00011-3

Shridhar, J., Ruchin, & Whig, P. (2014). Design and simulation of power efficient traffic light controller (PTLC). *2014 International Conference on Computing for Sustainable Global Development, INDIACom 2014*. 10.1109/IndiaCom.2014.6828157

Shrivastav, P., Whig, P., & Gupta, K. (2012). *Bandwidth Enhancement by Slotted Stacked Arrangement and its Comparative Analysis with Conventional Single and Stacked Patch Antenna*. Academic Press.

Shrivastav, P., Whig, P., & Gupta, K. (n.d.). *Bandwidth Enhancement by Slotted Stacked Arrangement and its Comparative Analysis with Conventional Single and Stacked Patch Antenna*. Academic Press.

Sinha, R., & Ranjan, A. (2015). Effect of Variable Damping Ratio on design of PID Controller. *2015 4th International Conference on Reliability, Infocom Technologies and Optimization (ICRITO)(Trends and Future Directions)*, 1–4.

Sinha, R., Whig, P., & Ranjan, A. (2015). Effect of Variable Damping Ratio on design of PID Controller. *2015 4th International Conference on Reliability, Infocom Technologies and Optimization: Trends and Future Directions, ICRITO 2015*, 4–7. 10.1109/ICRITO.2015.7359340

Soni, S. (2019). *A Comprehensive survey on Blockchain : Working, security analysis, privacy threats and potential applications*. Academic Press.

Srivastava, J., Bhagat, R., & Kumar, P. (2020). Analog inverse filters using OTAs. *2020 6th International Conference on Control, Automation and Robotics (ICCAR)*, 627–631.

Stephen, R., & Alex, A. (2018). A Review on BlockChain Security. *IOP Conference Series. Materials Science and Engineering*, *396*(1), 012030. Advance online publication. doi:10.1088/1757-899X/396/1/012030

Suner, A., Oruc, O. E., Buke, C., Ozkaya, H. D., & Kitapcioglu, G. (2017). Evaluation of infectious diseases and clinical microbiology specialists' preferences for hand hygiene: Analysis using the multi-attribute utility theory and the analytic hierarchy process methods. *BMC Medical Informatics and Decision Making*, *17*(1), 129. doi:10.118612911-017-0528-z PMID:28859640

Tandon, A. (2019). Challenges of Integrating Blockchain with Internet of Things. *Challenges of Integrating Blockchain with Internet of Things.*, *9*(9S3), 1476–1489. doi:10.35940/ijitee.I3311.0789S319

Thompson, B. (2021, August 28). *Blockchain Tutorial: Learn Blockchain Technology (Examples).* https://www.guru99.com/blockchain-tutorial.html

Tony, M., Wagner, M., Khoury, H., Rindress, D., Papastavros, T., Oh, P., & Goetghebeur, M. M. (2011). Bridging health technology assessment (HTA) with multicriteria decision analyses (MCDA): Field testing of the EVIDEM framework for coverage decisions by a public payer in Canada. *BMC Health Services Research*, *11*(1), 329. doi:10.1186/1472-6963-11-329 PMID:22129247

Uddin, M. A., Stranieri, A., Gondal, I., & Balasubramanian, V. (2021). A Survey on the Adoption of Blockchain in IoT: Challenges and Solutions. *Blockchain: Research and Applications*, *100006*(2). Advance online publication. doi:10.1016/j.bcra.2021.100006

van den Bogaart, E.H.A., Kroese, M.E.A.L., Spreeuwenberg, M.D., Ruwaard, D., & Tsiachristas, A. (2021). Economic Evaluation of New Models of Care: Does the Decision Change Between Cost-Utility Analysis and Multi-Criteria Decision Analysis. *Value in Health: The Journal of the International Society for Pharmacoeconomics and Outcomes Research*, *24*(6), 795-803. . doi:10.1016/j.jval.2021.01.014

van Til, J., Groothuis-Oudshoorn, C., Lieferink, M., Dolan, J., & Goetghebeur, M. (2014). Does technique matter; a pilot study exploring weighting techniques for a multi-criteria decision support framework. *Cost Effectiveness and Resource Allocation*, *12*, 22. . doi:10.1186/1478-7547-12-22

Velu, A., & Whig, P. (2022). *Studying the Impact of the COVID Vaccination on the World Using Data Analytics*. Academic Press.

Velu, A., & Whig, P. (n.d.). *Studying the Impact of the COVID Vaccination on the World Using Data Analytics*. Academic Press.

Velu, A., & Whig, P. (2021). Protect Personal Privacy And Wasting Time Using Nlp: A Comparative Approach Using Ai. *Vivekananda Journal of Research*, *10*, 42–52.

Velu, A., & Whig, P. (2021). Protect Personal Privacy And Wasting Time Using Nlp: A Comparative Approach Using AI. *Vivekananda Journal of Research*, *10*, 42–52.

Verma, T. (2019). A comparison of different R2R D/A converters. *International Journal of Sustainable Development in Computing Science, 1*(2).

Verma, T., Gupta, P., & Whig, P. (2015). Sensor controlled sanitizer door knob with scan technique. *Advances in Intelligent Systems and Computing*. doi:10.1007/978-3-319-13731-5_29

Vettoretto, N., Foglia, E., Ferrario, L., Arezzo, A., Cirocchi, R., Cocorullo, G., Currò, G., Marchi, D., Portale, G., Gerardi, C., Nocco, U., Tringali, M., Anania, G., Piccoli, M., Silecchia, G., Morino, M., Valeri, A., & Lettieri, E. (2018). Why laparoscopists may opt for three-dimensional view: A summary of the full HTA report on 3D versus 2D laparoscopy by S.I.C.E. (Società Italiana di Chirurgia Endoscopica e Nuove Tecnologie). *Surgical Endoscopy, 32*(6), 2986–2993. doi:10.100700464-017-6006-y PMID:29368286

Villanueva, V., Carreño, M., Gil-Nagel, A., Serrano-Castro, P.J., Serratosa, J.M., Toledo, M., Álvarez-Barón, E., Gil, A. & Subías-Labazuy, S. (2021). Identifying key unmet needs and value drivers in the treatment of focal-onset seizures (FOS) in patients with drug-resistant epilepsy (DRE) in Spain through Multi-Criteria Decision Analysis (MCDA). *Epilepsy & Behavior, 122*, 108222. doi:10.1016/j.yebeh.2021.108222

Villegas-ch, W., Palacios-pacheco, X., & Román-cañizares, M. (2020). *Integration of IoT and Blockchain to in the Processes of a University Campus*. doi:10.3390/su12124970

Wagner, M., Khoury, H., Bennetts, L., Berto, P., Ehreth, J., Badia, X., & Goetghebeur, M. (2017). Appraising the holistic value of Lenvatinib for radio-iodine refractory differentiated thyroid cancer: A multi-country study applying pragmatic MCDA. *BMC Cancer, 17*(1), 272. doi:10.118612885-017-3258-9 PMID:28412971

Wagner, M., Khoury, H., Willet, J., Rindress, D., & Goetghebeur, M. (2016). Can the EVIDEM Framework Tackle Issues Raised by Evaluating Treatments for Rare Diseases: Analysis of Issues and Policies, and Context-Specific Adaptation. *PharmacoEconomics, 34*(3), 285–301. doi:10.100740273-015-0340-5 PMID:26547306

Wagner, M., Samaha, D., Casciano, R., Brougham, M., Abrishami, P., Petrie, C., Avouac, B., Mantovani, L., Sarría-Santamera, A., Kind, P., Schlander, M., & Tringali, M. (2019). Moving Towards Accountability for Reasonableness - A Systematic Exploration of the Features of Legitimate Healthcare Coverage Decision-Making Processes Using Rare Diseases and Regenerative Therapies as a Case Study. *International Journal of Health Policy and Management, 8*(7), 424–443. doi:10.15171/ijhpm.2019.24 PMID:31441279

Wahlster, P., Goetghebeur, M., Kriza, C., Niederländer, C., & Kolominsky-Rabas, P. (2015). Balancing costs and benefits at different stages of medical innovation: A systematic review of multi-criteria decision analysis (MCDA). *BMC Health Services Research, 15*(1), 262. doi:10.118612913-015-0930-0 PMID:26152122

Wahlster, P., Goetghebeur, M., Schaller, S., Kriza, C., & Kolominsky-Rabas, P. (2015). Exploring the perspectives and preferences for HTA across German healthcare stakeholders using a multi-criteria assessment of a pulmonary heart sensor as a case study. *Health Research Policy and Systems, 13*(1), 24. doi:10.118612961-015-0011-1 PMID:25928535

Wang, J., Chen, H., Lin, X., Ji, C., & Chen, B. (2020). Multiple cross displacement amplification-a more applicable technique in detecting Pseudomonas aeruginosa of ventilator-associated pneumonia (VAP). *Critical Care (London, England), 24*(1), 306. doi:10.118613054-020-03003-4 PMID:32513206

Watson, M. (2018). Panel discussion on the application of MCDA tools. *Cost Effectiveness and Resource Allocation, 16*(Suppl 1), 40. . doi:10.1186/s12962-018-0130-y

Whig, K. K., & P. (2020). Macroeconomic Implications of the Monetary Policy Committee Recommendations: An IS-LM Framework. *ACTA Scientific Agriculture, 4*(2).

Whig, P. (2022). More on Convolution Neural Network CNN. *International Journal of Sustainable Development in Computing Science, 1*(1).

Whig, P., & Ahmad, S. N. (2011). On the Performance of ISFET-based Device for Water Quality Monitoring. *Int'l J. of Communications, Network and System Sciences, 4*(11), 709–719. doi:10.4236/ijcns.2011.411087

Whig, P., & Ahmad, S. N. (2013). A novel pseudo NMOS integrated CC -ISFET device for water quality monitoring. *Journal of Integrated Circuits and Systems*. https://www.scopus.com/inward/record.url?eid=2-s2.0-84885357423&partnerID=MN8TOARS

Whig, P., & Ahmad, S. N. (2014a). CMOS integrated VDBA-ISFET device for water quality monitoring. *International Journal of Intelligent Engineering and Systems*. https://www.scopus.com/inward/record.url?eid=2-s2.0-84901490722&partnerID=MN8TOARS

Whig, P., & Ahmad, S. N. (2014b). Simulation of linear dynamic macro model of photo catalytic sensor in SPICE. In *COMPEL - The International Journal for Computation and Mathematics in Electrical and Electronic Engineering* (Vol. 33, Issues 1–2). doi:10.1108/COMPEL-09-2012-0160

Whig, P., & Ahmad, S. N. (2015). Novel FGMOS based PCS device for low power applications. *Photonic Sensors*. doi:10.1007/s13320-015-0224-5

Whig, P., & Rupani, A. (2020). Novel Economical Social Distancing Smart Device for COVID19. *International Journal of Electrical Engineering and Technology, 2.*

Whig, P., Nadikattu, R. R., & Velu, A. (2022). COVID-19 pandemic analysis using application of AI. *Healthcare Monitoring and Data Analysis Using IoT: Technologies and Applications, 1.*

Whig, Priyam, & Ahmad. (2018). Simulation & performance analysis of various R2R D/A converter using various topologies. *International Robotics & Automation Journal, 4*(2), 128–131.

Whig, P. (2016). Modelling and Simulation of Economical Water Quality Monitoring Device. *Journal of Aquaculture & Marine Biology, 4*(6). https://doi.org/10.15406/jamb.2016.04.00103

Whig, P. (2017). Temperature and Frequency Independent Readout Circuit for PCS System. *SF J Material Res Let, 1*(3), 8–12.

Whig, P. (2019a). A Novel Multi-Center and Threshold Ternary Pattern. *International Journal of Machine Learning for Sustainable Development, 1*(2), 1–10.

Whig, P. (2019b). Exploration of Viral Diseases mortality risk using machine learning. *International Journal of Machine Learning for Sustainable Development, 1*(1), 11–20.

Whig, P. (2019b). Prediction of Smart Building Indoor Temperature Using IoT and Machine Learning. *International Journal of Machine Learning for Sustainable Development, 1*(4), 1–10.

Whig, P. (2019c). Machine Learning Based Techniques for Communication and Signal Processing Problem. *International Journal of Machine Learning for Sustainable Development, 1*(3), 1–10.

Whig, P. (2021). IoT Based Novel Smart Blind Guidance System. *Journal of Computing Science and Engineering: JCSE, 2*(2), 80–88.

Whig, P., & Ahmad, S. N. (2015). Novel FGMOS based PCS device for low power applications. *Photonic Sensors, 5*(2), 123–127.

Whig, P., & Ahmad, S. N. (2016). Modelling and simulation of economical water quality monitoring device. *Journal of Aquaculture & Marine Biology, 4*(6), 1–6.

Whig, P., & Ahmad, S. N. (2017a). Controlling the Output Error for Photo Catalytic Sensor (PCS) Using Fuzzy Logic. *Journal of Earth Science & Climatic Change, 8*(4), 1–6.

Whig, P., & Ahmad, S. N. (2017b). Fuzzy logic implementation of photo catalytic sensor. *Int. Robot. Autom. J, 2*(3), 15–19.

Whig, P., & Ahmad, S. N. (2018). Novel pseudo PMOS ultraviolet photo catalytic oxidation (PP-UVPCO) sensor for air purification. *Int Rob Auto J, 4*(6), 393–398.

Whig, P., & Ahmad, S. N. (2018a). Comparison analysis of various R2R D/A converter. *Int J Biosen Bioelectron, 4*(6), 275–279.

Whig, P., & Ahmad, S. N. (2019). Methodology for Calibrating Photocatalytic Sensor Output. *International Journal of Sustainable Development in Computing Science, 1*(1), 1–10.

Whig, P., & Naseem Ahmad, S. (2012). DVCC based Readout Circuitry for Water Quality Monitoring System. *International Journal of Computers and Applications, 49*(22), 1–7. https://doi.org/10.5120/7900-1162

Yang, C., Wang, Y., Hu, X., Chen, Y., Qian, L., Li, F., ... Chai, X. (2021). Improving Hospital Based Medical Procurement Decisions with Health Technology Assessment and Multi-Criteria Decision Analysis. *Inquiry, 58.* . doi:10.1177/00469580211022911

Zamora, B., Garrison, L.P., Unuigbe, A., & Towse, A. (2021). Reconciling ACEA and MCDA: is there a way forward for measuring cost-effectiveness in the U.S. healthcare setting. *Cost Effectiveness and Resource Allocation, 19*(1), 13. . doi:10.1186/s12962-021-00266-8

Compilation of References

Zheng, Z., Xie, S., Dai, H., Chen, X., & Wang, H. (2017). *An Overview of Blockchain Technology : Architecture*. Consensus, and Future Trends. doi:10.1109/BigDataCongress.2017.85

Zozaya, N., Martínez-Galdeano, L., Alcalá, B., Armario-Hita, J.C., Carmona, C., Carrascosa, J.M., Herranz, P., Lamas, M.J., Trapero-Bertran, M., & Hidalgo-Vega, Á. (2018). Determining the Value of Two Biologic Drugs for Chronic Inflammatory Skin Diseases: Results of a Multi-Criteria Decision Analysis. *BioDrugs*, *32*(3), 281-91. doi:10.1007/s40259-018-0284-3

About the Contributors

Pradeep Bedi received the B.Tech. degree in computer science and engineering from Uttar Pradesh Technical University (UPTU), Lucknow, India, in 2005 and M.Tech. in computer science and engineering from Guru Gobind Singh Indraprastha University (GGSIPU), Delhi, India, in 2009. He is GATE, UGC-NET qualified and currently pursuing Ph.D from Indira Gandhi National Tribal University, Amarkantak (Regional Campus Manipur). He started his academic career from Mahatma Gandhi Mission's College of Engineering and Technology in 2005 and served various reputed colleges and universities in India and abroad. Currently, he holds the position of assistant professor in the department of computer science and engineering, Galgotias University, Greater Noida, Uttar Pradesh, India. He has authored or co-authored over 40 technical papers published in national and international journals and conferences and also published 15 patents in India and abroad. He is a member of reputed professional bodies such as CSI, ACM etc. His research interests include applications of artificial intelligence, machine learning, deep learning and IoT in healthcare, automation, etc.

Ashima Bhatia is Assistant Professor (IT) in Vivekananda Institute of Professional Studies, Affiliated to GGSIPU, PhD (CSE) (Pursuing), M.Phil(Computer Science), MCA, B.Sc. (Industrial Chemistry), BLIS, PGDRTM. A competent professional in academics with almost more than 17 years of rich experience in academics and research in the varied areas of Computer Application / IT. Author of many book. Expertise in delivering lectures for PG and UG students through required inputs and also guiding the MCA / IT students for their industrial projects. Editorial Board Member of "International Journal of Research & Development in Technology and Management Sciences IJRDTM", "International Journal of Multidisciplinary Consortium" and "We School -Knowledge Builder - The National Journal". Assessor - IT/ITES of Level 1 and Level 2 for National Institute of Open Schooling for NVEQF Project - Haryana Government.

S. B. Goyal completed PhD in the Computer Science & Engineering in 2012 from India and served many institutions in many different academic and administrative positions. He is holding 19+ years experience at national and international level. He has peerless inquisitiveness and enthusiasm to get abreast with the latest development in the IT field. He has good command over Industry Revolution (IR) 4.0 technologies like Big-Data, Data Science, Artificial Intelligence & Blockchain, computer networking, deep learning etc. He is the first one to introduce IR 4.0 including Blockchain technology in the academic curriculum in Malaysian Universities. He had participated in many panel discussions on IR 4.0 technologies at academia as well as industry platforms. He is holding 19+ years' experience in academia at National & International level. He is serving as a reviewer or guest editors in many Journals published by Inderscience, IGI Global, Springer. He is contributing as a Co-Editor in many Scopus books. He had contributed in many Scopus/ SCI Journal/ conferences. Currently, Dr Goyal is associated as a Director, Faculty of Information Technology, City University, Malaysia.

Shama Kouser is working as a lecturer in the department of Computer science in Jazan University, Kingdom of Saudi Arabia. She has a enrich experience of working in IoT, Artificial Intelligence, and Machine Learning.

Jugnesh Kumar is working as a Director in St. Andrews Institute of Technology and Management, Gurugram, Haryana affiliated to the Maharshi Dayanand University, Rohtak, Haryana. He is an IT specialist in the area of machine learning, big-data. Dr Kumar is received academic cum professional degrees MCA, M.Tech. and PhD(CSE). He is holding 20+ year administrative experience in addition to academic expertise in the area of Database System, Mobile Computing, Software Engineering, Computer Architecture, Java programming, Computer Networking, Deep Learning etc. He had organized many conferences/ events at India level. He had published many research papers/ book chapters in the Scopus Journals/ International Conferences/ Edited books. He had got the grant of International Patent for eight years from Australia in data analytics.

Meghana P. Lokhande is an Assistant Professor in the Computer Engineering Department at Pimpri Chinchwad College of Engineering, Pune. She earned her MTech degree from Bharati Vidyapeeth Deemed University College of Engineering, Pune. Now she is doing a Ph.D. in Computer engineering. She has published papers in International and National journals.

Sushma Malik is working as Assistant Professor at Institute of Innovation in Technology and Management (IINTM), Affiliated to GGSIPU, New Delhi and she is also the research scholar of Shobhit Institute of Engineering & Technology (Deemed-to-be-University), Meerut-250110, India. She is sharing her rich knowledge and expertise in the field of academics for the past 10 years. She has a strong inclination towards both teaching and research. Her areas of interest include data mining, e-commerce, and software engineering. She has numerous research papers published in national as well as international journals. In addition, she has also published research papers in conferences and has attended several seminars.

Rahul Nadikattu has played a senior role throughout his experience working with "Natsoft Corporation". He is currently a senior research scientist with more than 10 years of experience in the IT field. As a senior and fellow member of highly reputed recognized organizations, he was invited to golden bridge awards, it is one among across the world to contribute directly in bringing the technology experts into the market, he was directly responsible for judging the talents for reputed universities from across the globe, his learnings and research publications talks about how AI can help state local government to identify engineering issues and implement a scalable engineering solution. As a senior scientist, He played a lead and critical role in implementing AI best practices to healthcare sectors bringing the security industry best practices into place.

Dipti D. Patil, PhD, is working as Associate Professor and Dean (Student Affairs) at MKSSS's Cummins College of Engineering for Women, Pune. Dr. Dipti has published many research articles in various national and international Journals and conferences. She has authored books in areas of Data Structures and Mobile healthcare. She is involved in developing healthcare system prototypes and for which she has filed various national and international patents. She is a patent holder for designing mobile healthcare system. Her areas of special interest include mobile healthcare, analytics, data science, artificial intelligence and Internet of Things. Dr. Patil is serving as member, board of Studies, IT for various institutes and universities. Dr. Patil is certified patent attorney of India. She is life member of professional bodies like CSI, ASI and ISTE.

Pavika Sharma is currently working as Assistant Professor in the ECE department at Bhagwan Parshuram Institute of Technology, GGSIPU, New Delhi. She has worked with Amity School of Engineering & Technology, Amity University, Noida at the Department of ECE, and Vice-Chancellor Office, Amity University Noida for 9 years. With more than 11 years of teaching and research experience, she has published 3 patents and more than 16 research papers in reputed peer reviewed journals and conferences. She has served as a reviewer of many reputed journals and conferences including IEEE Transactions on Intelligent Transportation Systems,

Future Generation Computer Systems, Elsevier, Annals of Operations Research, Parallel Processing Letters (PPL), Transactions on Asian and Low-Resource Language Information Processing and Physical Communication, Elsevier, etc. She has also served as session chair at Springer International conferences and was invited as a distinguished speaker at the National Science and Technology Entrepreneurship Board, Department of Science and Technology, Govt. of India. Her area of interest includes Physical Layer Design & Security, Beyond 6G, 7G, Internet of things, Smart Cities, MEMS Design, FPGAs, and ASIC Design.

Arun Velu has twelve years of experience in the Analytics and Data Science industry across consulting, marketing and financial services. He is currently working as the Director of Advanced Analytics at Equifax, leading the data and analytics team in supporting the B2C business of the company. His core skills include programming, project management, model development, and business intelligence using tools like SAS, SQL, Excel, Python, GCP, and Tableau. His area of expertise and research is developing predictive models and exploring application of business intelligence. He has developed logistic regression, random forest and Monte Carlo based predictive models for risk management and customer relationship management. He has worked in different geographies from Bangalore to New York to Atlanta and actively involved in recruitment and campus outreach programs in hiring talent and industry-academic partnership.

Pawan Whig did B.Tech in Electronics and Communication Engineering in 2005. After successfully completing his graduation he completed M.Tech in VLSI in 2008. His educational Journey is not stop here, he was awarded "Doctorate" from Jamia Millia Islamia . He has been working in the field of Electronics and Communication for the last 21 years. He is an editor and reviewer of several internationally refereed journals. He is designing and mentoring several projects in universities across India. He is member of international association of engineers Hong Kong, ISTE, IEEE, SCI, IEI and state student coordinator of Rajasthan of Computer Society of India (CSI). He published technical articles in more than 80 national and international journals. He has a wide area of research like Analog Signal Processing, Sensor Modeling, Water Quality Monitoring Applications and Simulation & design. He has invented a Low Power Water Quality Monitoring Device which is under Patent Process. He has proposed a SPICE Model for Novel Photo catalytic Sensor (PCS) which can be the area of interest for new researchers in the same field.

Index

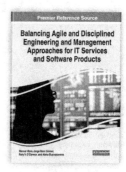

Ensure Quality Research is Introduced to the Academic Community

Become an Evaluator for IGI Global Authored Book Projects

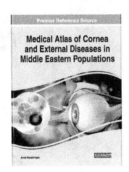
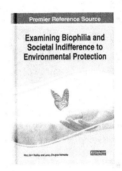
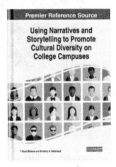
The overall success of an authored book project is dependent on quality and timely manuscript evaluations.

Applications and Inquiries may be sent to:
development@igi-global.com

Applicants must have a doctorate (or equivalent degree) as well as publishing, research, and reviewing experience. Authored Book Evaluators are appointed for one-year terms and are expected to complete at least three evaluations per term. Upon successful completion of this term, evaluators can be considered for an additional term.

If you have a colleague that may be interested in this opportunity, we encourage you to share this information with them.

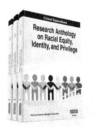
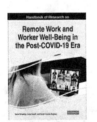

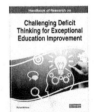